# Discovering Food

THIRD EDITION

HELEN KOWTALUK

GLENCOE
Macmillan/McGraw-Hill
New York, New York    Columbus, Ohio    Mission Hills, California    Peoria, Illinois

# Acknowledgements

The author and editors wish to express their deepest appreciation to Elizabeth Shipley-Moses, MS, RD, nutrition consultant, and Carri Whitaker, home economist, microwave consultant, for their invaluable suggestions, interest, and enthusiasm. We also wish to thank FDA, USDA, trade associations, and industry for providing information and assistance.

**Cover Design by Pat Allen**



Send all inquiries to:
GLENCOE DIVISION
Macmillan/McGraw-Hill
3008 W. Willow Knolls Drive
Peoria, Illinois 61614

**ISBN 0-02-663351-5**

Printed in the United States of America

3 4 5 6 7 8 9 AGH 99 98 97 96 95 94 93

# Credits

American Egg Board, 229, 231, 232
American Lamb Council, 217
American Plywood Association, 122
Arnold & Brown, 5, 24, 38, 60, 132, 147, 202, 231
Bair, Dot, 136
Ballard, James, 13, 24, 47
Bean, Roger B., 13, 19, 23, 63, 131, 243, 271
Black Star/Robin Moyer, 130
California Dry Bean Advisory Board, 189
Castle & Cook, 287
Chrysler, 17
Crickett Country Corner/Ann Garvin, 4, 7, 128, 135, 143
Crouser, Angela, 10, 37, 57, 80, 83, 84, 85, 86, 89, 90, 93, 95, 103, 105, 121, 123, 124, 125, 129, 135, 145, 147, 207, 208, 209, 211, 212, 218, 219, 274, 275, 279, 280, 289, 292
David R. Frazier Photolibrary, 4, 8, 11, 18, 19, 26, 39, 55, 60, 130
Davis Purity Bakery/Ann Garvin, 7, 290
Davis, Howard, 105
Dillard's Dept. Store/Brent Phelps, 141
Dudley-Anderson-Yutzy, 291
Esser, Stephen, 49
Garvin, Ann, 4, 5, 6, 7, 11, 12, 22, 23, 29, 30, 32, 33, 34, 36, 37, 40, 42, 43, 44, 46, 48, 60, 64, 66, 67, 68, 69, 70, 71, 76, 77, 78, 79, 80, 81, 84, 88, 89, 90, 91, 92, 93, 94, 95, 100, 101, 104, 106, 118, 120, 124, 125, 127, 128, 134, 135, 138, 140, 144, 146, 148, 149, 150, 157, 158,160, 162, 163, 164, 166, 171, 172, 176, 177, 179, 180, 184, 185, 187, 188, 190, 192, 195, 196, 201, 202, 203, 204, 205, 206, 210, 211, 212, 213, 215, 216, 221, 223, 226, 227, 228, 235, 236, 238, 241, 242, 244, 247, 248, 249, 250, 252, 254, 255, 256, 259, 261, 262, 264, 265, 267, 268, 270, 273, 275, 276, 279, 281, 283, 284, 286, 287, 288, 289, 290, 291, 293,
Grand Illusions/Rick Burdette, 1, 6, 142-143
Heringa, Dan/Economic Development and Tourism, Alaska, 31
Hutchings, Richard/Info Edit, 18
Idaho Dry Bean Commission, 189
Impact Communications, 5, 105
Jenkins, Mike, 58
Kansas Wheat Commission, 56
Kraft, 19
Manning, Eric, 144
McElwee, Bob, 13, 17, 51, 74, 118, 123
National Broiler Council, 197
National Fish & Seafood Promotional Council, 214
National Pork Producers Council, 6, 217, 243
National Turkey Federation, 197
Nebraska Dry Bean Commission, 183, 190
Noah Herman Sons, House of the 1990s/Roger B. Bean, 62, 220
PeoriArea Blind Center/Roger B. Bean, 103
Peterson, Judith, 10, 14, 27, 39, 50, 61, 62, 63, 81, 82, 101, 105, 106, 107, 108, 115, 152, 153, 154, 155, 156, 160, 161, 165, 167, 168, 169, 173, 174, 175, 176, 177, 182, 183, 185, 190, 192, 193, 194, 200, 201, 203, 224, 225, 230, 232, 236, 239, 245, 251, 253, 257, 258, 265, 272, 285
Phelps, Brent, 14, 17, 24, 29, 31, 44, 52, 55, 56, 58, 60, 61, 63, 75, 79, 80, 81, 82, 85, 86, 87, 94, 101, 102, 103, 104, 105, 106, 108, 109, 119, 123, 124, 125, 129, 148, 151, 153, 159, 161, 166, 167, 168, 170, 174, 176, 180, 181, 182, 184, 186, 189, 190, 197, 198, 199, 207, 209, 210, 217, 218, 219, 220, 222, 229, 234, 236, 238, 240, 243, 246, 249, 250, 257, 258, 259, 260, 263, 264, 266, 269, 270, 271, 277, 278, 282, 285, 286
PhotoEdit/M. Richards, 19
PhotoEdit/Mary Kate Denny, 21
PhotoEdit/McCarten, 20
PhotoEdit/Stephen McBrady, 54
Piggly Wiggly Market/Brent Phelps, 57, 61, 131, 174, 197, 208, 209
Purcell, Elizabeth, 9, 59, 127, 132, 288
Reynolds Metals Company/Ira Wexler, 17
Richwoods High School/Charles Hofer, 9, 117
Rubbermaid, 15, 114, 125, 144, 147
Schwartz, George, 34
Slater & Associates/ImageGate, 271, 173, 281, 289
Thompson's Food Basket/Arnold & Brown, 57
Thompson's Food Basket/Woodruff High School/Roger B. Bean, 51
U.S. Department of Agriculture, 217
U.S. Department of Commerce, 208
Underwriters Laboratory Inc., 67
United Fresh Fruit & Vegetable Assn., 161
Vergara, Carlos, 116, 139, 144
Woodruff High School/Arnold & Brown, 26
Woodruff High School/Roger B. Bean, 16, 18, 21, 25, 28, 35, 41, 51, 53, 117, 126, 131, 137, 178
Zehr, Duane R., 55, 57, 173, 286

# Contents

## Unit 1: Looking Ahead

## Unit 2: Nutrition

# Unit 3: Developing Skills

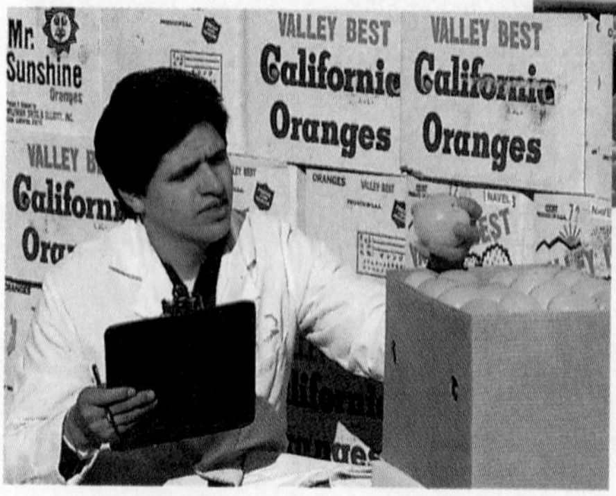


# Unit 4: Good Work Habits

# Unit 5: Mealtime

# Unit 6: Learning about Foods



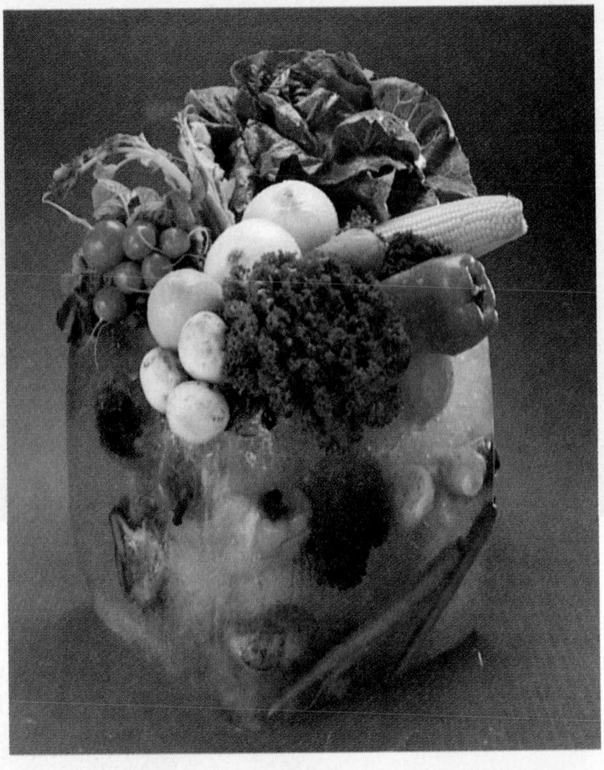

# Unit 7: Creative Combinations

# Unit 8: Baking



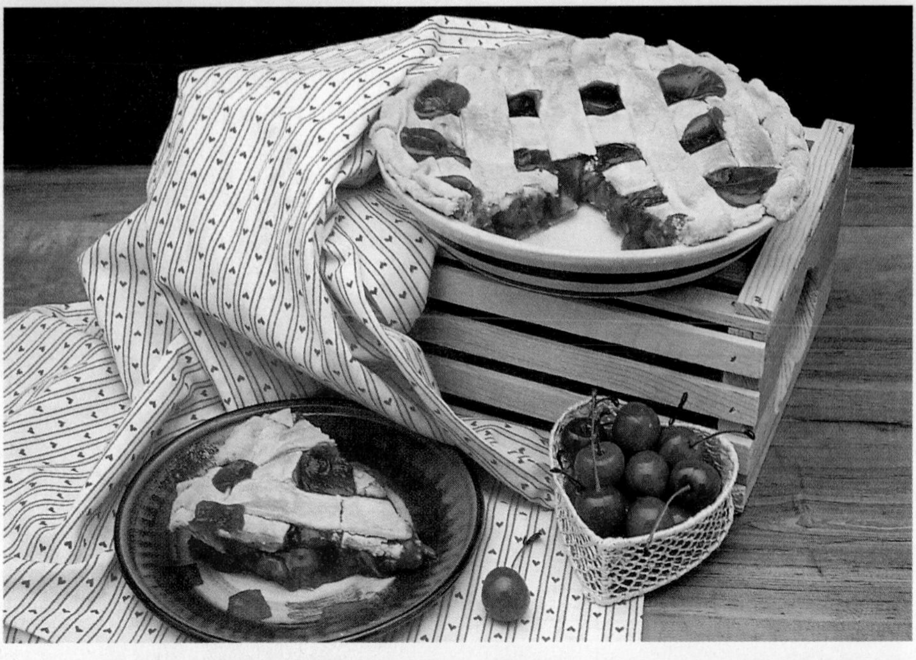

CHAPTER 1

# The Adventure of Food

**OBJECTIVES**

**Discover . . .**
- what you can gain from the study of food and nutrition.
- how to set and reach goals.

Why study food and nutrition? After all, you've been eating food all your life. As for preparing food, you can easily open a can or put a frozen meal in the microwave. What more do you need to know?

It's true that you can get by without knowing much about food. But with just a little more skill and knowledge, you can accomplish so much more.

## What Can You Gain from This Course?

You are about to start out on a great adventure—the study of food and nutrition. What do you think you will learn along the way? If you said "how to cook," that's only part of the answer. You may be surprised by all the ways this course can help you.

### Learning About Nutrition

One thing you will learn is how to choose nutritious, flavorful snacks and meals. Your body needs a variety of foods, including grains, dairy products, and fresh fruits and vegetables, to keep you healthy and active. Eating a variety of nutritious food every day can help you look and feel your best.

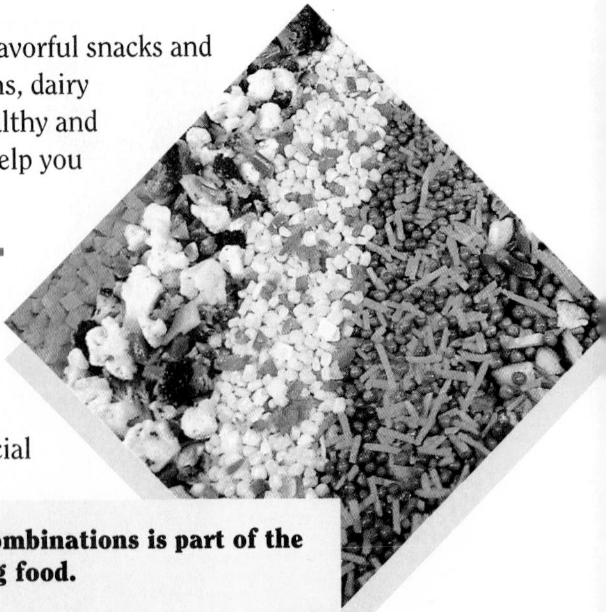

**Creating new combinations is part of the fun of preparing food.**

### Learning to Prepare Food

What's your favorite food? Pizza? Hamburger? Stir-fried chicken? All of these are made up of several different kinds of foods. The combinations of different foods and the way they are prepared give each dish a special flavor all its own. If you know how to prepare many different foods, you will have a greater variety of choices.

For instance, you can make a hamburger with plain ground beef. You can change the flavor by adding different foods to the meat before it is cooked—chopped onion or a little garlic. Instead of hamburgers, you can use the ground beef to make a casserole or a meat sauce for pasta or tacos.

That's the fun part of cooking—trying different food combinations and enjoying the variety. Once you learn basic food preparation skills, you will have knowledge that you can use throughout your life. You will be able to:

- Cook for yourself.
- Plan and prepare meals for your family.
- Entertain friends.
- Contribute to community service.

You may even find a rewarding career in the food industry.

## Developing Skills for Life

As you learn to choose and prepare food, you will also develop and reinforce other skills. They are skills that you can apply throughout your life in many ways. Some of these are:

- Using basic math.
- Reading, writing, speaking, and listening.
- Working as a team.
- Making decisions.
- Planning and organizing your work.
- Thinking critically and asking questions.

As you work through this course, think about the skills you are developing.

**Skills that you learn now can be useful at home, at school, and in the workplace for years to come.**

# Setting and Reaching Goals

One way to get the most out of this course is to set goals. A goal is like a target you aim at. Setting goals helps you see what you want to accomplish.

What are your own goals for this course? Take a moment to think about what you most want to learn. Write down your specific goals.

## Long-Term and Short-Term Goals

Working toward a goal is like climbing a staircase. You don't get to the top in one jump. Instead, you take one step at a time.

The small steps you take along the way are called *short-term goals*. A short-term goal is a task that can be accomplished in the near future. It helps you move toward your *long-term goal*, or what you want to accomplish farther in the future.

Why are short-term goals important? Every step you take, no matter how small, proves that you can be successful. As a result, you gain self-confidence. *Self-confidence* means your belief in your ability to succeed.

For example, perhaps one of your long-term goals is to prepare a nutritious, good-tasting meal for your family or friends. Your short-term goals would include:

- Learn basic skills, such as how to read a recipe and measure ingredients.
- Learn more about the types of food you will be preparing.
- Gain experience by preparing different recipes.

This book will help you learn one step at a time.

**Goals are reached one step at a time.**

## Stick With It

Remember the last time you tried to learn a new skill, such as skating or the latest dance style? It took a little while to learn the basic moves and then put them together. You had to practice until you could do them easily. It's the same with learning to choose and prepare food.

Don't be discouraged if the foods you make don't look like the pictures you see in magazines and cookbooks. Keep in mind that you're just learning. It takes time and practice to become skilled.

One way to measure your progress is to ask yourself:

- Am I giving my best effort?
- Am I getting closer to my goal?
- Have I learned from my mistakes?

If the answers are "yes," you can be proud of yourself.

**Success! Preparing food is an accomplishment to be proud of. The results are tasty, too!**

**Learning to prepare food is like learning to play a musical instrument—you have to start with the basics. With a little practice you'll be on your way.**

## Chapter 1 Review

### Check the Facts

1. Why is learning how to choose nutritious snacks and meals important?
2. Give at least three examples of how food preparation skills can help you.
3. Name at least three skills, other than food preparation, that this course can help you develop.
4. What is the difference between a short-term goal and a long-term goal? Give an example of each.
5. What is self-confidence? How does it relate to setting goals?
6. What three questions can help you measure your progress?

### Ideas in Action

1. Assume you are a reporter for your school or community newspaper. Write a short article giving reasons why everyone should study food and nutrition.
2. Discuss short-term and long-term goals you would like to achieve in this course.
3. Tell about an experience in which you could have used more knowledge about food and nutrition.

CHAPTER 2

# Managing Your Resources

**OBJECTIVES**

**Discover . . .**
- types of resources.
- how to use your resources wisely.
- steps in making good decisions.

A *resource* is something you can use to help you meet your goals. Using resources wisely to meet your goals is called *management*. Managing your resources is part of daily living. In this book, you will discover how to manage your resources as a part of good nutrition and food preparation.

## What Are Your Resources?

You have many different resources. They include:

**Personal resources.** You can use your own energy, knowledge, skills, and imagination to accomplish a great deal. Time is also a personal resource to be used wisely. Although you cannot always see or touch them, personal resources are among the most valuable.

**Material resources.** These include possessions such as tools, money, and food. Properly managed, food can be one of the most important resources in helping you to stay healthy. Still, think of food as being more than that. Well-prepared, flavorful food is to be enjoyed.

**Social resources.** Social resources come from other people. Your family and friends provide love, companionship, and support. They also have skills and knowledge that you can draw on. Many resources can be found in your community, such as hospitals, social service workers, libraries, places of worship, parks, museums, and restaurants. What others can you think of?

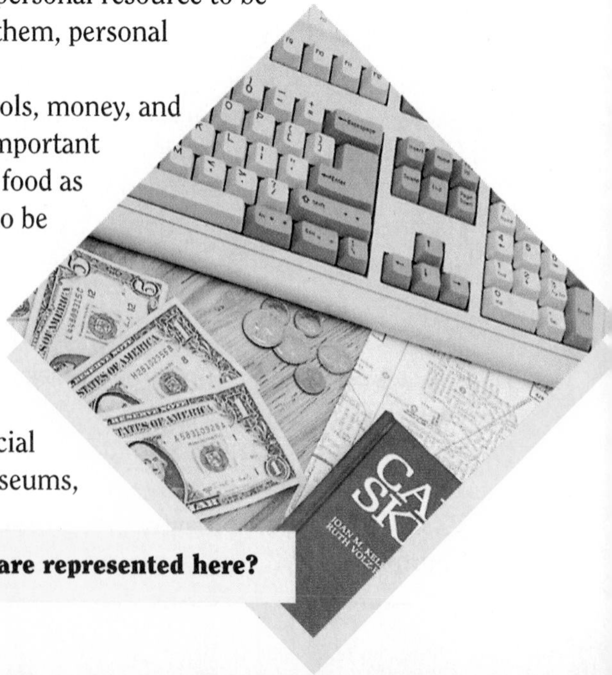

**What resources are represented here?**

**Natural resources.** *Natural resources* are materials that are provided by nature, such as air, fuel, water, and land. Life depends on natural resources—clean air to breathe, water to drink, and soil to grow food. Natural resources also help provide many conveniences. For example, automobiles, electrical appliances, and heating systems all use fuel.

**It's important to protect natural resources and use them wisely.**

# Using Resources Wisely

Resources can be very helpful, but they must be used wisely. Different situations call for different ways to manage resources.

## Increasing Resources

One way to manage resources is to increase the supply. Personal resources are among the easiest to increase. For example, you can add to your knowledge and skills by reading a book or taking a class. Eating right and staying healthy can give you more energy to get things done.

**How is this teen increasing her resources?**

## Conserving Resources

Some resources cannot easily be increased. You may have only a certain amount of money to last the week. There is only a limited supply of fresh water on the earth.

Conserving is a way to manage resources that are in short supply. Practicing conservation means using resources carefully instead of wasting them. To help your money last the rest of the week, for example, you can decide to spend it only on the things that are most important to you.

Conservation is especially important for natural resources. Many natural resources cannot be renewed. Once they are used up, they are gone forever. In Chapter 19 you will learn ways to conserve natural resources.

**Cleaning up a park is a way to share in the care of your community.**

## Substituting Resources

Another way to manage resources is to substitute one for another. For example, suppose you don't have enough time to prepare the lunch you had planned. What other resources could you substitute for time? You could...

- Eat at a restaurant (using money and a community resource).
- Ask a friend or family member to help you prepare the meal.
- Use your imagination and the food you have on hand. Perhaps you could come up with a different meal that would take less time to prepare.

**When time is short, you can use your other resources to plan and prepare a simple, nutritious meal. That's called being resourceful!**

## Making Decisions

As part of managing resources, you will often have to make decisions. Sometimes it may be a simple choice, such as whether to have orange juice or apple juice. Deciding on the best way to solve a problem or meet a goal can be more difficult. You can be more confident in making decisions if you follow these steps:

1. **Define the problem or goal.** Unless you know exactly what you are trying to do, it's very difficult to decide how to do it. For example, your problem may be that you always run out of money for snacks.
2. **Consider your resources.** Since money is in short supply, what other resources could help you?
3. **Think of possible solutions.** You might come up with these ideas for solving your snack problem:
   - Cut back on other expenses.
   - Make snacks at home and bring them to school.
   - Borrow money from friends at the end of the week.

4. **Compare the options.** What are the good and bad points of each plan? Remember to consider how the plan might affect other people. For instance, if you are thinking of bringing snacks from home, discuss your ideas with your family.

5. **Choose the best plan.** You might decide to add nutritious snacks to your family's weekly shopping list.

6. **Put your plan into action.** Many people are good at planning, but never carry out their plans. Take responsibility for making the snacks and packing them.

7. **Evaluate the results.** To *evaluate* means to judge how well you reached your goal. When you have carried out your plan, ask yourself whether you are happy with the results. How can you improve the plan?

**Here's one snack solution—tasty fresh fruit. What other ideas can you think of? Which would you choose and why?**

## Chapter 2 Review

### Check the Facts

1. What is a resource? How do resources relate to management?
2. Give an example showing how you use one of your personal resources wisely.
3. Identify two social resources and how they can benefit you.
4. What are three general ways to manage resources? Give an example of each.
5. Why is it important to conserve natural resources?
6. List the seven steps in decision-making.

### Ideas in Action

1. In small groups, select a personal or material resource. Create a public service announcement for a local radio station identifying some ways to best use that resource.
2. Discuss ways you can make good use of resources in foods class. How can you save time, money, food, water, and energy?
3. June and Kendra have been given $10 by their parents for food on Friday evening. Write a story showing how June and Kendra could use the decision-making process to plan how to use the money.

CHAPTER 3

# What About Careers?

**OBJECTIVES**

**Discover . . .**
- how to prepare now for a successful career.
- how to choose a career.
- different kinds of careers in the food industry.

This time of your life is a starting point for your future. Have you thought about the kind of career you want? A *career* is the work you choose to do for a long period or in a specific field.

You may not be able to decide now on the kind of career you want. But you can work on becoming the kind of person who will have a successful career. You can also learn about the many career choices available to you, including those related to food and nutrition.

## Preparing for the World of Work

No matter what kind of career you choose, all employers look for certain abilities. You can start now to develop these abilities. They are the foundation for a successful career.

**Be responsible.** Good employees take responsibility for their actions. When they are given an assignment, they follow through on it. If they see a job that needs to be done, they do it without having to be told. When they make a mistake—as everyone does at times—they admit it. Then they learn from it so that it will not happen again.

**Be willing to learn.** The learning process will continue throughout your lifetime. No matter where you work, you will need to keep up to date on new information, products, methods, and technology.

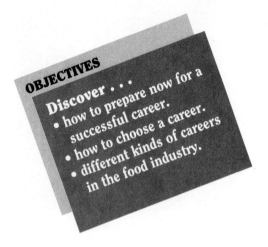

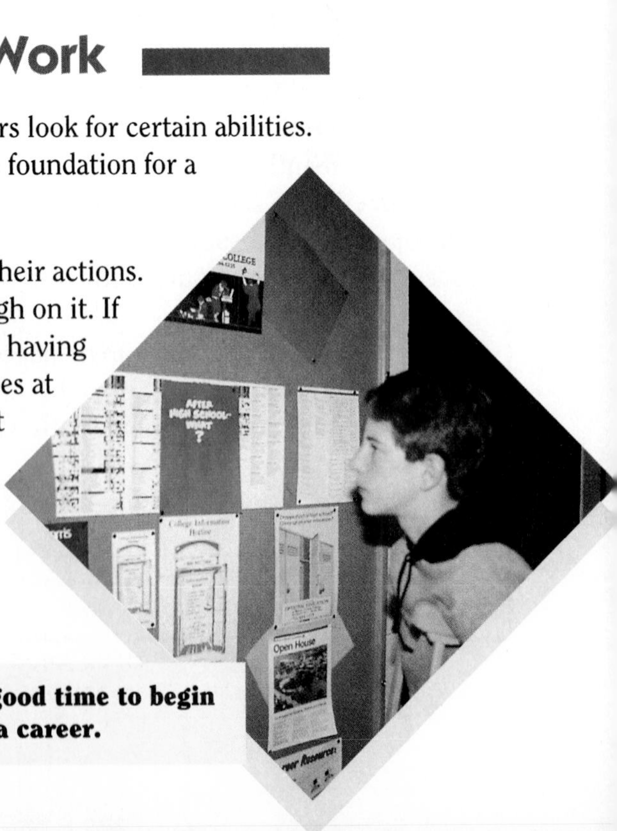


**Right now is a good time to begin thinking about a career.**

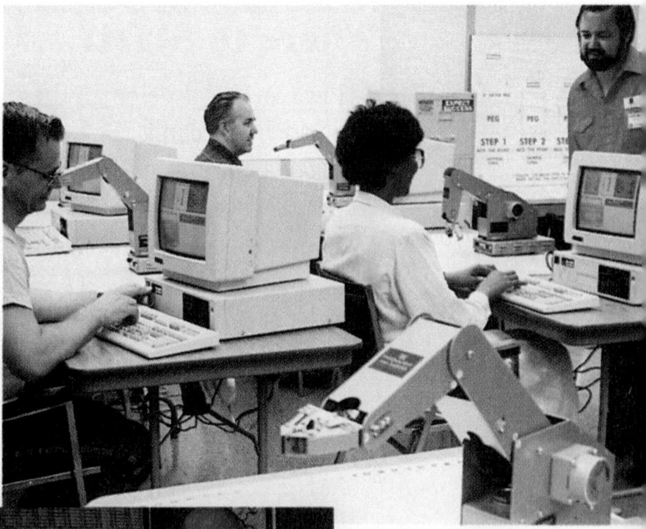

**These workers are learning to use a new computer system.**

**Develop good communication skills.** Listening, speaking, reading, and writing are essential. No matter what your job, you will be expected to understand instructions. You may also need to discuss ideas with co-workers, talk with and listen to customers, read reports, or write letters. Learn how to speak and write good, clear English so people can understand what you want to say.

**Can you see why communication skills are important on the job?**

**Know basic math skills.** Most jobs require at least basic math. For instance, you may have to fill out a time sheet showing the number of hours you worked on different tasks. If you are a checkout clerk in a supermarket, you need to know how to work a cash register. Even if you use a calculator or computer, basic math principles help you understand what to do.

**Most jobs require some math skills. Understanding basic math can help you be more confident.**

**Learn teamwork.** In most jobs, people work together to achieve a specific goal. Employers are impressed with people who work well on a team. They look for people who are willing to do their share of the work.

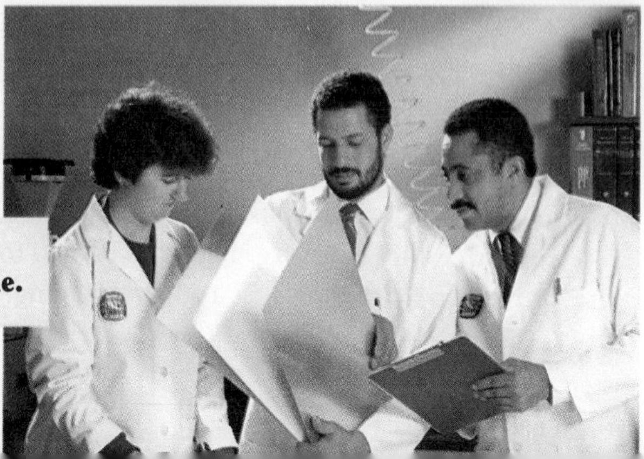

**A team of people working together can accomplish more than anyone can alone.**

## Where to Start?

How can you develop all these skills and qualities? You have many opportunities right now. You can...

- Make a commitment to your school studies.
- Spend time reading and learning on your own.
- Look for ways to practice communication skills, teamwork, and responsibility at home.
- Take part in school clubs or committees.
- Volunteer to help the community. You might clean up litter or read to the elderly, for example.

# Choosing a Career

Working is a way to earn income, but it can also provide personal satisfaction and enjoyment. The key is to find a career that fits you—your talents and abilities, your interests, your personality, your family life, and your goals.

It's a good idea to start learning about different careers. A guidance counselor can help you find information and think about what types of work might suit you. You might also want to talk to people in different fields. Ask them what their job is like and how they prepared for it.

**What are your talents and interests? How might they be useful on the job?**

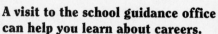

You will find that within each career area there are different job levels. Most people start with an *entry-level job*, one which does not require experience or a college degree. As you gain more training and education, you can work your way up the ladder to higher-paying jobs.

**A visit to the school guidance office can help you learn about careers.**

# Careers in the Food Industry

If you are interested in food and nutrition, why not consider turning that interest into a career? Many jobs related to food and nutrition are available. The following pages show just a small sampling.

## Careers in Food Production and Marketing

Do you ever think about how the food you see in the supermarket got there? It is the result of many people working to produce and market food. Perhaps you would enjoy being one of them.

The food you eat has its beginnings on a farm. Some farmers, like this couple, grow grains. Others grow fruits and vegetables or raise dairy herds for milk.

Hydroponic farming is a relatively new method. Plants are grown in water instead of soil.

After food is grown, it is processed—made ready for sale. Food processors employ thousands of people with many opportunities for advancement. One important job is inspecting food for quality before it is packaged, canned, or frozen.

Food marketing careers involve selling food. At supermarkets, you can find many entry-level jobs such as stocking shelves, working a cash register, or assisting customers with their bags. Your goal might be to become a supermarket manager like the one shown here. The manager directs and coordinates all the activities of the supermarket.

Other marketing careers include writing about food, arranging and photographing food, and helping to create advertisements. These are just some of the ways you can combine an interest in food and nutrition with other interests and abilities.

# Careers in Food Service

Today many meals are purchased and eaten away from home. Those meals are provided by workers in the food service industry.

If you are interested in food service, you might start with a job at a fast food restaurant. Experience in preparing or serving food can open the doors to success. You could eventually move up...

...to a job that requires more skill and training. The chef in this Japanese restaurant, for example, prepares food with creativity and showmanship. You might even start your own food service business.

Some food service workers are responsible for bringing the food from the kitchen to the customer. They may wait on tables, take orders at a counter, or serve food in a cafeteria. This worker must make sure that all the serving pans are always filled and at the right temperature.

Not all food service takes place in restaurants. Some food service workers, like this one, are employed by hospitals. Others prepare food for schools, nursing homes, airlines, company cafeterias, vending machines, banquets, and parties.

## Careers in Nutrition and Home Economics

If you enjoy home economics classes, you may want to continue your studies in college. Then you could choose from a variety of careers related to home economics.

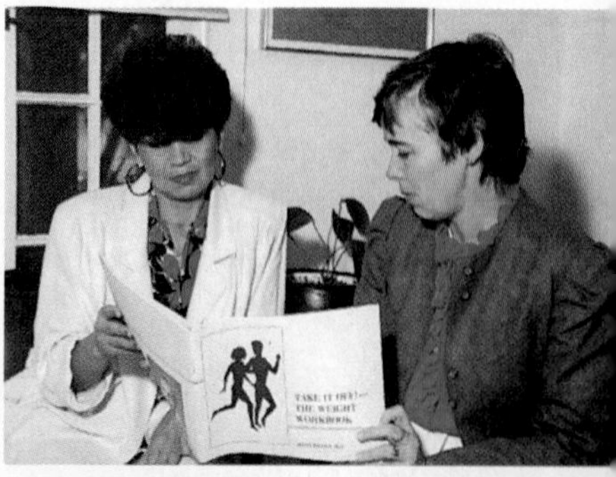

Nutritionists help people develop healthful eating habits. They teach individuals and families how to choose nutritious food and stay within their budget. They also evaluate food service systems in hospitals and nursing homes.

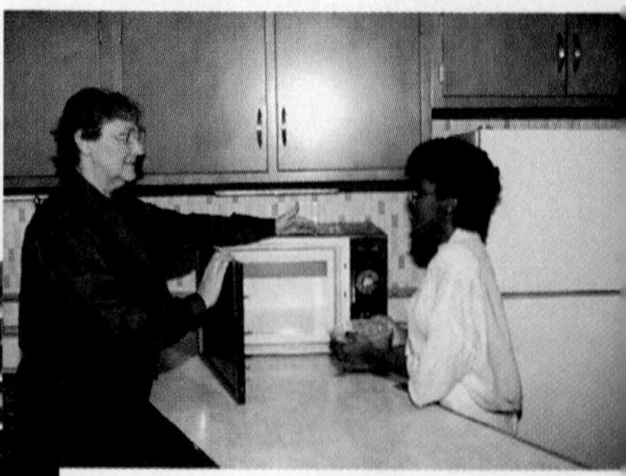

Perhaps teaching is for you. Home economics teachers instruct students in nutrition principles, food preparation, and good consumer practices.

Some home economists work as researchers. They may develop new products, test new chemicals to be added to food, or make new discoveries about nutrition.

## Chapter 3 Review

### Check the Facts

1. Identify five qualities that are a foundation for a successful career. Give an example showing why each quality is important.
2. List at least four ways you can develop the skills and qualities that make employees successful.
3. What is an entry-level job? Give an example.
4. Name at least three careers in food production and marketing.
5. List at least three different job opportunities in the food service industry.
6. Give at least two examples of home economics-related careers.

### Ideas in Action

1. Discuss the importance of basic abilities such as communicating clearly and taking responsibility. If a worker does not have those abilities, how might job performance be affected? How would employers, co-workers, and customers be affected?
2. With a partner, develop a list of questions to ask employers about various careers related to foods, nutrition, and home economics.
3. In small groups, design an informational exhibit for your school career fair showing careers related to foods, nutrition, and home economics.

CHAPTER 4

# Wellness—Your Goal For Life

**OBJECTIVES**

**Discover . . .**
- the meaning of wellness.
- healthy habits that lead to wellness.
- how to plan your personal wellness program.

Many people today are emphasizing wellness. *Wellness* means good health—not just physical, but emotional and mental as well. It also means taking responsibility for your own health.

People interested in wellness make choices that help them become and stay healthy. They know that it's much easier to keep the human body well than it is to cure an illness, even a minor one.

## Good Habits for Life

The health habits you establish now will affect the quality of your life for years to come. You can't control every aspect of your health. But by practicing wellness, you will be doing what you can to live a long, healthy life.

A wellness plan includes:
- Choosing and eating nutritious food.
- Exercising regularly.
- Getting plenty of sleep.
- Learning to handle stress.
- Avoiding harmful substances such as alcohol, tobacco, and other drugs.

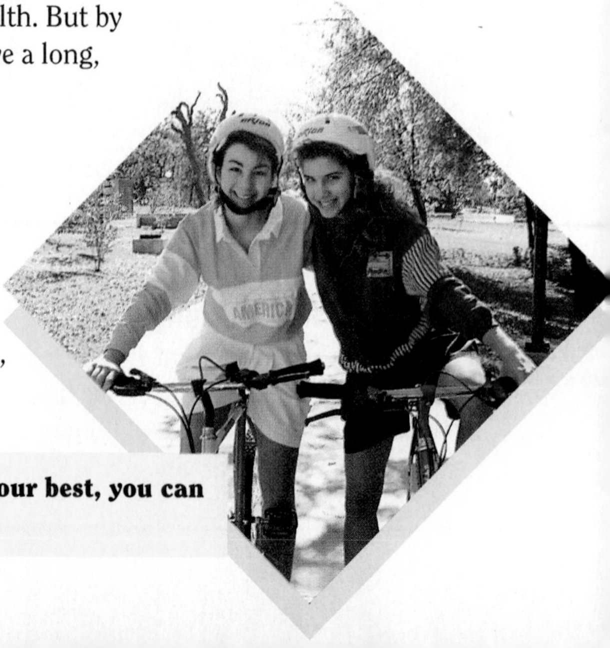


**When you feel your best, you can enjoy life more.**

## Choose Nutritious Food

When people eat, they usually think of the food as satisfying their hunger or giving them pleasure. Food also provides the body with nutrients. *Nutrients* are chemicals in food that the body needs to work properly. The body uses nutrients for three main purposes:

**To provide energy.** Your body uses energy all the time, even when you are sleeping. Nutrients help provide the body with the energy it needs.

**To build and repair cells.** Good nutrition helps the body grow, which it does by building new cells. A healthy body is also constantly replacing cells that are worn out or damaged.

**To regulate body processes.** Breathing, digesting food, and building red blood cells are examples of the many processes that happen continuously in the body. These processes cannot take place properly without the chemicals provided by nutrients.

**As you read further in this book, you will discover how to choose nutritious food for good health.**

## Get Plenty of Sleep

Sleep is essential to good health. When you sleep, your body gets rid of waste products that you have collected in your muscles during the day. It also builds up a fresh supply of energy for your day's activities. During sleep, the body mends and builds new cells more quickly. That's why people who are ill need extra sleep.

Teens often need more sleep than others because of growth and changes occurring in teen bodies. Your clue to the amount of sleep you need is how you feel when you wake up in the morning. If you are getting enough sleep, you will wake up easily and feel alert all day.

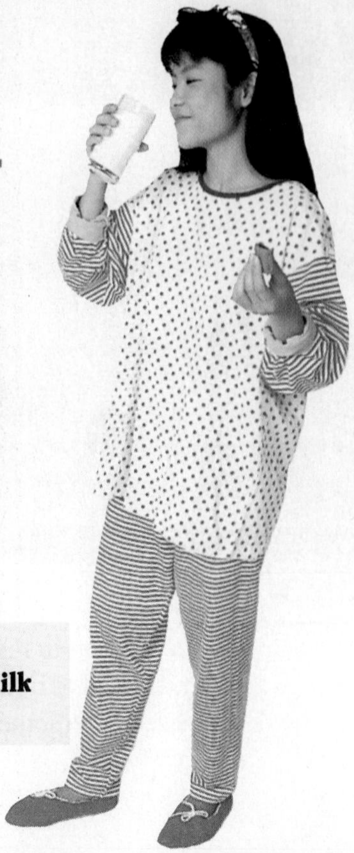

**Do you ever have trouble getting to sleep? A small snack, such as skim milk and a cookie, may help.**

## Exercise Regularly

Exercise is essential to good health. It firms and tones your muscles, including the heart. It can help you sleep better at night and feel more alert during the day.

Different types of exercise benefit you in different ways. A good exercise program includes activities that help improve:

**Strength.** When you force your muscles to work hard at pushing or pulling, they become stronger. Examples of ways to build strength include push-ups, chin-ups, lifting weights, and using strength-building machines.

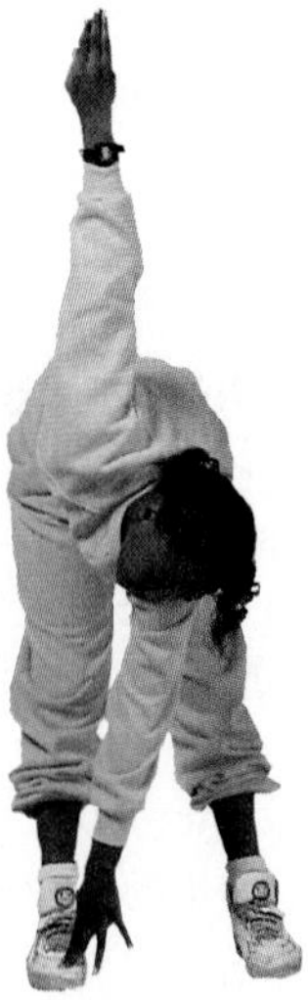

**Flexibility.** Stretching exercises help make your muscles and joints more flexible. Stretching muscles correctly helps prevent injury from other activities.

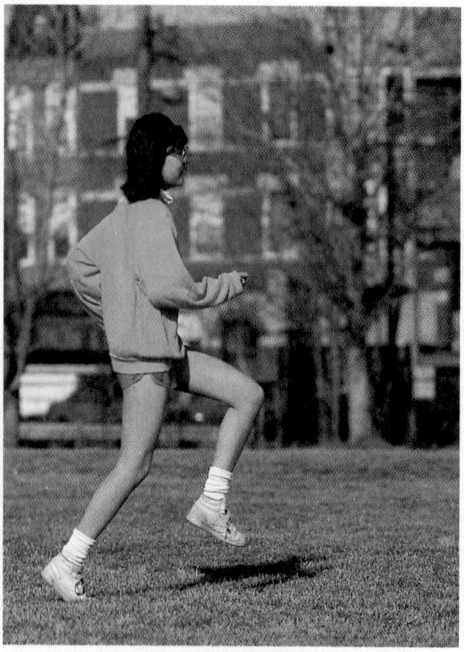

**Endurance.** Endurance is your ability to continue a physical activity for a long period of time. Activities such as running or bicycling build endurance in two ways. First, they train your muscles to work longer before tiring. Second, they are *aerobic* (uh-ROE-bik) exercises. This means they help the body use and take in more oxygen than it normally does. As a result, the heart and lungs work more efficiently. Other aerobic activities include brisk walking, climbing stairs, and aerobic dancing. For the most benefit, exercise vigorously for at least 20 minutes three to five times a week.

In addition to regular exercise sessions, look for ways to become more active every day. Instead of riding an elevator, walk up a flight or two of stairs. If you're watching television, do some stretching exercises at the same time.

## Learn to Handle Stress

Have you ever felt nervous or tense before a test, during a big game, or when meeting someone new? If so, you were feeling stress. *Stress* is emotional and physical tension. It is caused by changes and events in your life and the way you react to them.

Stress is not necessarily bad. It can give you the energy to face a challenge and do your best. However, if stress gets out of control, it can affect your body and your health. For example, being angry or upset can cause you to lose sleep. Negative emotions can also make it hard for your body to digest food.

Stress cannot be avoided—it's part of life. The secret is to learn to handle stress. Although you can't always control what happens in your life, you can control the way you react. For example, some people become angry when they have to wait in line. Others relax and accept the situation.

You can learn to react positively to stressful situations. Here are some suggestions:

- Develop a positive attitude. Look for the good instead of the bad.
- Set reasonable goals and break them into small steps.
- Develop a sense of humor. Laughter helps relieve tension and can help you see the situation in a more positive way.
- Take time out every day for rest and recreation. Visit with a friend, go to a movie, or spend time on a hobby.
- Talk your problems over with a close friend, relative, or counselor.
- Work off your tensions. Any kind of physical activity, such as taking a walk or cleaning out your closet, can help.

**Spending time with friends is a great way to relieve stress. How do you handle the stress in your life?**

## Avoid Harmful Substances

One of the major responsibilities of your wellness program is to avoid using harmful substances. These include:

**Tobacco.** Using tobacco increases the risk of developing a serious disease later in life. Smoking has been linked to cancer, heart disease, lung disease, and other health problems. Chewing tobacco has been linked to cancer of the mouth.

**Alcohol.** Alcohol is a drug that can affect your judgement and reactions. Heavy use can cause liver damage and death. Drinking and driving is a major cause of auto accidents. As a result, innocent victims are injured or killed.

**Other drugs.** Drugs such as marijuana and cocaine can damage your health permanently and even lead to death.

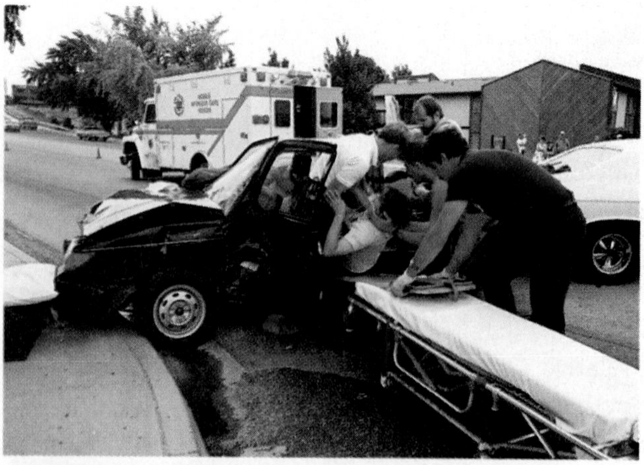

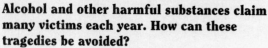

**Alcohol and other harmful substances claim many victims each year. How can these tragedies be avoided?**

**Misused medicines.** What about over-the-counter medicines or drugs a physician prescribes? These can be helpful if taken according to directions. If used incorrectly, they can be dangerous.

**Other harmful substances.** Almost any substance may be harmful if used for something other than its intended purpose. For example, inhaling spray from aerosol cans is dangerous.

Alcohol, tobacco, and other drugs won't make you popular or solve your problems for you. They only create more problems—not just for the user, but for society. Drugs interfere with work and school and can tear families apart. Many drugs are illegal.

When it comes to harmful substances, you have the power to choose. No one can force you to take them. The decision is yours. You have the power to say "NO" to drugs.

# Your Personal Wellness Program

Now that you know the basics of wellness, think about your own habits. Are you doing your best to stay healthy? What changes could you make to improve your wellness?

Right now is a good time to put a wellness plan into action. It's easier to develop good health habits while you're young than to try to change them when you're older.

Before you begin, you may want to discuss your ideas with a health professional. He or she can give you advice about nutrition, exercise, and other parts of your plan.

Remember, you can make choices that lead to wellness. It's never too early to begin planning for good health for the rest of your life.

## Chapter 4 Review

### Check the Facts

1. In your own words, define wellness.
2. Name five elements included in a good wellness plan.
3. What are nutrients? Name three ways the body uses nutrients.
4. Why is sleep essential to good health?
5. What three types of exercise are included in a good exercise program? Give an example of each.
6. What is stress? What causes it?
7. Name at least five ways to react positively to stress.
8. Name four substances known to be harmful to health.
9. Why should harmful substances be avoided? Identify at least three reasons.

### Ideas in Action

1. In small groups, create a commercial promoting one or more elements of a good wellness plan. If possible, videotape your commercial to share with other classes.
2. Brainstorm specific ways teens, in general, can improve their wellness. What are some ways to encourage teens to make healthful changes in their lives?
3. Assume you are an advice columnist for the school newspaper. Write a reply to this letter: "I've been having a hard time concentrating in school lately. I'm tired all the time. Because my schedule is so busy, I often have to skip meals. My grades are starting to slip. Help! What can I do?"

CHAPTER 5

# How Nutrients Work for You

**OBJECTIVES**

**Discover . . .**
- the nutrients and what they do for you.
- food sources of nutrients.
- facts about nutrient supplements.

As you learned in Chapter 4, eating nutritious food is an important part of staying healthy. You have learned that food provides nutrients, which are chemicals the body needs to work properly.

When you eat, your body breaks down the food into liquid through the process known as digestion. As food is digested, nutrients are absorbed into the blood.

What are the different types of nutrients? What does each one do for you? Read on to find out.

## The Nutrient Team

Nutrients work as teams. Each nutrient has certain jobs to do in the body. One nutrient cannot work a miracle. But if a nutrient is missing, it can keep the rest of the team from working. Think of a football team. Each player has a specific job to do as part of the teamwork. If one of the players is missing or doesn't do the job, the team breaks down.

So far, over 40 nutrients have been discovered. Scientists continue to look for other nutrients or new facts about known nutrients.

All of these nutrients can be grouped into a few basic types. They include carbohydrates (car-bow-HIGH-drayts), proteins (PRO-teens), fats, vitamins, and minerals. Fiber and water are also essential for good health.

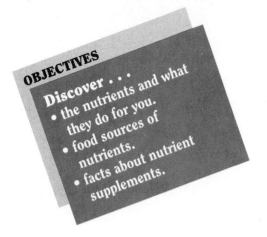

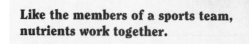

**Like the members of a sports team, nutrients work together.**

# Carbohydrates

*Carbohydrates* are starches and sugars. They come mostly from plant foods, such as fruits, vegetables, legumes, and grains. They are your body's main source of energy.

Carbohydrates also help your body use protein and fat efficiently. If you don't eat enough carbohydrates, your body uses proteins and fat for energy. That means they can't do their regular jobs.

There are two types of carbohydrates: simple and complex.

## Simple Carbohydrates

*Simple carbohydrates* are known as sugars. Sugars are found naturally in small amounts in some foods, such as fruits, vegetables, and milk.

Foods such as candy, soft drinks, cookies, jams, and jellies contain large amounts of added sugar. They are high in calories and provide few other nutrients. A balanced diet includes only a small amount of added sugars.

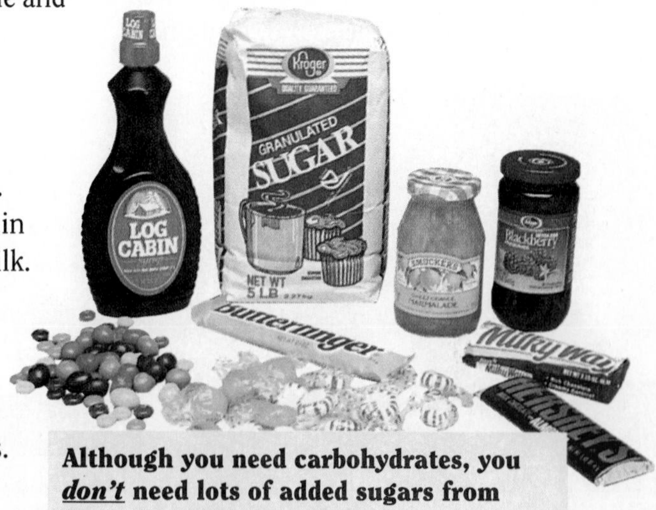


**Although you need carbohydrates, you *don't* need lots of added sugars from foods like these.**

## Complex Carbohydrates

*Complex carbohydrates* are also known as starches. For good health, you should eat lots of complex carbohydrates each day. Good food sources include:

- Dry beans and peas.
- Other starchy vegetables, such as potatoes and corn.
- Rice, grits, pasta, oatmeal, and cornmeal.
- Breads and cereals.

All of these foods supply not only complex carbohydrates but also other nutrients, such as vitamins and minerals.

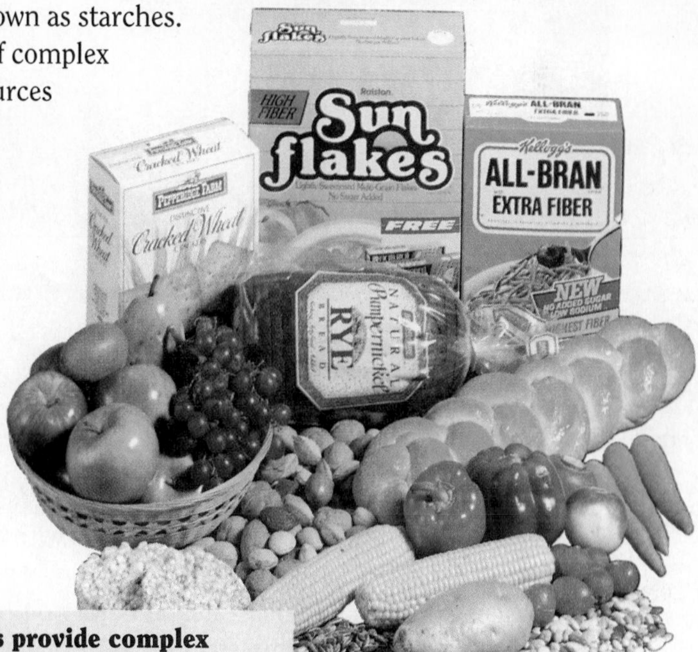


**Which of these foods provide complex carbohydrates? Which are natural sources of simple carbohydrates?**

# Proteins

*Proteins* are substances that the body uses to build new cells and repair injured ones. They are necessary for growth and to help you to fight off disease.

Proteins are made up of *amino acids*. You can think of amino acids as building blocks that combine to make different kinds of protein.

So far, 22 amino acids have been discovered. Of these, the body can make 13. The other 9 are called essential amino acids because the body must get them from food.

Proteins in food are either complete or incomplete, depending on the kind of amino acids they contain.

- *Complete proteins* contain all the essential amino acids in the right amounts. Foods from animal sources, such as meat, poultry, fish, eggs, and dairy products, are complete proteins.

- *Incomplete proteins* lack one or more of the essential amino acids. Foods from plant sources are incomplete proteins. Dry beans, dry peas, grains, and nuts have more protein than other vegetables and fruits.

You can get complete protein from plant foods by combining them in the right way. Combine cooked dry beans or peas with a grain product, nuts, or seeds. For example, serve cooked dry beans with bread or rice. The two foods may be combined during the same meal or eaten at different times of the day.

You can also get complete protein from plant foods by eating some animal protein with them. Macaroni and cheese is an example.

# Fats

Why do you need fats? Fats supply chemicals called essential fatty acids. You need these for healthy skin, healthy cells, and other bodily functions. In addition, fat transports some vitamins. It also keeps food in your stomach longer so you don't feel hungry as quickly.

Your body stores fat as a reserve supply of energy. This stored fat also insulates you from heat and cold and cushions vital organs. Your body makes this fat from any extra amounts of carbohydrate, protein, and fat that you eat.

Most people eat much more fat than the small amount they need. Butter, margarine, and oils are all fats. Fat is also hidden in many foods, such as meat, fish, poultry, eggs, dairy products, nuts and seeds, and baked goods.

**Sometimes it's easy to see fat, like butter on bread. However, many foods, such as these, contain hidden fat.**

## Cholesterol

*Cholesterol* is a fat-like substance that helps the body carry out its many processes. Your body makes all the cholesterol it needs.

High levels of cholesterol in the bloodstream are linked with heart disease. For this reason, health experts advise eating less cholesterol in foods.

Cholesterol is found only in foods from animal sources: meat, poultry, fish, egg yolks, and dairy products. It is not found in any foods from plant sources.

**Scientists have found that a certain type of fatty acid—found in some fish, such as salmon and mackerel—appears to help protect against heart disease. This may explain why natives of North Arctic, whose diets include lots of fish, tend to have a low rate of heart disease.**

## Saturated and Unsaturated Fats

The level of cholesterol in the blood is also affected by the types and amounts of fats that are eaten.

**Saturated fats** are usually solid at room temperature. They tend to raise the amount of cholesterol in the blood. Saturated fats are present in all animal foods and in the tropical oils: coconut, palm and palm kernel. Of all the animal meats, fish tends to have the least amount of saturated fats.

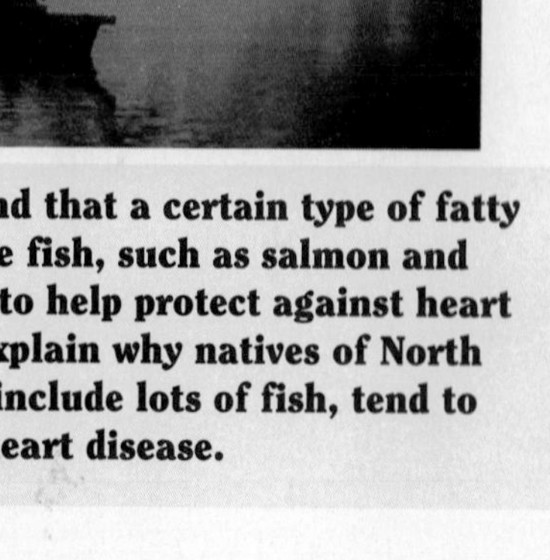

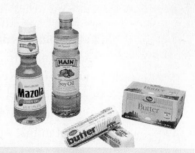

**Which of these fats are more highly saturated?**

**Unsaturated fats** are usually liquid at room temperature. They are found mainly in vegetable oils, except the tropical oils. They tend to help lower the amount of cholesterol in the blood.

**Hydrogenated oil** is oil that has been turned into a more solid fat. In the process, it becomes more saturated.

Health experts advise people to eat less fat of any kind. The fat that is eaten should be mainly unsaturated.

## Vitamins

Vitamins are chemical mixtures found in many types of foods. Vitamins themselves do not provide energy or become a part of the body. Instead, they help carbohydrates, proteins, fats, and minerals work properly. If you don't get enough vitamins, you may eventually develop poor health.

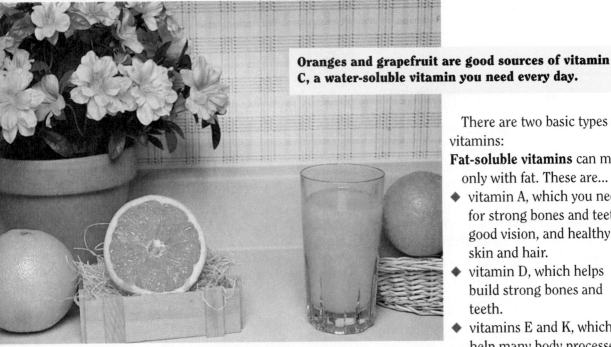

**Oranges and grapefruit are good sources of vitamin C, a water-soluble vitamin you need every day.**

There are two basic types of vitamins:

**Fat-soluble vitamins** can mix only with fat. These are...

- vitamin A, which you need for strong bones and teeth, good vision, and healthy skin and hair.
- vitamin D, which helps build strong bones and teeth.
- vitamins E and K, which help many body processes.

**Water-soluble vitamins** can mix only with water. Most cannot be stored by the body, so you need to be sure you eat foods containing these vitamins every day. The water-soluble vitamins are...

- vitamin C, which helps you build and maintain a healthy body, fight infection, and heal wounds.
- B vitamins, which help your body get energy from carbohydrates and help keep nerves and muscles healthy. They include riboflavin, thiamine, niacin, $B_6$, $B_{12}$, and folate.

## Minerals

Like vitamins, minerals are found in a wide variety of foods. Later on in this book you will learn which vitamins and minerals are found in specific foods.

Your body uses minerals for many processes. The minerals also become a part of the human body—cells, fluids, muscles, and bones.

Here are some of the minerals you need:

**Calcium and phosphorus** work together, along with vitamins D and A, to help you build strong bones and teeth. They also help keep other parts of the body healthy.

**Iron** works with protein to make sure that your red blood cells carry oxygen to all parts of your body.

**Potassium and sodium** are needed for keeping the water balance in your body. Potassium is also needed for a normal heartbeat.

**Dairy products and green, leafy vegetables, like many other foods, provide minerals.**

Your body also needs small amounts of many other minerals. These include copper, iodine (EYE-uh-dine), magnesium (mag-NEE-zee-um), manganese (MANG-guh-neez), selenium (suh-LEE-nee-um), and zinc.

## Water

Water is essential for life. The human body can live a long time without many other nutrients, but only a few days without water.

Health experts recommend drinking 6 to 8 glasses of water a day. This includes beverages that contain water, such as fruit juice. That amount, plus the water that is found in foods you eat, will replace the amount that you lose every day through breathing, perspiration, and waste.

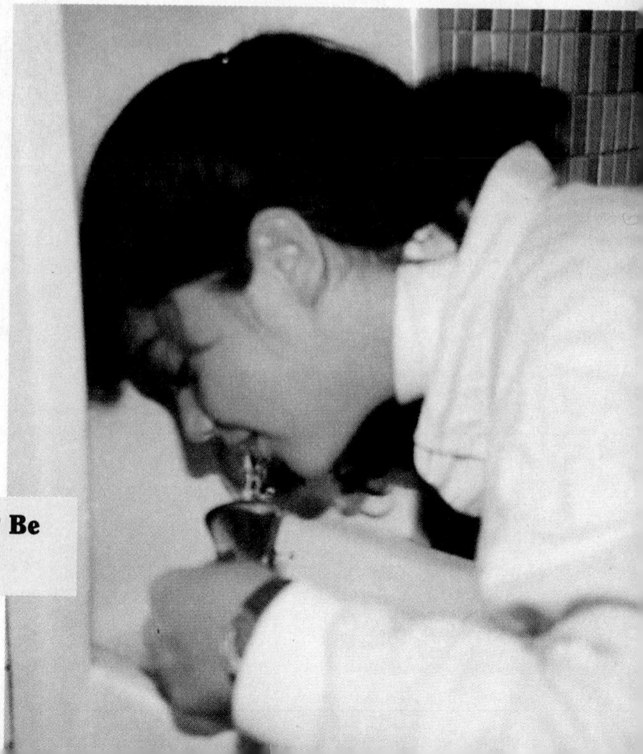

**How much water do you drink throughout the day? Be sure you get plenty.**

## Fiber

*Fiber* is a mixture of plant materials that do not break down completely during digestion. Good sources of fiber include:

- Fruits and vegetables, especially those with edible skins and seeds.
- Dry beans and peas.
- Whole-grain breads, cereals, and other products.
- Nuts and seeds.

**Whole-grain cereals help provide the fiber you need each day.**

Fiber is an important part of a healthy diet. One type, called insoluble fiber, is needed for a healthy digestive system. It is found mainly in whole-grain products, such as wheat bran. Another type, called soluble fiber, is found in fruits, vegetables, dry beans and peas, and some grains, such as oats. Some studies show that soluble fiber may help lower the level of cholesterol in the blood. Researchers are studying other possible benefits of fiber.

# How Much of the Nutrients Do You Need?

The body needs a certain amount of each nutrient. The exact amount depends on the individual. For example, a baby, a 14-year-old girl, and a 50-year-old man need different amounts of nutrients.

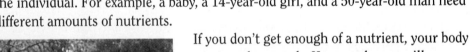

If you don't get enough of a nutrient, your body cannot work properly. You may become ill.

What happens if you get too much of a nutrient?

- Extra amounts of carbohydrates, proteins, or fat are turned into body fat.
- Some vitamins and minerals are stored by the body. Large amounts can create a health problem.
- The body may get rid of some extra vitamins and minerals as waste.

**Your nutrient needs depend on your age, how active you are, and whether you are male or female.**

Researchers have developed standards that give the recommended amounts of certain nutrients. These amounts are called the Recommended Dietary Allowances (RDA). They are used mainly by health professionals.

How can you make sure you are getting the right amounts of each nutrient? The easiest way is to follow the simple guidelines explained in the next chapter.

## Nutrient Supplements

Nutrients occur naturally in food. Many are also available in the form of supplements, such as pills, powders, and liquids.

A physician or dietitian may recommend supplements for specific health reasons. For example, people who are allergic to milk may need to take a supplement.

Most people, however, do not need supplements. If you eat a wide variety of nutritious food, you should be able to get all the nutrients you need. Supplements can be a waste of money because the body may just get rid of the extra nutrients.

## Chapter 5 Review

### Check the Facts

1. What are the basic types of nutrients? Name at least one function and one source of each.
2. Describe the difference between simple and complex carbohydrates.
3. Why are some protein foods considered incomplete?
4. Explain the difference between saturated and unsaturated fat.
5. Name at least two fat-soluble and two water-soluble vitamins.
6. Identify two possible benefits of including fiber in the diet.
7. Is there any advantage to taking in more nutrients than your body needs? Explain.
8. Does everyone need to take nutrient supplements? Why or why not?

### Ideas in Action

1. In small groups, prepare the script for a radio or TV commercial convincing people of the importance of nutritious food. Present your commercial to the class using music or other media to help make your point.
2. Discuss reasons why teenagers often develop poor eating habits. How can attitudes about eating be changed?
3. Assume you are an investigative reporter for a well-known newspaper. Write an article on the pros and cons of nutrient supplements.

CHAPTER 6

# What Are Food Guides?

**OBJECTIVES**

**Discover . . .**
- the purpose of food guides.
- how the Dietary Guidelines for Americans can guide your food choices.
- how to use the Daily Food Guide.

Nutrition experts study how the food you eat affects your health. Their findings are used to develop *food guides*—simple guidelines to help you make healthy food choices. Following these guidelines can help you stay healthy and perhaps even improve your health.

There are many different kinds of food guides. Two of the most commonly used have been developed by the U.S. government. They are the Dietary Guidelines for Americans and the Daily Food Guide.

## What Are the Dietary Guidelines?

You can make more healthful food choices by following six simple rules listed in the Dietary Guidelines. They are:

**Dietary Guidelines for Americans**

1. Eat a variety of foods.
2. Maintain healthy weight.
3. Choose a diet low in fat, saturated fat, and cholesterol.
4. Choose a diet with plenty of vegetables, fruits, and grain products.
5. Use sugars only in moderation.
6. Use salt and sodium only in moderation.

These guidelines are for healthy Americans, ages 2 years and over. They are not for younger children and infants, who need different amounts of food.

On the following pages are some ideas to help you understand and use the Dietary Guidelines.

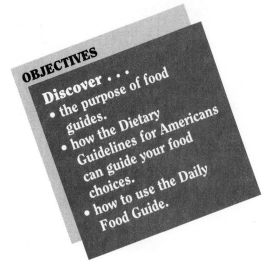

**Food guides can help you eat right for good health.**

## Variety Is Important

Why is it important to eat a variety of foods? First, it insures getting the nutrients you need. No single food can supply all nutrients in the right amounts.

Variety also makes eating more fun. Think of food as an adventure in eating. Try new foods regularly and look for different ways to prepare familiar foods. You may discover a delicious taste treat.

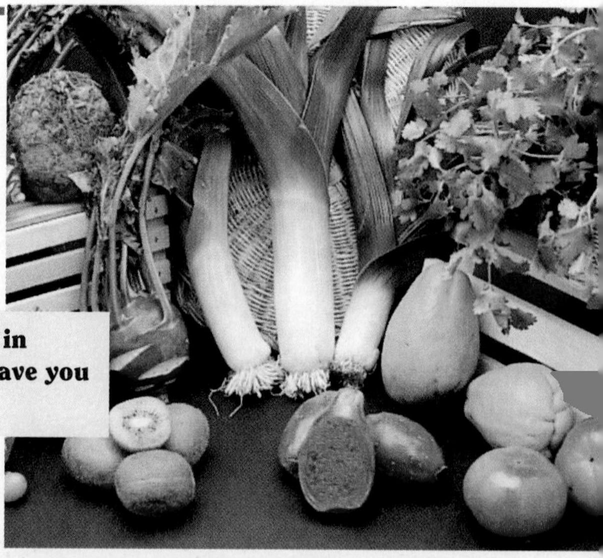

**Think of food as an adventure in eating. Try new foods often. Have you ever tasted any of these?**

## Maintaining a Healthy Weight

Health experts have studied how people's weight is related to their health. They believe that weighing too much or too little creates a greater risk of health problems.

Reaching and maintaining a healthy weight is a matter of energy balance. As you learned in Chapter 4, food provides energy for your body. Your body uses the energy for all its activities. The energy supplied by food and the energy your body uses are both measured in calories. The balance between the two affects your weight.

**Food and activity calories balance.** If you eat the same number of calories you use during the day, your energy balances. Your weight stays the same.

**Not enough food calories.** If you use more calories during the day than you eat, your energy doesn't balance. If this keeps up over time, you lose weight.

**Too many food calories.** If you eat more calories than your body can use, your energy doesn't balance. You have more energy than you need. Your body turns the extra energy into fat and stores it for future use. If this keeps up, you gain weight.

## What Weight Is Right for You?

**Regular exercise can help you reach and maintain a healthy weight.**

Your physician can tell you whether your weight is within a healthy range. Remember that at your age, you are probably growing taller and adding muscles to your body. It's normal for you to gain weight.

Some people try to lose weight in unhealthy ways. For example, they may eat very little or only a few types of foods. Remember, your body needs food for more than just energy. You need a variety of foods to supply important nutrients. You also need a certain number of calories each day just to stay healthy.

If you need to lose weight, your physician or a nutritionist can give you a plan for doing so. A healthy weight loss plan includes eating sensible amounts of nutritious foods. To change your energy balance, become more active. You might try going for a walk each day or joining an exercise class.

## Balancing Carbohydrate, Fat, and Protein

What is the right balance of carbohydrate, fat, and protein in a healthful diet? Health experts recommend that:

- At least 55% of all the calories you take in should come from carbohydrates.
- No more than 30% of all the calories you take in should come from fats. Most of these should be unsaturated rather than saturated.
- About 15% of all the calories you take in should come from protein.

These goals apply to food chosen over several days. They do not apply to a single meal or food.

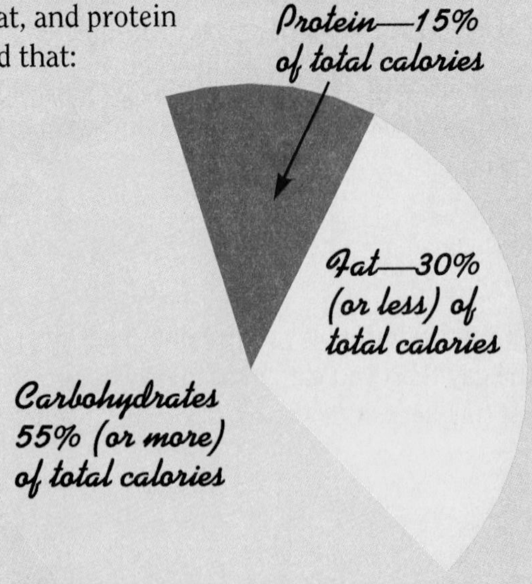

## Fats, Cholesterol, and Your Health

The third Dietary Guideline recommends choosing a diet low in fat, saturated fat, and cholesterol. Why? With a low-fat, low-cholesterol diet, there is less risk of certain serious health problems, such as heart disease and cancer.

In addition, a high-fat diet could cause you to gain too much weight. That's because fat is higher in calories than carbohydrate or protein. One gram of fat has 9 calories, while a gram of carbohydrate or protein has 4 calories.

Most people in this country eat more fat than is recommended. (See the box on the opposite page.) How can you cut down on fats?

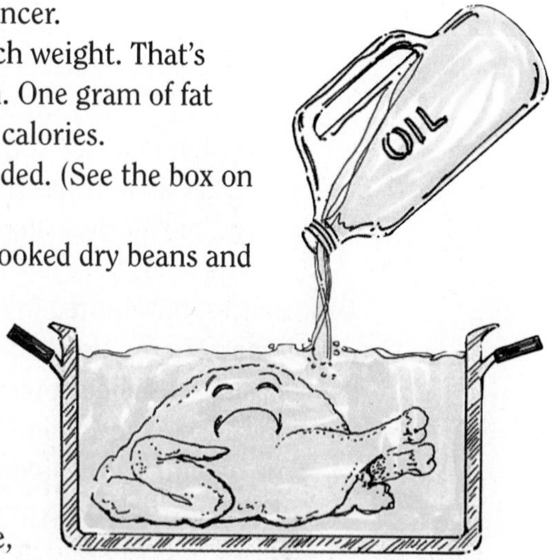


- Choose low-fat foods, such as skim milk, lean meat, and cooked dry beans and peas. (As you study different kinds of food in this book, you will learn more about making low-fat choices.)
- Read labels. Compare the amount of fat in foods you buy.
- Choose cooking methods that add little or no fat. For example, baked chicken is lower in fat than fried chicken.
- When eating, use only small amounts of butter, margarine, sour cream, salad dressings, and other fats.

## Why Vegetables, Fruits, and Grain Products?

The fourth Dietary Guideline recommends choosing a diet with plenty of vegetables, fruits, and grain products. Why? One reason is that these foods are high in carbohydrates.

Most people in this country do not eat enough carbohydrate-rich foods. Instead, they eat more protein than they need and too much fat. By simply eating more vegetables, fruits, and grain products, you can go a long way toward bringing your diet into a more healthful balance. Vegetables, fruits, and grain products are also good sources of vitamins, minerals, and fiber.

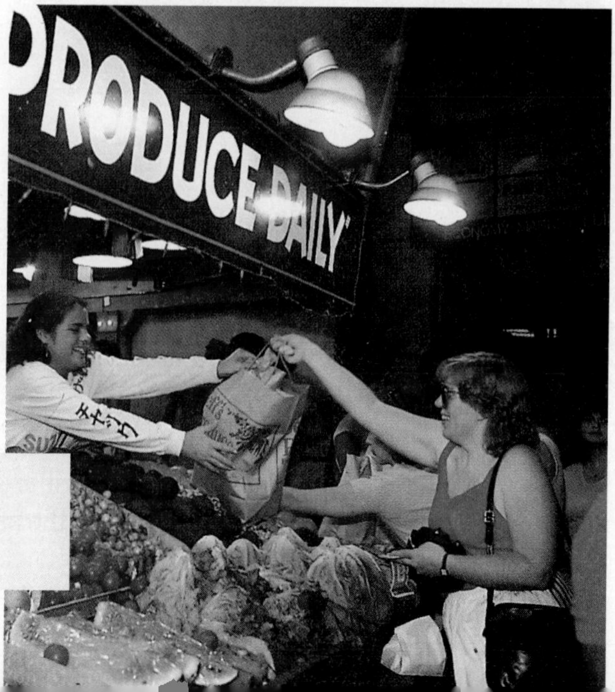


**How could you add more fruits, vegetables, and grain products to your daily meals and snacks?**

## Sugars and Nutrient Density

As you learned in Chapter 5, sugars are simple carbohydrates. Some sugars occur naturally in foods such as fruits, vegetables, milk, and grains. Other foods, such as candy or sweetened cereals, contain large amounts of added sugar.

The fifth Dietary Guideline is "Use sugars only in moderation." This tells you that foods high in added sugar should be eaten only occasionally or in small amounts. Why? The answer has to do with *nutrient density*—a way of relating the amount of energy, or calories, supplied by a food with the nutrients it provides.

Some foods have low nutrient density. This means they are relatively high in calories, but limited in important nutrients. They are not good sources of complex carbohydrates, protein, fiber, vitamins, or minerals. Foods with a high nutrient density are good sources of these nutrients.

Compare a lean hamburger patty with a candy bar. Both have about 200 calories. The hamburger is high in protein, B vitamins, and iron. The candy bar is not high in any nutrients except sugar and fat. Which has a higher nutrient density? You're right if you said the hamburger.

Sugary foods often have a low nutrient density. If you eat too many of these foods, you may not get enough of the nutrients you need. You may also gain too much weight.

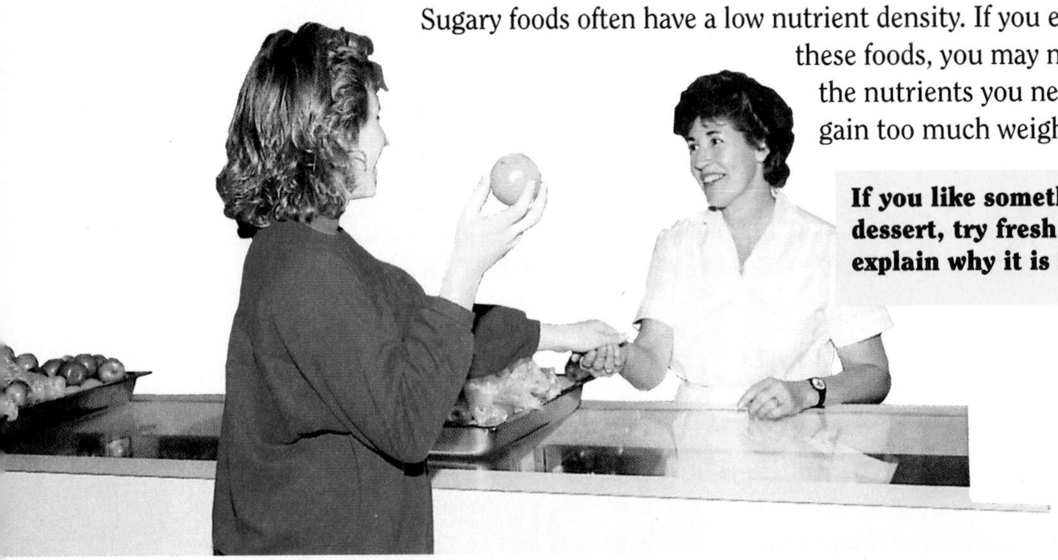

**If you like something sweet for dessert, try fresh fruit. Can you explain why it is a good choice?**

To cut down on sugar, use less at the table. When you buy foods, read the list of ingredients on food labels. Look for any of the names listed below. They are all sugars.

◆ sucrose ◆ brown sugar ◆ raw sugar ◆ dextrose ◆ fructose ◆ maltose
◆ honey ◆ syrup ◆ corn sweetener ◆ molasses ◆ high-fructose corn syrup

Are any of these sugars the first or second ingredient listed? Does the list include several of them? In either case, the product is high in sugar.

## Salt and Sodium

The sixth Dietary Guideline is "Use salt and sodium only in moderation." Eating too much sodium is believed to be linked to high blood pressure. Most Americans eat more salt and sodium than they need. Processed foods provide most of the sodium. It is also found in table salt.

How can you eat less salt and sodium?

- Try not to add salt to food when you eat.
- Use as little salt as possible in cooking. With foods such as vegetables, meats, soups, and stews, you can usually omit salt or cut down on the amount. Try flavoring with pepper or herbs instead.
- Limit processed foods such as canned soups, instant foods, and frozen dinners. When you do use these foods, compare labels. Choose ones lower in sodium.
- Use only small amounts of highly salted foods, such as crackers, pretzels, nuts, mustard, and pickled foods.

**There are many ways to flavor foods without using salt.**

# What Is the Daily Food Guide?

A second tool for choosing food is called the Daily Food Guide. It gives you a general pattern for daily food choices.

The Daily Food Guide organizes foods into five main groups, shown on the next two pages. It also tells you how many servings you need each day from each food group.

Each of the food groups provides some, but not all, of the nutrients you need. No one food group is more important than another. For good health, you need them all.

# The Daily

## Breads, Cereals, Rice, and Pasta

6 to 11 Servings

**What Is a Serving?**

- 1 slice of bread
- ½ cup cooked cereal, rice, or pasta
- 1 ounce ready-to-eat breakfast cereal

**Key Nutrients**

In general, foods in this group are a good source of:

- Carbohydrates
- B vitamins
- Minerals
- Fiber

## Vegetables

3 to 5 Servings

**What Is a Serving?**

- 1 cup leafy raw vegetables, such as lettuce or spinach
- ½ cup all other vegetables, cooked or chopped raw
- ¾ cup vegetable juice

**Key Nutrients**

In general, foods in this group are a good source of:

- Carbohydrates
- Vitamins, especially vitamins A and C
- Minerals, such as iron and magnesium
- Fiber

## Fruits

2 to 4 Servings

**What Is a Serving?**

- A medium whole fruit, such as an apple or banana
- ½ cup of chopped, cooked, or canned fruit
- ¾ cup of fruit juice

**Key Nutrients**

In general, foods in this group are a good source of:

- Carbohydrates
- Vitamins, especially vitamins A and C
- Minerals, such as potassium
- Fiber

# Food Guide

## Meats, Poultry, Fish, Dry Beans and Peas, Eggs, and Nuts

**2 to 3 Servings**

The total amount of these servings should equal 5 to 7 ounces of cooked lean meat, poultry, or fish per day.

**What Is a Serving?**

- Count 2 to 3 ounces of cooked lean meat, poultry, or fish as a serving. A 3-ounce serving of meat is about the size of an average hamburger.
- The following equal 1 ounce of lean meat:
  ½ cup cooked dry beans
  1 egg
  2 Tbsp. peanut butter

**Key Nutrients**

In general, foods in this group are a good source of:

- Protein
- B vitamins
- Minerals, such as iron and zinc

## Milk, Yogurt, and Cheese

**2 to 3 servings**

- 3 servings for teenagers, young adults to age 24, and women who are pregnant or breastfeeding
- 2 servings for most other people

**What Is a Serving?**

- 1 cup milk or yogurt
- 1½ ounces of ripened cheese
- 2 ounces of process cheese

**Key Nutrients**

In general, foods in this group are a good source of:

- Protein
- Vitamins
- Minerals, especially calcium

# Using the Daily Food Guide

Fats, oils, and sweets are not part of any of the food groups. Use them sparingly.

The Daily Food Guide makes healthy eating simple. As long as you eat the recommended number of servings from each group, you are probably getting the right balance of nutrients.

Some foods don't fit into any of the five main food groups. They are grouped together as "Fats, Oils, and Sweets." These foods include salad dressings and oils, cream, butter, margarine, sugars, soft drinks, candies, and sweet desserts. Most people should use them in very small amounts.

## Food Mixtures

Many of the foods you eat each day are mixtures, such as pizza. How do these fit into the Daily Food Guide?

Mixtures contain foods from several groups. For instance, pizza has a crust made from grain, a sauce made from tomatoes, and assorted toppings which may include cheese, meat, and vegetables. It contains foods from four of the five food groups, all except the Fruit Group.

Pizza is an example of a food mixture. What others can you think of?

When you add up your servings for the day, think of a food mixture in terms of its separate parts. Estimate how many servings from each food group the food provides.

## How Many Servings Are Right for You?

In the Daily Food Guide groups, the number of servings is given as a range. The number of servings right for you depends on your age, your physical condition, how active you are, and whether you are male or female.

Almost everyone should have at least the lowest number of servings in the ranges. Most teenage girls would need the number of servings in the middle of the range. Teenage boys may need the highest number of servings, especially if they are active.

## Choosing Foods from the Daily Food Guide

The Dietary Guidelines and the Daily Food Guide work together as a team. You are also part of the team. You are responsible for choosing healthful foods in each food group.

Use the Dietary Guidelines to help you make the proper choices from the Daily Food Guide. Remember to:

- Choose a variety of foods from within each group. All the foods in a group do not contain the same kinds or amounts of nutrients. For example, one day your choices from the vegetable group might include carrots, lettuce, and broccoli. The next day you might choose spinach, tomatoes, and corn.
- Choose nutrient-dense foods low in fat, saturated fat, cholesterol, sugar, and sodium.

## Chapter 6 Review

### Check the Facts

1. What is the purpose of food guides? How are they developed?
2. Name the Dietary Guidelines and tell why each one is important.
3. Identify four ways to reduce the amount of fat in your diet.
4. What is nutrient density? Name three foods that have high nutrient density and three foods that have low nutrient density.
5. List the five main groups included in the Daily Food Guide.
6. Name at least two nutrients provided by each food group.
7. What is the benefit of using the Daily Food Guide?
8. How can you determine the number of servings you need from each food group?

### Ideas in Action

1. Discuss the relationship between diet and health. How does food affect your physical health? In what ways can developing healthful eating habits now benefit you in the future?
2. With a partner, use the Daily Food Guide and the Dietary Guidelines to plan meals and snacks for one day for each of the following individuals:
   - Jennifer, an eighth grade girl active on the track team.
   - Hans, a seventh grade boy who manages the school football team.
   - Cicily, a high school junior who would like to lose ten pounds to achieve a healthier weight.

CHAPTER 7

# Making Healthful Food Choices

**OBJECTIVES**

**Discover . . .**
- what affects your food choices.
- how to tell the difference between food fact and fiction.
- how to evaluate and improve your food choices.

Throughout the day, you make many food choices. Even if your meals are prepared for you, you still decide whether or not to eat them. How healthful are your food choices? This chapter will help you find out.

People sometimes believe that healthful foods don't have a good flavor. The truth is, healthful foods are tasty and fun to eat. Even more important, they can help you look and feel good, give you the energy you need to do your best, and help you grow into a healthy adult.

## What Affects Your Food Choices?

What makes you choose the foods you eat? You might say it's because you enjoy the flavor. That's just part of the answer. Your food choices are also affected by:

**Your lifestyle.** The patterns of your daily life influence the food you eat. For example, if you are always on the go, you are more likely to eat meals that can be prepared and eaten quickly.

**Your priorities and values.** Many people today place a high priority on good health. They look for nutritious, low-fat foods.

**Your family and culture.** Many of your food likes and dislikes begin at home. You may love the way your family prepares chicken and refuse to eat it any other way. On the other hand, you may dislike certain vegetables because your family dislikes them. Perhaps you have a favorite dish that is part of your cultural heritage.

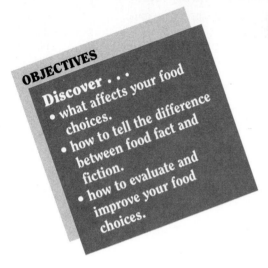

**What are some of your favorite foods?**

**Your friends.** Do you enjoy going out with friends for a snack? When a group gets together, food is usually an important part of the activities. People within a group often eat the same kind of food.

**Trends and technology.** New developments affect the choices you have. The next time you are at a supermarket, notice how many different products for the microwave oven you see. Before the microwave oven was introduced, none of these choices were available.

**How do other people influence the food choices you make?**

**Advertising.** Have you ever had a craving for a candy bar or fast-food burger because you saw it on TV? Advertisements appear in a wide variety of places—in newspapers and magazines, on television and radio, and on buses and trains. Advertising's main goal is to sell the product, whether it's nutritious or not.

# Food Fact and Fiction

Information about food and nutrition is everywhere. You can pick up a magazine or newspaper and find recipes and shopping advice. A friend may tell you about a great new diet that will make you lose weight or gain muscle. And of course, there are advertisements for hundreds of products, each claiming to be the best.

Even news reports can be confusing. Almost every week you can read or hear about new studies of food and health. A particular food may seem to be a "miracle cure" one day, then dismissed as worthless or even harmful the next. Sometimes it may seem as though nothing is safe to eat.

How can you find your way through all this confusion? Use your thinking skills and decision-making ability to evaluate the information.

## Making Sense of Claims and Information

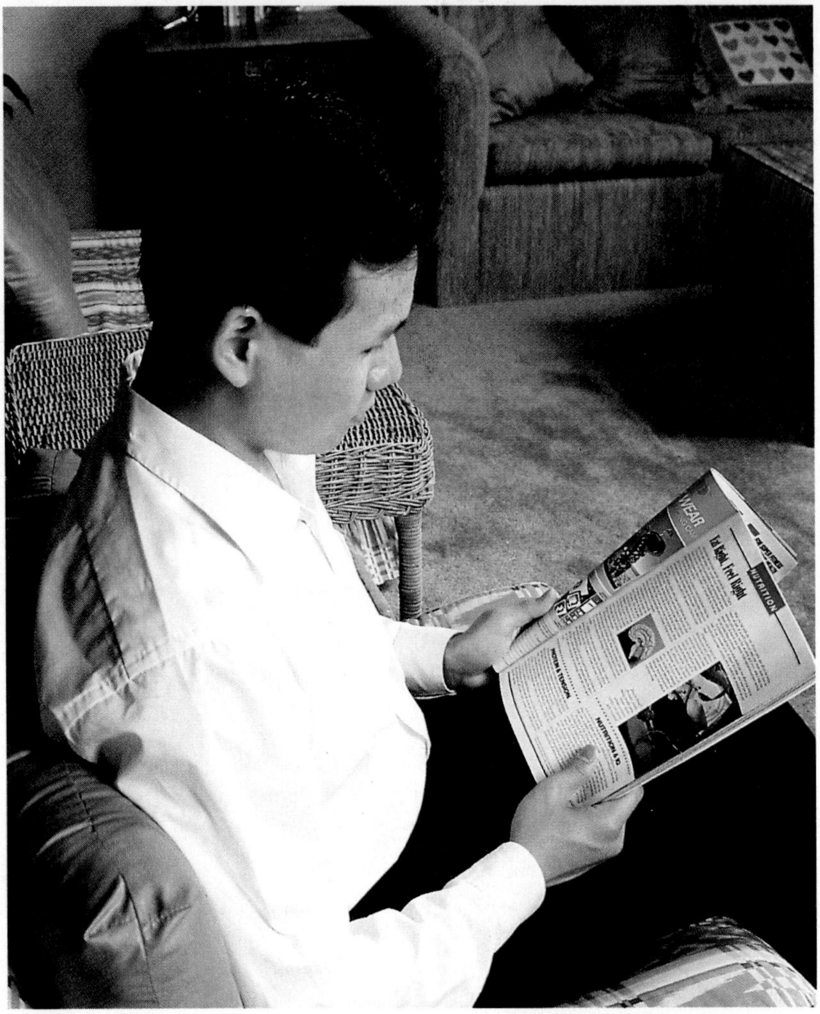


**Think carefully about what you read. Is it fact or just a theory? How reliable is the source?**

- Think critically about the claims being made. Ask yourself whether they fit in with what you already know about food and nutrition. For instance, a snack may claim that it gives you the fiber you need for good health. The truth is, all fruits, vegetables, and whole-grain products supply fiber. By eating a variety of these foods every day, you can get all the fiber you need.
- Consider the kinds of foods being promoted. Are they healthful foods, or are they high in fat, sugar, or sodium? How expensive are they?
- Realize that news reports are often based on the early results of just one study. More studies must be done before researchers can agree on the results and on what they mean for you.

If you're still confused, how can you get the facts? Good sources of information include:

- A physician or school nurse.
- A home economics teacher.
- A registered dietitian or a nutritionist.
- Guidelines from an official source, such as the Dietary Guidelines for Americans and the Daily Food Guide.

# Evaluating Your Choices

How do you make the right food choices? Begin by taking a look at the food choices you make now. Everyone makes both good and poor food choices throughout the day. Focus on the good choices. Then work at replacing poor food choices with better ones.

## What Do You Eat?

There are many ways to keep track of what you eat. You can write down all your food choices and use charts or even computer software to evaluate them. However, it's not necessary to go to all that trouble every day. Just take a few moments to review your food choices.

At the end of the day, think about what you ate. Also think about the food you have eaten for the past few days. Did you get enough servings from each of the food groups? Did you follow the Dietary Guidelines?

Don't worry if your diet isn't "perfect" every day. By getting into the habit of reviewing your food choices regularly, you can balance your choices over several days. If you miss some servings from one of the food groups one day, just be sure you choose those foods the next day.

Two keys words to remember are variety and moderation. As you know, variety helps you get all the nutrients you need from different types of foods. Moderation simply means avoiding extremes. It doesn't mean you have to completely give up favorite foods that are high in fat, sugar, or sodium. Just eat them less often and in smaller amounts.

**Think about all the food choices you make during a typical day. How good are your choices overall? How can you improve them?**

## When Do You Eat?

When you evaluate your food choices, also think about the type of meal pattern you follow. A *meal pattern* refers to how many meals and snacks are eaten throughout the day and when they are eaten.

Most people eat three basic meals a day—in the morning, at midday, and in the evening—and perhaps a snack or two. Some, however, prefer to eat smaller meals more often. For instance, they may eat six very small meals instead of three larger ones.

Are you so busy with school and other activities that you don't take time to eat? Skipping meals can be harmful to your health. Your body may not get the nutrients it needs. As a result, you may feel tired and dragged out. Also, at the next meal, you may be so hungry you eat more than you really need.

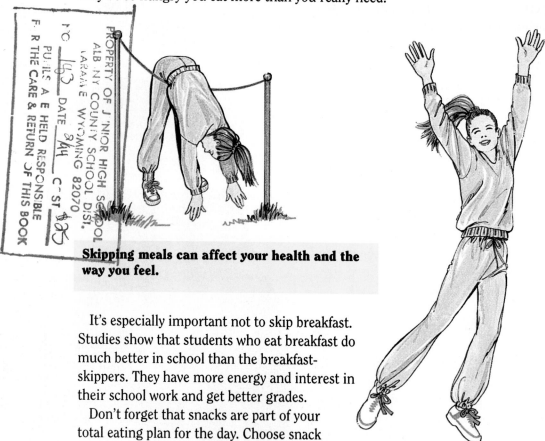

**Skipping meals can affect your health and the way you feel.**

It's especially important not to skip breakfast. Studies show that students who eat breakfast do much better in school than the breakfast-skippers. They have more energy and interest in their school work and get better grades.

Don't forget that snacks are part of your total eating plan for the day. Choose snack foods that will fit in with your healthful eating plan. You'll find ideas for nutritious snacks in Chapter 36.

## Where Do You Eat?

After reviewing your food choices, you may discover that where you eat makes a difference in the kinds of choices you make. Thinking about different eating situations can help prepare you to make better choices.

## Choices at Home

How do today's busy lifestyles affect the choices you have when eating at home?

Many meals are prepared and eaten at home. Different families handle meal preparation in different ways. For example, family members may prepare meals together or take turns.

When family members have busy schedules, there may be times when they are on their own for meals. Perhaps you are sometimes in this situation. If so, think about your resources and the choices available to you. Should you snack on whatever you find in the kitchen? Have a pizza delivered? Go to a friend's house? Pop a frozen meal in the microwave?

After taking this course, you will have another resource—the knowledge and skills to prepare a simple, nutritious meal on your own. You will also be better able to evaluate your options. You can use your decision-making skills to choose the best option in terms of time, money, and nutrition.

## Choices Away from Home

At school, you can buy nutritious foods in the cafeteria or bring them from home. Either choice is more healthful than buying candy and soft drinks from a vending machine.

Another place where you make food choices is the supermarket. Chapter 8 will give you tips for smart shopping.

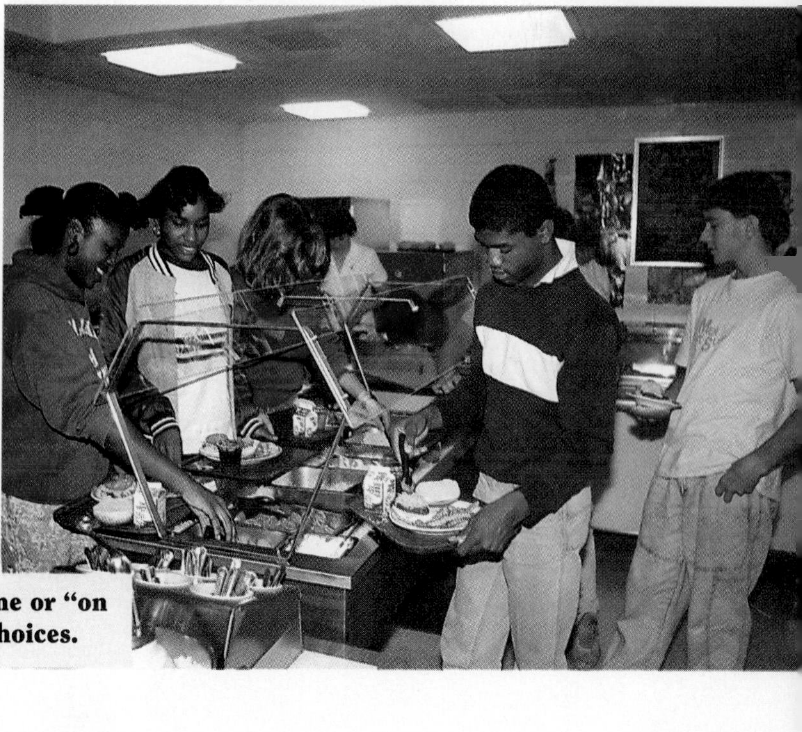

**How often do you eat away from home or "on the run"? Look for nutritious food choices.**

## Eating in Restaurants

Today many restaurants, including fast-food places, are providing choices for health-conscious customers. Still, following the Dietary Guidelines and the Daily Food Guide when eating out can be tricky. Here are some tips:

**Sometimes eating out is a special occasion. What if you decide to splurge on a high-fat meal or sugary dessert? Make up for it by eating healthfully the rest of the time.**

- Look for signs or leaflets that tell you about the nutrition of each menu item.
- Choose low-fat items if they are available. Some examples might be a salad with low-calorie dressing, baked or broiled chicken instead of fried, and a plain baked potato.
- If you don't know how a menu item is prepared or what it includes, ask.
- Ask for items to be prepared without high-fat or high-sodium toppings, such as mayonnaise or tartar sauce.
- Remember to balance your restaurant meal with other food eaten during the day. For example, if the menu doesn't include fresh fruit, have an extra serving at another meal.

# Meeting Individual Needs

People's needs for food and nutrients differ. One reason is that everyone goes through a life cycle. You have already moved from babyhood to childhood to the teen years. All along the way, your food needs changed. They will continue to change slightly as you grow older.

Some people have a health concern, such as diabetes, that affects the kind and amount of food they can eat. They follow a special diet prescribed by a physician or a nutritionist.

Some people are vegetarians. They do not eat any animal foods. Vegetarians need to carefully balance the types of foods they eat to be sure they are taking in all the necessary nutrients. If you choose to be a vegetarian, discuss the matter with your home economics teacher, a physician, or a nutritionist. They can help you make healthful food choices.

## Food for Athletes

Athletes often believe that more protein, vitamins, and minerals will help them perform better. However, studies show that they can get enough of these nutrients just by making healthful food choices.

Athletes do have some special needs. Because they use so much energy, they need lots of carbohydrates. Complex carbohydrates, such as breads, cereal, pasta, rice, and potatoes, are the best sources. Athletes also need plenty of water to replace the water lost during strenuous activity.

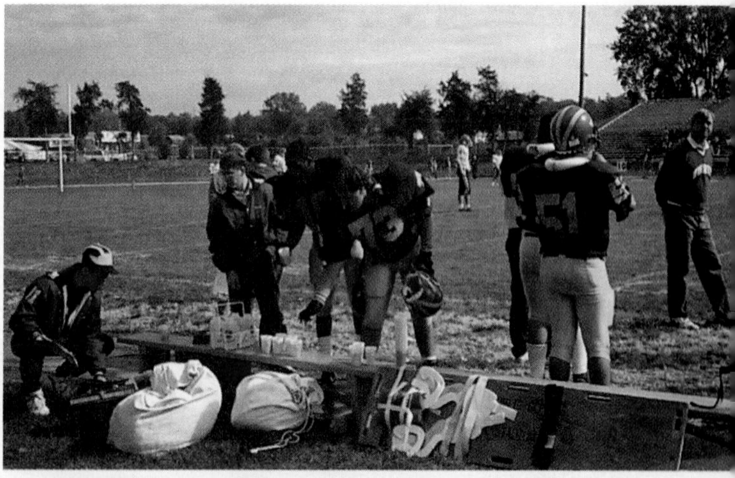

**Athletes need a balanced diet with plenty of carbohydrates and water.**

# It's Up to You

How can you improve your choices? Think about what you eat, where, and when. Consider your individual needs. Then use your management skills to come up with a plan.

Remember, wherever and whenever you eat, you have the power to choose. Because you make your own decisions, you can control your daily food choices. Will you make healthful food choices? It's all up to you!

## Chapter 7 Review

### Check the Facts

1. Name six influences on your food choices. Give an example showing how your choices might be affected by each.
2. How can you decide whether information about food and nutrition is accurate? Suggest at least three different ways.
3. Name two benefits of reviewing your food choices every few days.
4. What is a meal pattern?
5. Identify at least four ways to make healthful food choices when eating out.
6. List at least two ways individual needs are a consideration when making food choices.

### Ideas in Action

1. Brainstorm healthful food choices for teen athletes.
2. Conduct a slogan contest promoting healthful food choices for your school. Prizes for the best slogan may include a free school lunch or an invitation to a healthful meal in the foods classroom.
3. Develop a personal checklist for evaluating your own food choices.
4. In small groups, write a flyer to help other teens make wise food choices. Include healthful tips found in the chapter. If possible, distribute flyers at your school.

CHAPTER 8

# Shopping for Food

**OBJECTIVES**

**Discover . . .**
- how to plan your food shopping.
- how to use food labels and other consumer information.
- how to shop wisely.

If you are like most teens, you shop for food fairly often. It may be just to get snacks for you and your friends, or you may buy food for your entire family.

Shopping for food is more than just going to the supermarket. It means using your management skills to plan ahead, get information, and make wise decisions. That way, you will make the most of your time and money. You will get the best nutrition and quality in the food you buy.

## Plan Your Food Shopping

Before you shop, several important decisions need to be made. How much can you spend? Where and when will you shop? What will you buy?

### Consider Your Budget

Most families decide on a specific amount to spend on food each month. Before you go shopping, talk with other family members about your food budget.

The cost of food depends on many factors, such as the weather, the time of year, and the costs of packaging and transportation. Many nutritious foods are inexpensive. With careful planning, you can have appealing and nutritious meals on a limited budget.

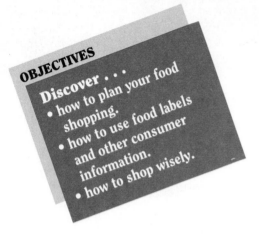

**Shopping skills can help you get the most for your money.**

## Where Will You Shop?

Depending on where you live, you may be able to choose from several kinds of food stores.

**Food stores differ in the selection of items they carry and how they are displayed.**

**Supermarkets** have a great variety of foods attractively displayed. Many offer extra services.

**Discount or warehouse stores** are similar to supermarkets, but food is often displayed in cardboard boxes. Prices are usually lower.

**Co-ops** require you to pay a membership fee. The co-op buys food in large quantities and sells it at low prices to its members.

**Convenience stores** are smaller and usually more expensive than supermarkets.

Compare food stores in your area. Choose a store that is clean, sells good quality food, and offers a good selection. Decide whether you are willing to pay more for convenience and service. If you decide to shop at several stores, be sure it is worth the extra time, effort, and expense.

## When Will You Shop?

How often you buy food depends on your schedule and the amount of storage space you have at home. In most cases, making many trips to the store during the week takes extra time and energy. It's usually more efficient to plan ahead and make one major shopping trip.

Try to shop when the store is not crowded. Avoid shopping when you're hungry. Hungry shoppers often buy more than they need to.

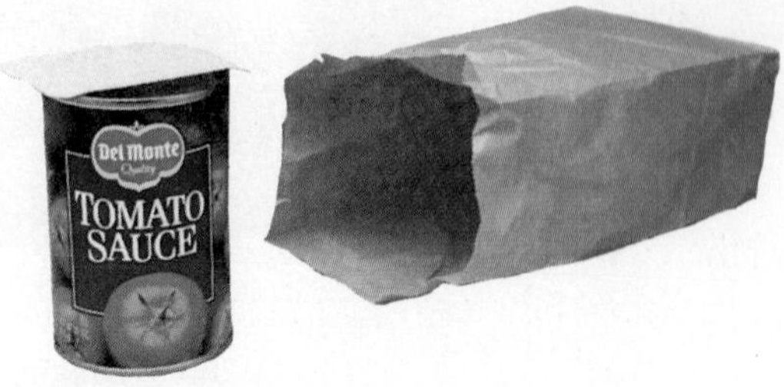


**How do frequent shopping trips waste resources?**

# What Will You Buy?

Have you ever stopped to think about the many different forms of food that are available? For example, you can buy fruit that is fresh, canned, or dried.

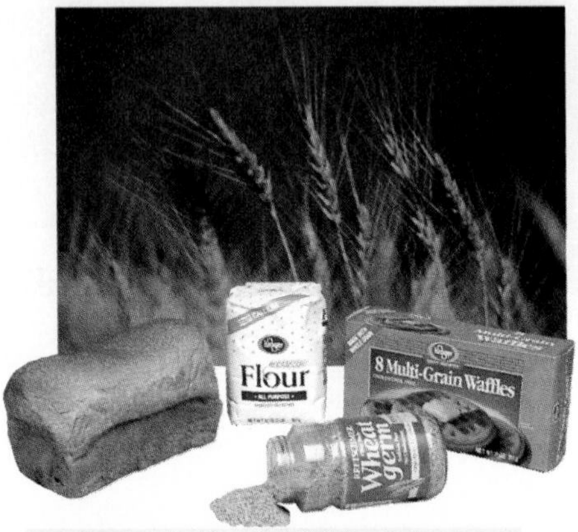


**Food processing turns raw wheat into products you can buy in the store.**

Different forms are available because of different processing methods. *Processing* includes all the steps that are taken to prepare and package food for sale.

Foods may be processed for several reasons, such as:

- To make them safer to eat or drink.
- To make them easier to use.
- To lengthen the time they can be stored.
- To add nutrients or put back nutrients that have been lost. Foods with added nutrients are called *enriched* or *fortified*.
- To turn the food into a particular product. For example, wheat is processed to make flour and breakfast cereal.

## Convenience Foods

Foods that have been processed to make them more convenient to store or use are called convenience foods. The choices range from canned tomato sauce to mashed-potato mix to a complete frozen meal.

In today's fast-paced world, it's tempting to use many convenience foods. There are, however, other points to consider besides speed and simple preparation:

- As food is processed, it loses nutrients. Labels can help you compare the nutritional value of foods.
- Most convenience foods are high in sodium. Many are also high in sugar and fat.
- Convenience foods often cost more. Compare prices.

**Convenience foods are more highly processed than fresh foods. What are the advantages and disadvantages of using the convenience forms?**

It's fine to use some convenience foods, as long as you choose wisely. However, if most of the foods you eat are highly processed, it's difficult to follow the Dietary Guidelines. You need other foods, such as fresh fruits and vegetables, for good health.

# Make a List

Making a shopping list is one of the most important steps in buying food. When you make the list:

- Plan the meals and snacks you are going to prepare. (Chapter 20 gives tips for meal planning.)
- As you plan, consider what foods you already have and need to use up. Check supermarket ads in the newspaper to see what foods are on sale.
- Use your plan to make a list of the foods you need to buy.
- Check your supply of staples—basic foods that you always keep on hand, such as flour and milk. Add them to the list if needed.
- If you clip and save coupons, look through them to find any you may be able to use on this trip.

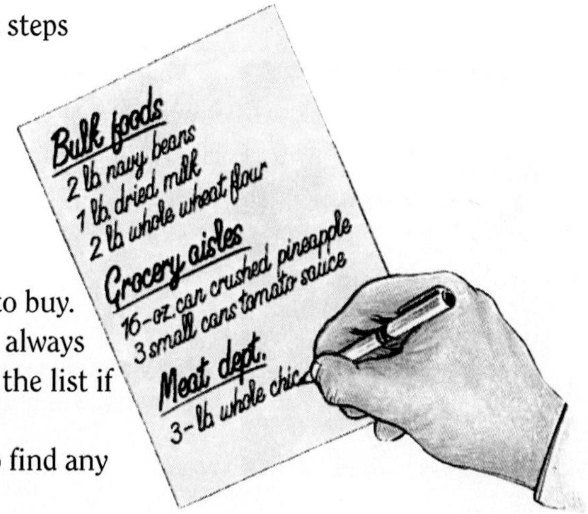


## Organize Your List

An orderly list helps speed your shopping. Group items on your list according to the areas of the store, such as:

**Grocery** section—canned, bottled, boxed, and packaged foods that can be stored at room temperature.

**Bulk foods**—unpackaged grocery items kept in large bins. You use a scoop to put the amount you want into a bag. Foods such as flour, dry beans, and dried fruits are sold this way in some stores.

**Produce**—fresh vegetables and fruits.

**Refrigerated** cases—dairy products, juices, and fresh meat, poultry, and fish.

**Frozen** foods.

**Delicatessen (deli)**—hot and cold ready-to-eat foods.

**Supermarkets are divided into specialty departments. Learning the layout of stores where you shop can help save you time.**

# Understanding Consumer Information

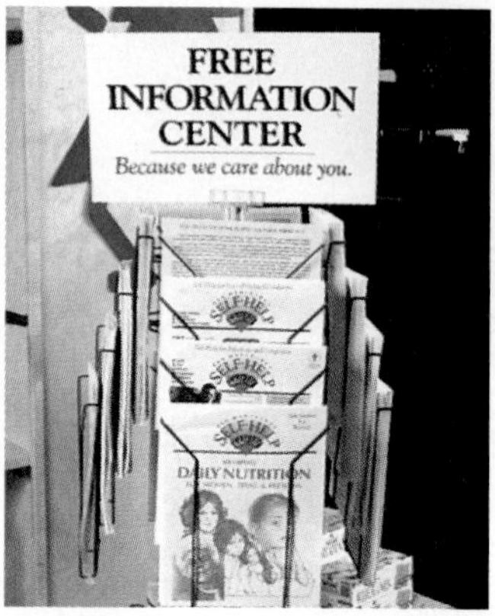


When you go to the store, you will find several types of information for consumers—shoppers like you. Unit pricing, open dating, and food labels can help you get the best value for your food dollar.

**Many supermarkets offer information, recipes, and coupons. Take advantage of these helpful extras.**

## Unit Pricing

**Which of these packages has a lower unit price?**

Many stores help customers by posting the unit price of items. The *unit price* is the cost per ounce, pound, item, or other unit of measure. For instance, a can of pineapple weighing 8 ounces might cost 56 cents. The unit price would be 7 cents per ounce.

Unit pricing helps you compare the cost of items so you can find the most economical size and brand. If the store doesn't give the unit price, you can figure it out yourself. Divide the price of the item by the number of ounces or other unit. Do the same for other brands or sizes and then compare the unit price for each.

## Open Dating

**How does open dating help shoppers?**

Some food packages have a date stamped on them to help you know whether the food is fresh. For example, the package may say "sell by May 31" or "best if used by June 8." This is called open dating. Look for it on foods such as dairy products, bakery items, and grocery items.

Open dating cannot guarantee the quality of the product. Quality is affected by the way the food has been handled and stored. For example, if fresh milk is stored at an improper temperature, it may lose quality before the date stamped on the package.

# Food Labels

Food labels give you valuable information for making wise choices. Here is a typical example.

***Description***
Read this part of the label to make sure you are getting the product you want.

***Picture of product***

***Quantity***
"Net weight" means the weight of the food itself, not including the package.

***Ingredients***
Ingredients are listed by weight, from the most to the least. Reading the list of ingredients can help you avoid foods you do not want or cannot eat.

***Nutrition information***
Many labels show how many calories the food has and how much of certain nutrients. The calories and nutrients are listed for just one serving.

***Directions***
The label may tell how to store or prepare the food.

***Manufacturer or distributor***

***UPC symbol***
The Universal Product Code (UPC) is used with computerized checkout systems. A scanner "reads" the bars to identify the item. The price is then rung up automatically.

When you read labels, watch out for terms that may be confusing or misleading. For example, "light" may mean that the food is low in fat or calories, or just that it is light in color or texture. When you see terms like this, use the ingredients list and nutrition label to get the facts.

The federal government regulates food labels. New regulations may change the information that must be included on labels.

# Your Shopping Trip

When you get to the store, follow your shopping list. Avoid *impulse buying*—buying an item you don't need just because it seems appealing at the moment.

However, keep your plan flexible. Look for unadvertised specials that could save you money.

**Store displays are designed to encourage impulse buying.**

## Comparison Shopping

**Compare before you buy. Decision-making skills can help you choose which product you want.**

You can find the best values by using comparison shopping. Compare the unit prices and nutrition of:

**Different forms of food.** Fresh green beans may be a better buy than frozen this week. At another time of year the reverse may be true.

**Different brands.** Name brands are nationally advertised. The price you pay for the food includes the cost of advertising. You can often save money by buying products with the store's own brand name on the label. *Generic* products, which have a plain label, are even less expensive.

**Different sizes.** Larger sizes often have a lower unit price than smaller sizes, but not always. Also consider whether you will actually use the larger amount before it spoils. If not, you waste food and money.

## Choosing Quality Foods

Always buy food that is in good condition. Poor quality food wastes money. You will find information about buying specific types of food in Units 6, 7, and 8. In the meantime, here are some general guidelines.

- Avoid containers that are damaged in any way. Give damaged containers to a clerk.
- Be sure refrigerated items feel cold when you buy them.
- Make sure frozen food packages are frozen hard. Ice crystals may mean that the food has thawed and refrozen.
- Buy refrigerated and frozen foods last. Otherwise they will start to get warm as you shop.

**Don't buy damaged packages. Give them to a store clerk.**

## More Shopping Tips

- Be considerate. Don't block traffic by leaving your cart in the middle of the aisle.
- Handle food carefully so you do not damage it. If you choose an item and then change your mind, put it back where it belongs.
- Don't open packages. If packages of meat or produce contain more than you want, ask a store clerk for help.
- Put raw meat and poultry packages in a plastic bag. That will help keep the juices, which may contain harmful germs, from dripping on other foods in your cart.

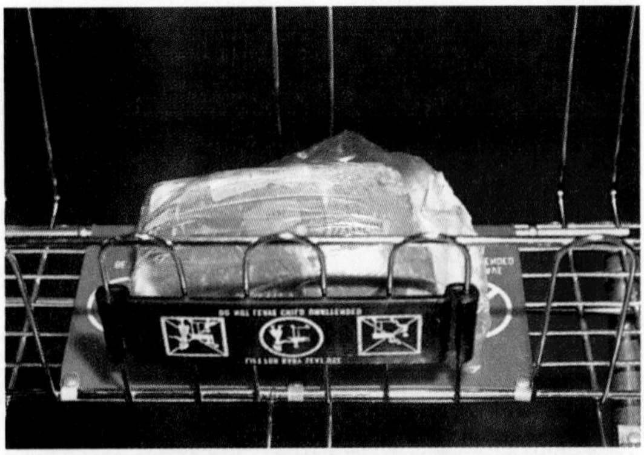

**Be sure meat juices do not drip on other foods, such as fresh fruits and vegetables.**

## After Shopping

After shopping, bring the food home immediately and store it. If you do errands on your way home, food may begin to lose its quality. For instance, frozen food may start to thaw. In Chapter 17 you will learn how to store food properly to keep it safe and fresh.

## Chapter 8 Review

### Check the Facts

1. Name two benefits of using your management skills wisely when shopping for food.
2. What should you consider when deciding where to shop for food?
3. Identify at least two factors that help determine the best time to shop for food.
4. List five reasons foods may be processed.
5. Name two advantages and two disadvantages of using convenience foods.
6. What steps should you follow when preparing a shopping list?
7. Name at least five types of information found on food labels.
8. Name five quality guidelines to follow when buying food.

### Ideas in Action

1. Alisa is buying canned peaches for the family dessert. The 16-oz. can costs $.94, while the 32-oz. can costs $1.39. Determine the unit price of each to help Alisa decide which would be the better buy.
2. Assume you write a column for consumers in a local newspaper. A reader writes in: "I always overspend my food budget and find I often forget to buy the things I need. When I am at the store, I often buy items on impulse. What can I do to improve my food shopping habits?" Write your response based on information in the chapter.
3. Discuss how open dating benefits consumers.

CHAPTER 9

# Using Kitchen Appliances

**OBJECTIVES**

**Discover . . .**

- large and small appliances you can use in food preparation.
- how to use and care for these appliances.

Appliances are some of the resources found in the kitchen. They can help make food preparation easier and faster. Large appliances, such as ranges and refrigerators, are usually kept in one place. Small appliances, such as toasters, can be used wherever there is an electrical outlet.

## Ranges

A range provides heat for cooking food. Most ranges are powered by gas or electricity. A basic range is a single unit that includes a cooktop with heating units, an oven, and a broiler.

**Cooktop.** The temperature of the gas burners or electrical heating elements can be adjusted with dials or push buttons.

**Oven.** In a *conventional oven,* hot air circulates around the pan in the oven. The food cooks on the outside first. As the heat moves to the center of the food, the inside cooks. You can set the oven control to a specific temperature.

**Broiler.** The heating unit is located at the top of the broiler compartment. Food cooks by direct heat flowing downward. The broiler may be in the oven or in a separate compartment.

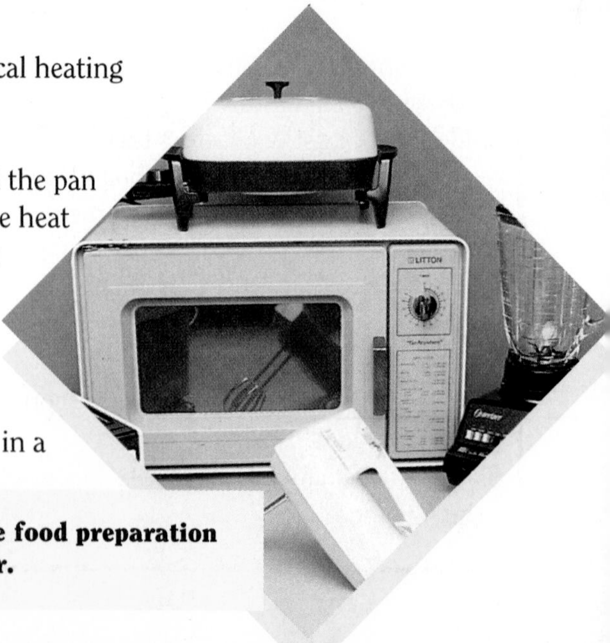


**Appliances make food preparation easier and faster.**

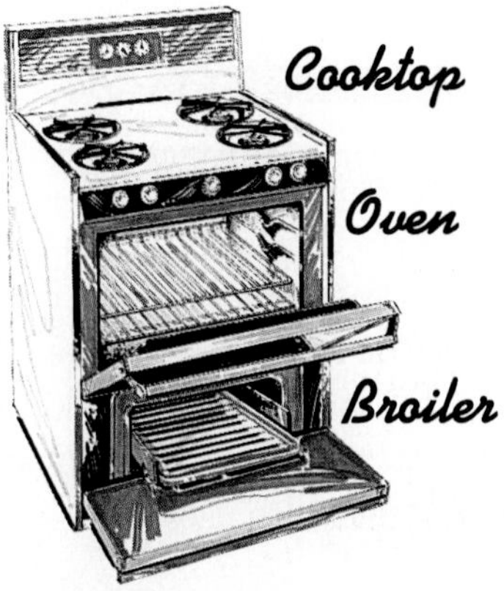


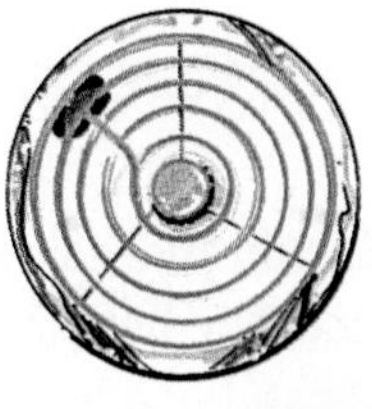

**Does your cooktop have electric heating elements or gas burners?**

**Heat flows upward and circulates around the pan in a conventional oven.**

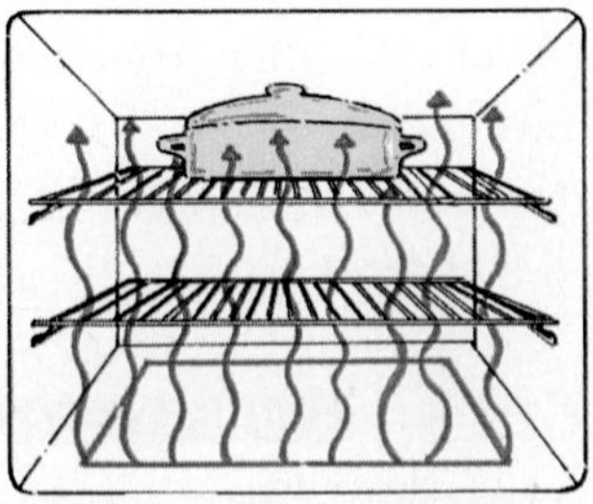

**In a convection oven, fans circulate hot air at high speeds to cook foods more quickly.**

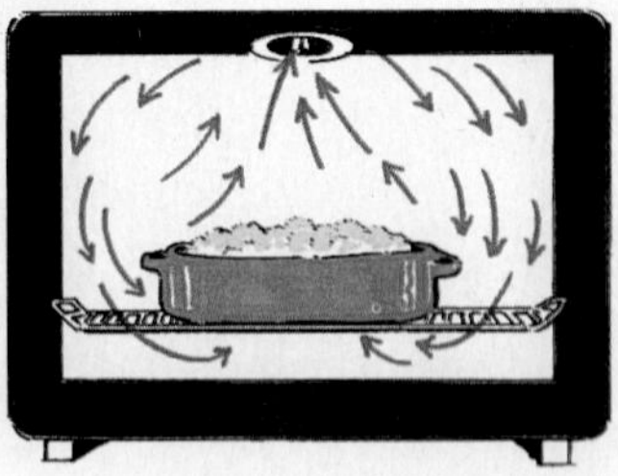

There are many variations on the basic range. For example:

- Some ranges have more than one oven.
- Different types of ovens may be included in a range. Some ranges have a built-in microwave oven (see page 64). Another type is a *convection oven.* This is similar to a conventional oven except that fans circulate the air at high speed. It will cook many foods faster than a conventional oven, but not as fast as a microwave oven.
- The cooktop and the oven may be separate units that are built into kitchen cabinets.

## Use and Care of the Range

Before using any appliance, read the owner's manual. It gives information about safe use and care. Here are some tips for using ranges:

- Match the pan size to the size of the heating element or burner flame. Otherwise, heat is wasted.
- Use pans with flat bottoms. They will not tip over easily.
- Turn the surface unit off before you remove a pan.
- Adjust oven racks to the correct positions before turning on the heat.
- When you open the oven door, stand to one side. This way hot air and steam escaping from the oven won't burn you.
- Wipe up any spills after the range has cooled.

# Microwave Ovens

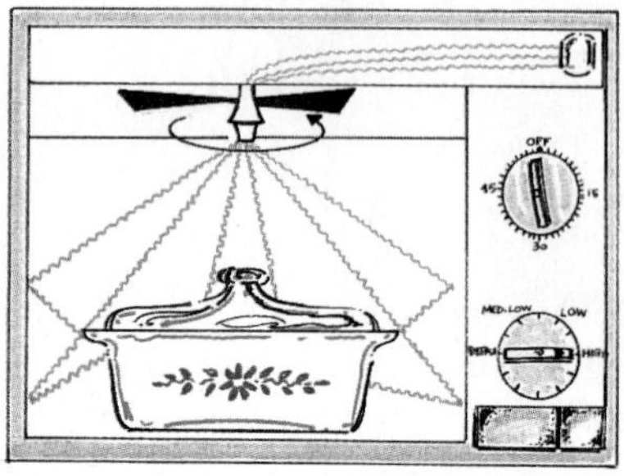

A *microwave oven* cooks with tiny waves of energy called microwaves. The microwave energy causes the molecules in the food to vibrate against each other. This causes friction, which produces the heat that cooks the food. The food cooks on the outside and inside at the same time. This speeds up the cooking process, so most foods cook much faster than in a conventional or convection oven. This faster cooking time also uses less energy.

Microwave ovens vary in size and in the amount of electrical power they use. Maximum cooking power can range from 500 to 700 watts. The higher the power, the faster the oven will cook.

You will learn about using microwave ovens in Chapter 15.

# Refrigerator-Freezers

Refrigerator-freezers store food at cold temperatures. There are two basic types:

**Two-door model.** One door is for the refrigerator, the other for the freezer. The freezer may be at the top, side, or bottom. It is cold enough to freeze fresh foods as well as store those already frozen.

**One-door model.** This type has only one outer door. Inside there is a small freezer section with a lightweight inner door. The freezer section is cold enough to store already frozen foods up to two weeks. It is not cold enough to freeze fresh foods well.

## Use and Care of the Refrigerator-Freezer

Every time you open the refrigerator or freezer door, cold air escapes. The motor comes on to lower the temperature again. To save energy and maintain the proper temperature, keep the door open for as short a time as possible. Decide what you need ahead of time and take the food out all at once. Then close the door right away.

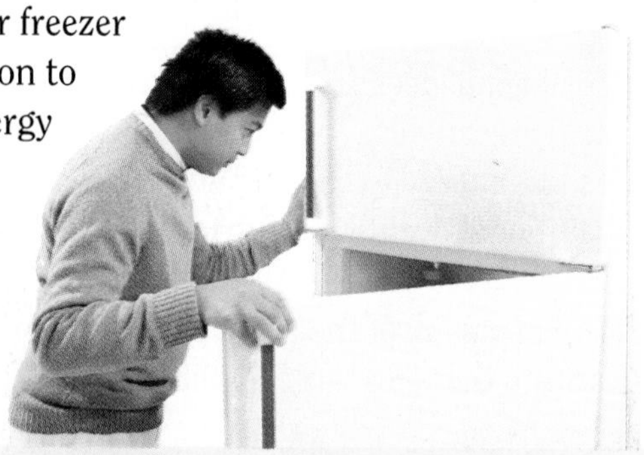

**Don't leave the refrigerator door open while you make up your mind.**

Never cover the shelves of the refrigerator or freezer to keep them clean. If you do, cold air won't be able to circulate properly.

Don't overload the refrigerator or food may spoil. The refrigerator compartment works most efficiently when it is about three-quarters full. However, the freezer compartment works most efficiently when it is full.

Keep the refrigerator-freezer clean. Spills and dirt breed germs. Be sure the containers you put in are clean and wipe up spills immediately. Every few weeks, clean the inside of the refrigerator-freezer thoroughly with baking soda and warm water. The outside can be cleaned with mild detergent and water.

With some refrigerator-freezers, you must periodically remove food from the freezer and allow built-up frost to melt. Follow the directions in the owner's manual.

**An overloaded refrigerator may not be able to keep food cold enough.**

**When frost builds up, the freezer has to work harder and use more energy.**

# Small Appliances

Small appliances are available to help with almost any kitchen job. Many small appliances can help you save energy when cooking a small amount. For example, it takes less energy to bake a potato in a small toaster oven than in a large conventional oven. An electric skillet uses less energy than a burner on an electric range.

Here are some of the more common small appliances. Think about how you could substitute them for large appliances.

**Slow cooker.** Cooks food slowly at low temperatures. A main dish can be prepared in the morning and be ready to eat in the evening.

**Electric skillet.** Does many different cooking jobs. The heat can be set at a specific temperature.

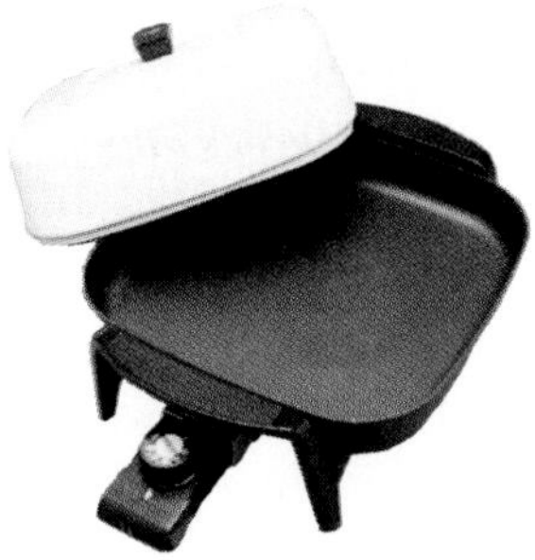

**Toaster.** Toasts bread. Comes in two- and four-slice sizes.

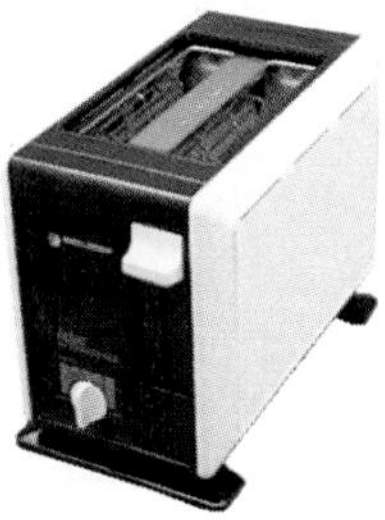

**Toaster oven.** Can be used as a toaster or as an oven. Some models include a broiler.

**Mixer.** Beats and mixes food. Available as a lightweight portable mixer or a heavier model on a stand.

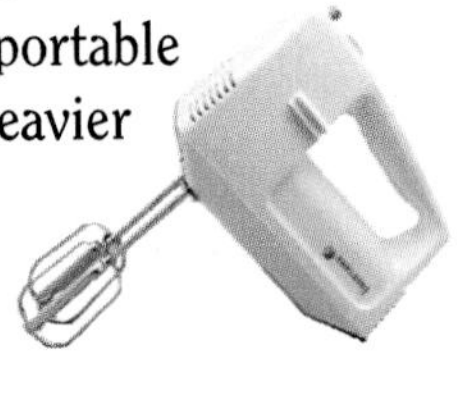

**Blender.** Cuts, grates, chops, minces, blends, and liquifies food quickly.

**Food processor.** Cuts, chops, and slices a wide variety of foods. Can also be used for mixing ingredients and kneading dough.

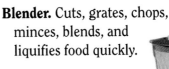

## Use and Care of Small Appliances

Always read and follow the manufacturer's directions carefully. Electricity can give you a shock or start a fire if misused. Refer to the guidelines on page 109 for using electricity wisely. Here are some additional tips:

- Turn the appliance off before plugging it in or unplugging it.
- Always unplug a mixer before putting the beaters in or removing them. Otherwise, the mixer might be turned on accidentally while your fingers are holding the beaters.
- Clean appliances after each use. Unplug them first.
- Do not put an appliance into water unless it is labeled "immersible." You can damage the appliance and create a safety hazard.
- If you get a shock from an appliance, unplug it immediately. Have it repaired.

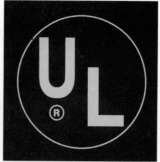

**Look for the UL label. It shows appliances have been tested for safety.**

## Chapter 9 Review

### Check the Facts

1. What are the three main parts of a range? Briefly describe how each part works.
2. Name two differences between a conventional oven and a convection oven.
3. List three tips for use and care of a range.
4. List two benefits of cooking food in a microwave oven.
5. Aside from the number of doors, what is the difference between a two-door refrigerator-freezer and a one-door model?
6. Give four guidelines for use and care of a refrigerator.
7. List at three safety rules for using small appliances.

### Ideas in Action

1. You are the extension home economist for your county. Develop a radio public announcement describing tips for saving energy when using the range and refrigerator.
2. Discuss some pros and cons of buying and using small appliances. What should consumers think about before buying a small appliance? Are some small appliances better than others? Which small appliances do you think are most useful? Least useful?
3. Suppose your lab group has the opportunity to buy two small appliances to use in your kitchen. Your selection needs to be made carefully because you must use these appliances all year. Brainstorm all the preparation needs you can think of. What two appliances would meet your needs most effectively? Why did you choose them?

CHAPTER 10

# Know Your Equipment

**OBJECTIVES**

**Discover . . .**
- some of the equipment you can use for food preparation.
- what the equipment looks like.
- what the equipment is used for.

When you prepare food, you need certain kinds of equipment to help you work easily, successfully, and safely. This chapter will help you learn what equipment is best suited for specific jobs. You will learn about equipment for measuring, cutting, mixing, cooking, and baking.

Remember, these are not the only items needed in a kitchen. For example, you need an apron to protect your clothes from food spots and stains. Potholders and oven mitts protect your hands when working with hot pans. Cleanup equipment also belongs in every kitchen.

## Measuring Tools

The cups and spoons you use daily for eating vary in size. They should not be used for measuring ingredients. For a recipe to turn out right, you need accurate measurements. The amounts given in recipes are based on these standardized measuring cups and spoons. You will learn more about them in Chapter 13.

**Dry measuring cups.**
Used to measure dry and solid ingredients. A basic set includes at least four measuring cups in different sizes.

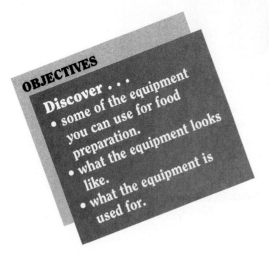

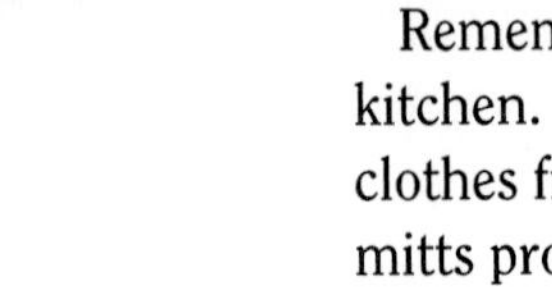

**Each tool used in the kitchen has a specific purpose.**

**Liquid measuring cup.** Made of plastic or glass. Has extra space at the top so liquids can be carried without spilling. Has a pouring spout. Comes in different sizes.

**Measuring spoons.** Used to measure liquid or dry ingredients. A basic set includes at least four spoons in different sizes.

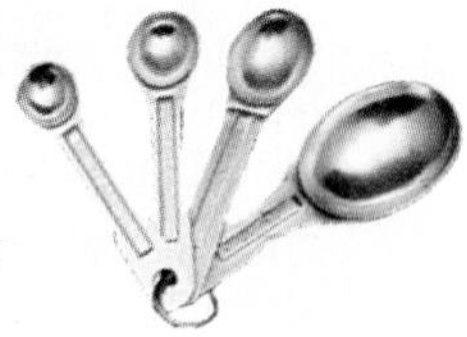

# Cutting Tools

These tools help you cut food into smaller pieces. Each is designed for a particular cutting task. Match the right tool to the job. When knives are kept properly sharpened, they cut more easily and cause fewer accidents than dull ones.

**Cutting board.** Protects countertop or table while cutting. For food safety, use one made of hard plastic. Wooden cutting boards can harbor germs.

**Grater.** Grates food into tiny pieces.

**Peeler.** Removes the peel from fruits and vegetables.

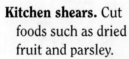

**Chef's knife.** For quick slicing, dicing, and chopping of foods.

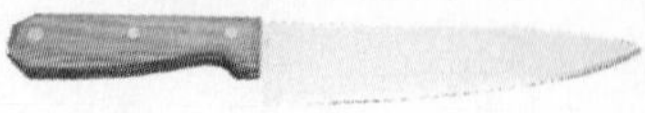

**Kitchen shears.** Cut foods such as dried fruit and parsley.

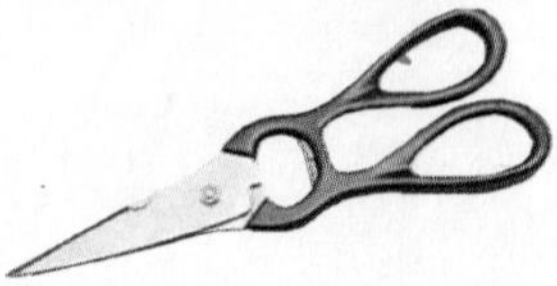

**Utility knife.** All-purpose knife. Cuts and slices many foods, such as fruits and vegetables.

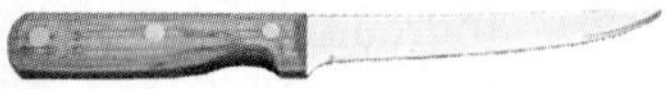

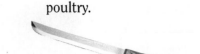

**Slicing knife.** Slices meat and poultry.

**Serrated knife.** Has serrated (sawtooth) edge. Cuts bread and cakes easily.

# Mixing Equipment

This equipment is used for mixing ingredients by hand. You can also mix ingredients with electric appliances, such as a mixer or blender.

**Sifter.** Adds air to flour and other dry ingredients while mixing them. Removes lumps and large pieces.

**Mixing bowls.** Made of pottery, glass, or metal. Come in different sizes.

**Wooden spoon.** Beats, mixes, stirs.

**Wire whisk.** Beats, blends. Especially good for beating egg white mixtures.

**Rotary beater.** Used for light beating, such as beating eggs or pancake batter.

**Pastry blender.** Cuts shortening into flour when making pastry and biscuits.

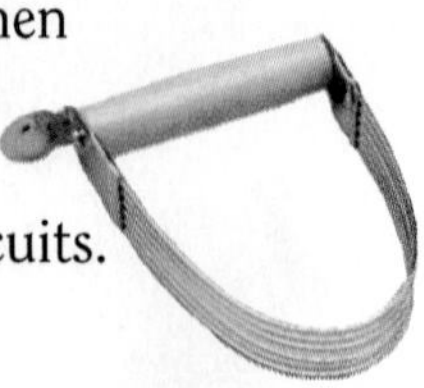

# Cooking and Baking Tools

These tools help you to handle food when you cook and bake. Some tools are designed for use with pans that have a nonstick finish. Such tools are made of plastic or of metal coated with plastic. They don't scratch the finish on the pan.

**Rubber scraper.** Removes food from spoons, sides of bowls, pans, jars, and cans.

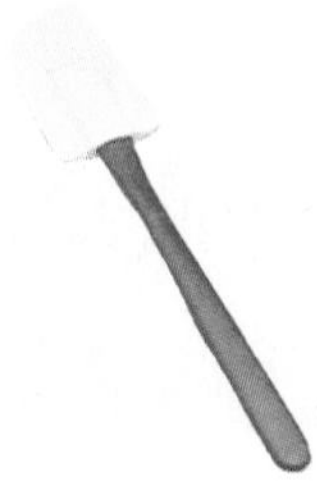

**Spatula.** Levels off dry or solid ingredients when measuring. Loosens baked goods from pans.

**Basting spoon.** Bastes or lifts food. Has a long, heatproof handle.

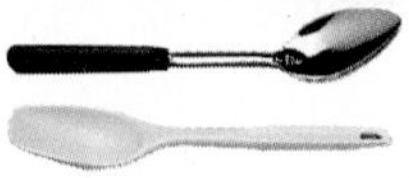

**Slotted spoon.** Drains liquid from food.

**Utility fork.** Lifts or turns food.

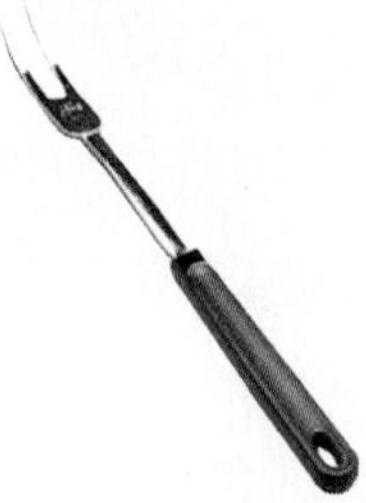

**Tongs.** Lift and turn hot food without piercing it.

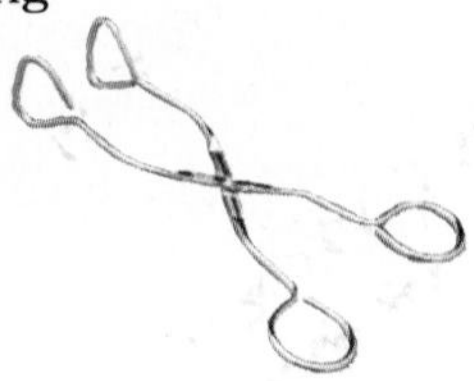

**Ladle.** Used to dip liquid, such as soup, from pan to bowl or cup.

**Turner.** Lifts and turns food, such as pancakes and hamburgers.

**Meat thermometer.** Inserted into roast or poultry. Measures internal temperature to show when food is cooked.

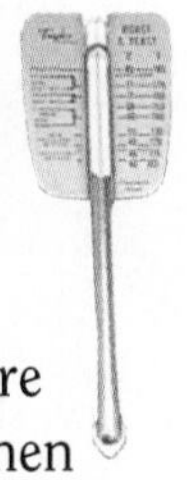

**Rolling pin and cover.** Rolls out dough for pie crust, biscuits, cookies. Cover keeps dough from sticking to the rolling pin.

**Wire cooling racks.** Hold hot food, such as cakes, breads, and cookies, while cooling.

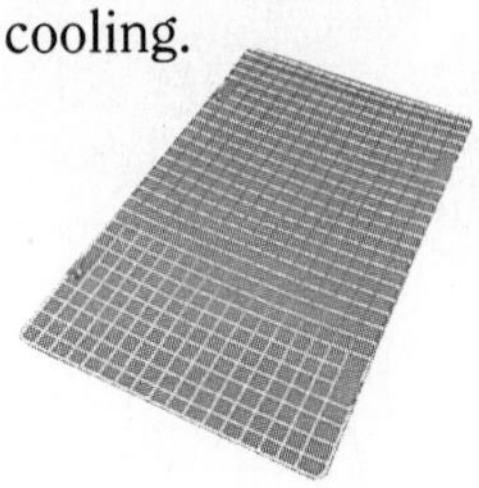

**Colander.** Drains liquid from foods such as cooked spaghetti.

# Cookware

Cookware refers to the wide variety of pans used for cooking and baking. Some cooks have a few basic pieces. Others have special cookware for preparing many different foods.

Cookware is made of various materials. Metal, enamel-coated metal, and glass-ceramic cookware can usually be used on top of the range or in the oven. Pottery and some glass cookware is meant for oven use only. Even some plastic cookware is now ovenproof. Microwave ovens have special cookware needs. You will learn about those in Chapter 15.

Here are the basic types of cookware you should know:

**Saucepans and pots.** Saucepans have one long handle. Pots have two small handles. Both styles come in assorted sizes and usually have matching covers.

**Steamer basket.** Used for steaming food, especially vegetables. Inserted into a pot or pan to hold food above boiling water.

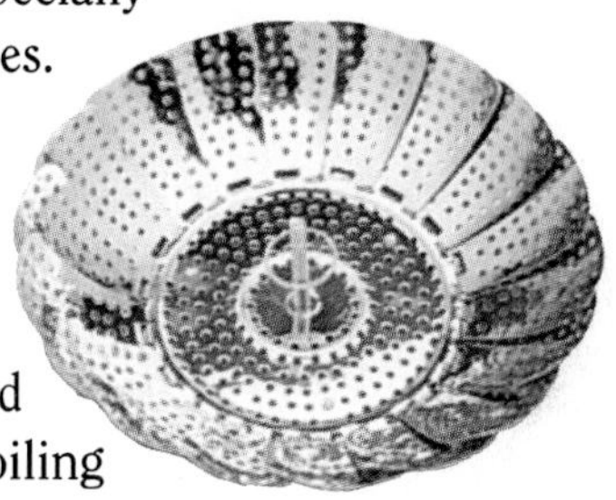

**Skillets.** Also called frypans. Made of metal or glass. Size is usually indicated by the diameter. Some have nonstick finish. Some have matching covers.

**Casseroles.** For baking foods and food combinations. Made of many different materials—glass, pottery, stoneware, glass ceramic. Usually measured by quart or liter sizes.

**Baking pans.** Usually made of metal or ovenproof glass. They come in a wide variety of shapes and sizes, depending on the product to be baked. Baking pans include pie pans, cake pans, cookie sheets, and loaf pans.

*Glass Loaf Pan*

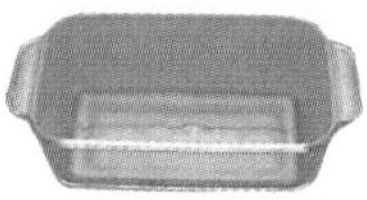

*Cake Pans*

*Glass Pie Plate*

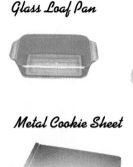

*Metal Cookie Sheet*

*Metal Muffin Tin*

**Roasting pans.** Shallow pans with handles on both ends. They usually have a roasting rack on the bottom to hold the meat or poultry out of the juices.

## Chapter 10 Review

### Check the Facts

1. Give an example of how using proper kitchen equipment can help you work more easily or more safely.
2. Explain why standard measuring equipment should be used when measuring ingredients.
3. Why should knives be sharpened regularly?
4. What knife would you choose for slicing bread? How can you recognize this type of knife?
5. What is a wire whisk used for?
6. What is the difference between saucepans and pots?

### Ideas in Action

1. You have an opportunity to equip a new kitchen but are limited to 30 pieces of equipment. Use this chapter to develop a list of the equipment you would choose. Compare your list with your classmates. How were your equipment choices similar and different? Why did you choose the equipment you did?
2. Perform a measuring experiment. Measure one cup of flour in a two-cup liquid measuring cup. When you have the right amount, carefully pour the flour into a one-cup dry measuring cup. How do the measurements compare? Did you have too much flour or too little when you measured it in the liquid measuring cup? What does this tell you about using the proper equipment for each task?

CHAPTER 11

# Reading Recipes

**OBJECTIVES**

**Discover . . .**

- **the information given in a recipe.**
- **what basic food preparation terms mean.**

Have you ever had a taco with too much hot pepper or a dry, tough hamburger? What went wrong?

The secret of successful food preparation is knowing how to use recipes correctly. A *recipe* is your guide to help you prepare a certain food. It explains how to put the right amounts of food and seasonings together in just the right way. If you understand the terms used in recipes and follow directions exactly, you can create many delicious dishes.

## What a Recipe Tells You

Recipes can be written in different styles. However, all recipes should include the same basic information:

**Ingredients.** *Ingredients* are the foods in a recipe. Look for specific details, such as "finely chopped onion" or "light brown sugar."

**Amounts.** The recipe should tell you exactly how much you need of each ingredient. You will learn about units of measurement and their abbreviations in Chapter 12.

**Directions.** Are there clear, step-by-step instructions for preparing the recipe?

**Pan or container.** Be sure to use the type and size called for so the recipe will turn out right.

**Temperature.** You may need to know how to set the controls for the oven or other appliances.

**Time.** You may need to know how long to cook or chill the food, for example.

**Yield.** The *yield* is the amount the recipe makes or the number of servings.

**It's fun to look through cookbooks and choose a recipe you'd like to prepare.**

*Broiler Cheesies*

*3 slices bread*
*3 slices American cheese*
*3 slices tomato (each ¼ inch thick)*

*Set oven temperature to broil. Arrange slices of bread on broiler pan. Place one slice cheese on each piece of bread. Broil 2-3 minutes until cheese is melted. Top each broiler cheesie with a slice of tomato. Serve hot. Yield: 3 servings.*

**Here's an example of a recipe. Can you find all the information you need?**

# Following Recipes

Before you begin to prepare food, look at the recipe carefully. If it's not clear and complete, choose a different one.

Some recipes are flexible—they can be varied according to your taste. After you prepare a stew, for example, you might decide to use a little more onion and less celery next time. You could also experiment with herbs and spices to give the stew a different flavor. That can be part of the fun of cooking.

However, some recipes cannot be changed as easily. That's true of most baked goods, such as breads, cakes, and cookies. For best results, follow these recipes exactly.

**Experienced cooks often enjoy experimenting to come up with their own variations on recipes. It may take several tries before they are satisfied.**

What if you don't have an ingredient called for in the recipe? Many cookbooks have a substitution chart. The chart may suggest ingredients that can be used in place of the one you're missing. Keep in mind that the results will probably be a little different.

# Basic Terms and Techniques

Here are some of the most common terms and techniques used in food preparation. Become familiar with them. They can help you use recipes more easily and successfully.

## Techniques for Cutting Foods

When cutting foods, always use sharp tools and a cutting board. If you cut directly on a kitchen counter or table, you can damage the surface. A plastic cutting board is durable and easy to clean.

Here are some cutting terms you should be familiar with:

**Pare.** Use a peeler or paring knife to cut a very thin layer of peel from fruits or vegetables.

**Slice.** Cut into thin, flat pieces.

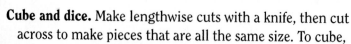

**Cube and dice.** Make lengthwise cuts with a knife, then cut across to make pieces that are all the same size. To cube, make the cuts about ½ inch (13 mm) or more apart. To dice, make the cuts about ¼ inch (6 mm) apart.

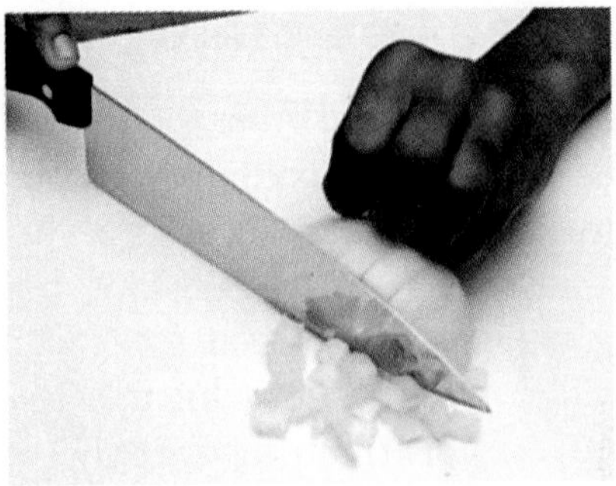

**Chop and mince.** Use a knife, food chopper, kitchen shears, or food processor. To chop, cut food into small irregular pieces. The recipe may tell you what size. To mince, keep chopping until the food pieces are as small as possible.

**Shred.** Cut food into long, thin pieces by rubbing it on the coarse surface of a grater. You can also use a food processor, a knife (to shred lettuce or cabbage), or two forks (to shred cooked meat).

**Grate.** Rub food on a grater to make very fine particles. Many graters have small holes for grating and larger holes for shredding.

**Puree** (pure-RAY *or* pure-EE). Put food through a blender, food processor, food mill, or strainer so that it becomes a smooth, thick mass.

## Techniques for Combining Foods

A variety of bowls, spoons, and other tools are used to combine ingredients. The different terms help you know what tool to use and how quickly and completely to combine the ingredients.

**Stir.** Use a wooden or metal spoon and a circular or figure-8 motion. Stirring may be done to combine ingredients or to distribute heat evenly.

**Mix or combine.** Both these terms usually mean to stir different ingredients together.

**Blend.** Mix ingredients together thoroughly until they are completely uniform. You can use a spoon, wire whisk, or electric blender.

**Beat.** Use a spoon or wire whisk with an over-and-over motion; a rotary beater; or an electric mixer. When beating different ingredients together, continue until the mixture is smooth. Whole eggs or egg whites are often beaten until they take on the desired color and texture.

**Cream.** This usually refers to combining shortening and sugar. Beat them together using a spoon, rotary beater, or electric mixer until soft, smooth, and creamy.

**Whip.** Some ingredients, such as cream, can be whipped to add air and increase volume. Beat very rapidly with a beater, mixer, or wire whisk.

**Fold in.** This is a very gentle way to combine two mixtures, such as beaten egg whites and batter. Use a wooden spoon or rubber scraper. Cut straight down through the mixture, across the bottom, then up and over. Do not lift the spoon or scraper out of the mixture. Give the bowl a quarter turn. Repeat until the mixture is well blended.

**Cut in.** This is a way to mix shortening and flour. Use a pastry blender or two knives and a cutting motion.

**Toss.** Tumble a mixture, such as a salad, very lightly with a spoon and fork.

## Cooking Terms

There are many different ways to cook food. You will learn more about cooking techniques in Chapters 14 and 15. For now, here are some cooking terms you might see in recipe directions.

**Preheat.** Turn on an appliance, such as an oven or electric skillet, ahead of time so that it will be at the right temperature when you put in the food.

**Brown.** Cook food briefly until the surface turns brown. You can brown food in a skillet with a little hot fat, in the oven, or in a broiler. Use the method called for in the recipe.

**Boil.** When a liquid is heated to boiling, bubbles constantly rise to the surface and break.

**Simmer.** A simmering liquid is not quite hot enough to boil. Bubbles form slowly and break before they reach the surface.

## Other Recipe Terms

Here are additional terms you may see in recipes.

**Baste.** To brush or pour liquid over food as it cooks. Basting keeps the food from drying out. Melted fat, sauces, or meat drippings may be used.

**Chill.** Refrigerate food until it is cold.

**Grease.** Some recipes call for a greased pan. Spread a thin layer of unsalted shortening in the pan or use a cooking spray.

**Drain.** Remove excess liquid by pouring it off or by placing food in a strainer or colander.

**Garnish.** Decorate a food or dish with a small, colorful food such as parsley or a lemon slice.

## Chapter 11 Review

### Check the Facts

1. Name seven types of information found in a recipe.
2. What should you do if you don't have an ingredient a recipe calls for?
3. When is it necessary to use a cutting board? Why?
4. Explain the differences between these terms: cube, dice, chop, mince.
5. What does "creaming" refer to? How is it done?
6. What is the difference between boiling and simmering?
7. Explain how to baste food.

### Ideas in Action

1. Look through cookbooks and magazines for six recipes. Examine the recipes carefully. Do they provide all of the information you need? Choose one recipe and rewrite the directions to make them more clear and complete. Include all information you think is necessary. You may need to check other recipes for ideas.
2. In class, take turns acting out the techniques described in this chapter. You may use tools as props, but you must act out the motions without speaking. See if the other class members can guess what techniques are being demonstrated.

CHAPTER 12

# Recipe Math

**OBJECTIVES**

**Discover . . .**

- two basic systems of measurement.
- units of measurement commonly used in recipes.
- how to increase and decrease recipes.

Food preparation and math go hand in hand. Basic math skills can help you understand the units of measure given in recipes. They can also help you to make changes in a recipe.

## The Math of Measuring

Some people—perhaps you—speak more than one language. Measurement also has different "languages." They are called the customary system and the metric system.

The *customary system* is the one most commonly used in the United States. The *metric system* is the standard system in most of the world. It is also used by scientists and health professionals in this country.

You will find it useful to learn both systems of measurement. Some recipes give measurements in the customary system, others in the metric system. In this book, both systems are used.

It's seldom necessary to convert measurements from one system to the other. Just use the correct measuring equipment. For example, if a recipe gives metric units, use metric measuring tools.

Different units of measure can be compared using equivalents. For example, 12 inches is the *equivalent* of, or the same as, one foot.

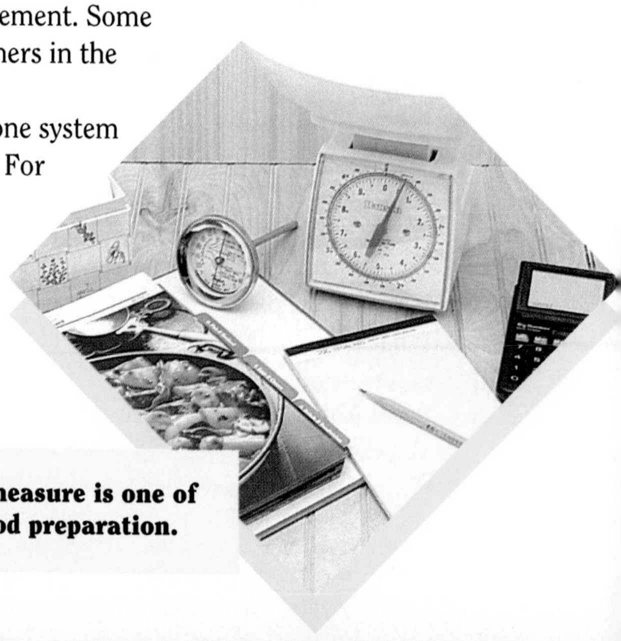

**Understanding units of measure is one of the keys to successful food preparation.**

## Weight

Weight refers to how heavy or light an ingredient is. Scales are used to measure weight. Many food packages are labeled according to how much they weigh.

Here are basic units for measuring weight and their abbreviations or symbols:

**Customary system:** • ounce (oz.) • pound (lb.)

**Metric system:** • gram (g) • kilogram (kg)

| Weight Equivalents | | |
|---|---|---|
| **Customary Measure** | **Customary Equivalent** | **Approximate Metric Equivalent** |
| 1 oz. | | 30 g |
| 1 lb. | 16 oz. | 500 g |
| 2 lb. | 32 oz. | 1 kg or 1000 g |

## Volume

Volume refers to the amount of space an ingredient takes up. Many recipe ingredients are measured by volume using measuring cups and spoons.

Basic units for measuring volume include:

**Customary:** • teaspoon (tsp.) • tablespoon (Tbsp.) • fluid ounce (oz.) • cup (c.) • pint (pt.) • quart (qt.) • gallon (gal.)

**Metric:** • milliliter (mL) • liter (L)

Notice that the term "ounces" is used in two different ways—to measure weight and volume. Keep in mind that the two kinds of ounces are not the same. When a recipe calls for ounces, be sure you understand whether you are to measure by weight or by volume.

### *Customary Equipment*

*Liquid Measure*

*Measuring Spoons*

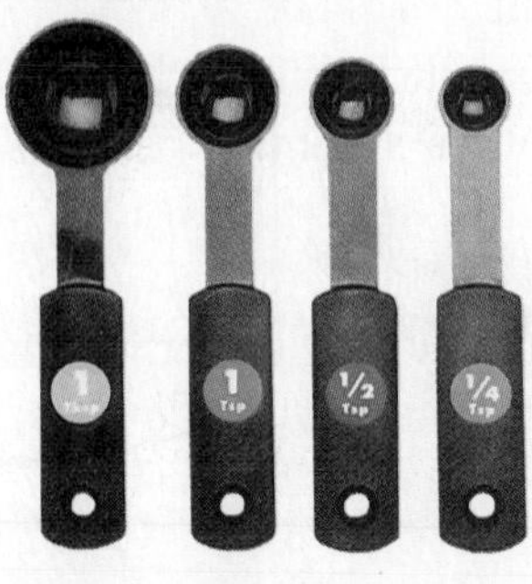

*Dry Measures*

*1 cup, ½ cup, ⅓ cup, ¼ cup*

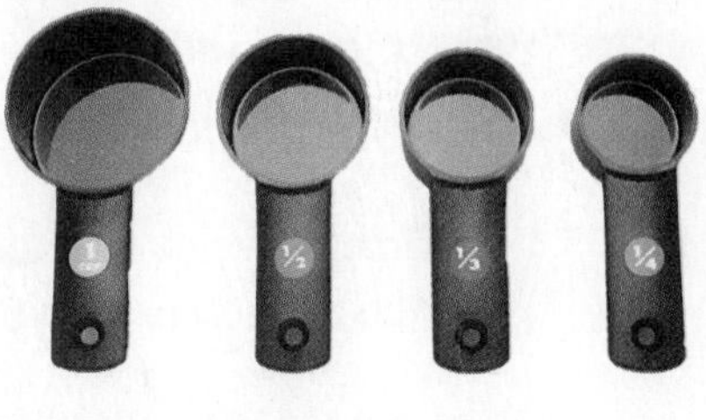

## Metric Measures

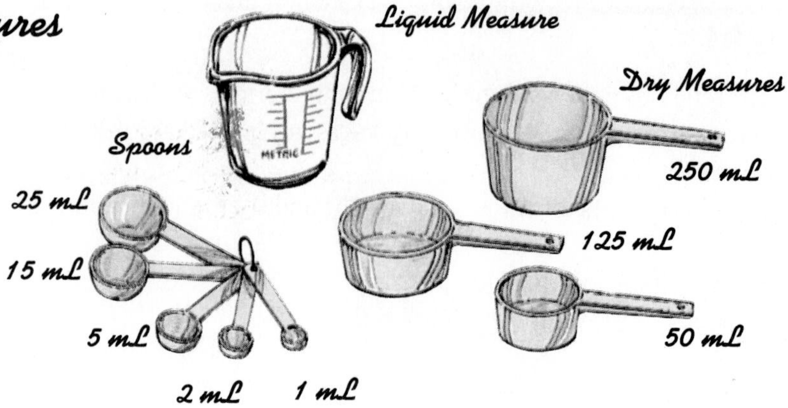


| Volume Equivalents | | |
|---|---|---|
| **Customary Unit** | **Customary Equivalent** | **Approximate Metric Equivalent** |
| Dash | Less than ⅛ tsp. | Less than 0.5 mL |
| ¼ tsp. | | 1 mL |
| ½ tsp. | | 2 or 3 mL |
| 1 tsp. | | 5 mL |
| 1 Tbsp. | 3 tsp. | 15 mL |
| 1 fluid oz. | 2 Tbsp. | 30 mL |
| 1 cup | 8 fluid oz. or 16 Tbsp. | 250 mL |
| 1 pt. | 2 cups or 16 fluid oz. | 500 mL |
| 1 qt. | 2 pt. or 4 cups or 32 fluid oz. | 1 L or 1000 mL |
| 1 gal. | 4 qt. | 4 L |

## Other Measurements

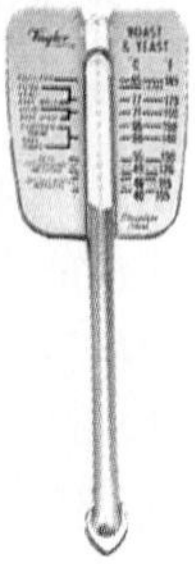

**Temperature.** In the customary system, temperature is measured in degrees Fahrenheit (°F). In the metric system, temperature is measured in degrees Celsius (°C). Many thermometers show both types of degrees.

**Length.** Recipes sometimes include length measurements. For example, you may need to know the length and width of a pan or the size of a vegetable. The customary system measures length in inches (in.), while the metric system uses millimeters (mm) or centimeters (cm).

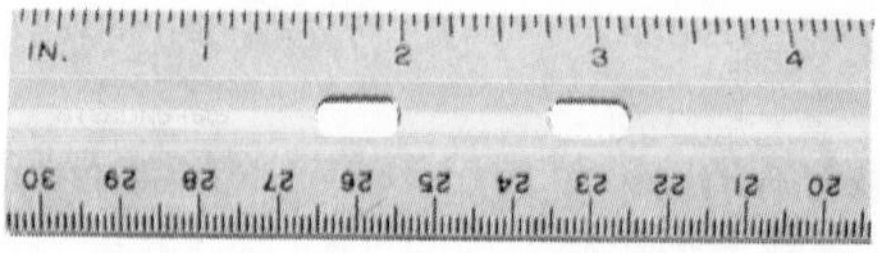

**Time.** A recipe may tell you how long something has to cook, measured in minutes, seconds, or hours.

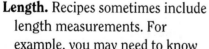

# Increasing or Decreasing Recipes

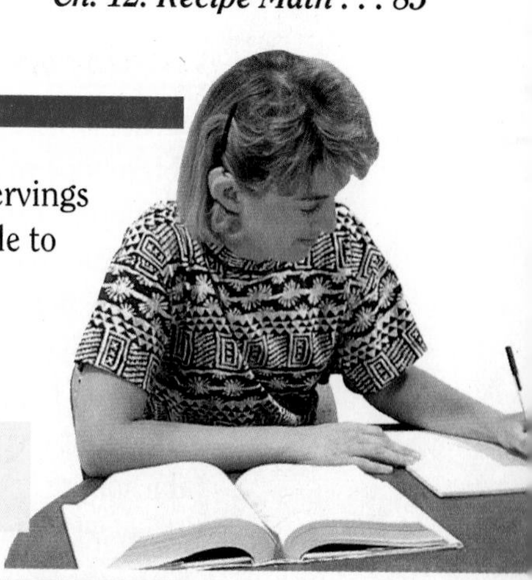

As you learned in Chapter 11, the yield of a recipe tells how many servings it will make. What if you want more or fewer servings? You may be able to change the yield by increasing or decreasing the recipe.

**Why might you need to adjust a recipe for a different number of servings?**

## How Many Servings Do You Want?

The first step is to decide how many servings you want. This is called the desired yield.

Suppose you need enough pasta salad for seven people. The recipe yields four servings. Should you increase the recipe to make seven servings? You could, but the calculation for eight servings would be easier. You decide that eight servings is your desired yield.

## Calculating the New Amounts

To adjust a recipe, you must multiply the amount of each ingredient by some number. In this case, you want eight servings of pasta salad instead of four. You would multiply the amount of each ingredient in the recipe by two.

How do you know what number to multiply by? Use the formula:

**desired yield ÷ original yield = number to multiply by**

The same formula works whether you are increasing or decreasing a recipe. Suppose a recipe makes 12 servings of tuna casserole. How would you adjust it to make four servings? You would have to multiply each amount in the recipe by $\frac{1}{3}$ (because $4 \div 12 = \frac{1}{3}$).

Before you start to prepare the recipe, figure out all the new amounts and write them down. Otherwise, you would have to stop and calculate each time you had to measure something. You might forget to change one of the amounts.

**Don't rely on your memory when adjusting a recipe. You might mistakenly use the amount specified in the recipe instead of the new amount you meant to use.**

## Converting Amounts

When you adjust a recipe, you may have to convert an amount (such as 1 tablespoon) to an equivalent measure (such as 3 teaspoons). Converting an amount to different units often makes calculating and measuring easier.

For example, the recipe for tuna casserole calls for ½ cup of milk. If you multiply ½ by ⅓, you get ⅙ cup. A measurement like this is awkward to use. Your measuring cup does not have a marking for ⅙ cup.

Instead, begin by converting ½ cup into tablespoons. Look at the volume equivalent chart on page 84. One cup is 16 tablespoons, so ½ cup equals 8 tablespoons.

Now when you multiply by ⅓, you get:

$$8 \times \frac{1}{3} = \frac{8}{3} = 2\frac{2}{3} \text{ Tbsp.}$$

But how do you measure ⅔ tablespoon? Break the tablespoon down into smaller measures. Remember, one tablespoon equals 3 teaspoons. Therefore, ⅔ of a tablespoon is 2 teaspoons. To measure the milk for the tuna casserole, you measure 2 tablespoons plus 2 teaspoons!

## What If It Doesn't Come Out Even?

Sometimes an amount can't be decreased easily. For example, you might end up with an amount like " ½ egg." What should you do then?

With mixtures such as casseroles, stews, salads, or soups, exact amounts usually are not critical. You could probably use a whole egg instead of a half in a casserole and still get successful results.

**Some ingredients, like an egg, can't be divided easily.**

However, decreasing the recipe for a baked product, such as cookies, cake, or bread, may pose a problem. These baked products depend on exact amounts of ingredients in specific relation to each other. If you have to round off amounts or can change only some of them, the recipe may not work.

If a recipe can't be increased or decreased easily, think of another way to solve the problem. Instead of trying to prepare just half of a recipe, perhaps you could prepare the entire amount and freeze half to use later.

## Use the Right Size Equipment

Remember to consider how increasing or decreasing a recipe will affect your equipment needs. Suppose you double a recipe for brownies. Will you need a larger mixing bowl? What will you bake the brownies in? If you use a larger pan, they will take longer to bake. You may want to divide the mixture into two pans of the same size and shape.

When you decrease a recipe, cook the food in a smaller pan. Otherwise, it may cook too fast or dry out.

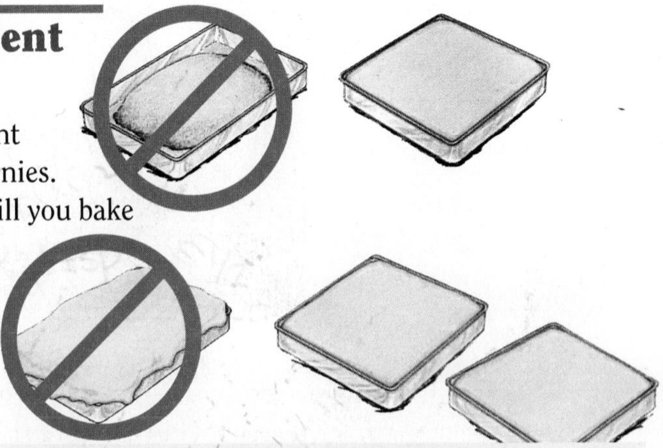

**The depth of food in the pan affects how fast it will cook. Use pans that are the right size for the recipe, not too large or too small.**

## Chapter 12 Review

### Check the Facts

1. Name two systems of measurement. Which is most common in the U.S.? In the world?
2. List two basic units for measuring weight in each measuring system.
3. How many tablespoons equal one cup? How many teaspoons equal one tablespoon?
4. When increasing or decreasing a recipe, what formula is used to calculate the new amount of each ingredient?
5. A recipe calls for 1 Tbsp. cinnamon. If you are cutting the recipe in half, how much cinnamon do you need?
6. Why can't all recipes be decreased successfully?

### Ideas in Action

1. Discuss the pros and cons of the metric system. Which system would make it easier to increase or decrease a recipe? Why?
2. Select a recipe from this textbook or a cookbook. Increase it to make three times as many servings. Remember to convert amounts, if needed, so they are easier to measure. Include any changes in equipment and procedure that would be needed.
3. Follow the directions for activity 2, but this time cut the original yield in half. Do you think decreasing the recipe will cause any problems? If so, why? What could you do to solve or avoid the problem?

CHAPTER 13

# Basic Measuring Methods

**OBJECTIVES**

**Discover . . .**
- **how to measure dry ingredients.**
- **how to measure liquid ingredients.**
- **how to measure solid fats.**

One of the secrets of successful food preparation is measuring ingredients accurately. Too much or too little of an ingredient can make a big difference.

You have already learned about customary and metric units of measure. You also know how to make calculations for increasing and decreasing a recipe. Now you will learn how to work with measuring cups and spoons to make sure that you have just the right amount of each ingredient.

## Measuring Dry Ingredients

When you measure dry ingredients, they usually should be level with the top of the measuring cup or spoon. Otherwise the measurement will not be accurate.

*Level* 

*Heaping* 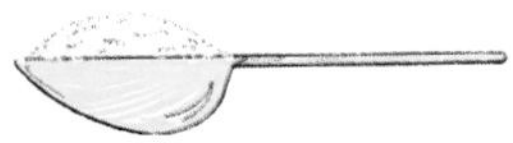

**Unless the recipe calls for a "heaping" amount, the measurement should be level.**

Measuring spoons are used for small amounts. For larger amounts, use dry measuring cups. They are designed so that you can easily level off the ingredient.

**Always measure carefully to be sure you use the exact amount needed.**

**To measure dry ingredients . . .**

1. Hold the cup or spoon over waxed paper or over the ingredient's container. If any spills over, it will be caught by the paper or the container instead of going into your recipe.

2. Fill the cup or spoon to the top and slightly overflowing. Do not pack the ingredients into the measuring utensil unless the recipe says so. Also, do not try to shake the ingredients down or tap the cup to make more room.

3. Use a straight edge, such as a spatula, to level off the top of the cup or spoon.

## Measuring Flour

Some recipes call for sifted flour. To *sift* means to put a dry ingredient through a fine sieve or sifter in order to separate the particles.

Spoon the flour into the sifter. You can sift onto waxed paper or directly into the measuring cup. After you measure the amount you need, return any remaining flour to its original container.

Whole-grain flours, such as whole wheat and rye, should not be sifted. Just stir them with a spoon before measuring.

## Measuring Sugar

Brown sugar requires a special measuring technique. Spoon the sugar into the cup. Use the back of the spoon to pack the sugar into the cup. Continue adding and packing until slightly overfilled. Level off with a spatula. When you turn the measuring cup upside down to empty it, the brown sugar should come out holding the shape of the cup.

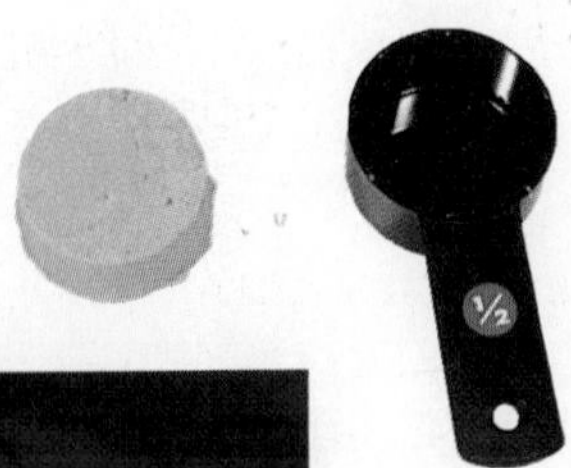


Other sugars should be measured in the normal way. If sugar is lumpy, put it through a strainer before measuring. Press out the lumps with a spoon.

# Measuring Liquid Ingredients

For liquids, such as milk, water, oil, or honey, use a liquid measuring cup. It has extra space at the top to help prevent spilling and a spout for pouring. Often customary amounts are marked on one side and metric on the other.

**To measure liquids . . .**

1. Place the cup on a flat, level surface, such as a table or counter.

2. Slowly pour the liquid into the cup.

3. Check the measurement at eye level. To do this, you will have to stoop down so that you can look straight through the side of the cup.

▲ This allows you to read the exact amount of liquid in the cup. If you look down on the cup, you will not get an accurate measurement.

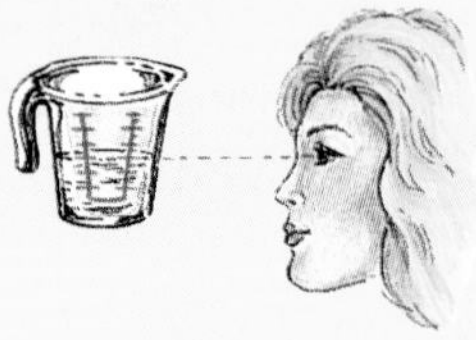

Syrup and honey are thick and sticky. When measuring them, you can grease or oil the liquid measuring cup so they will flow out more easily. You may need to use a rubber scraper to get all the liquid out of the cup.

For small amounts of liquids, use measuring spoons. Hold the spoon away from the mixing bowl or pan in case of spills. Fill the spoon just to the brim.

**Hold the cup or spoon away from the mixing bowl. That way, if you happen to pour out too much of the ingredient, the extra won't fall into the bowl.**

# Measuring Solid Fats

Solid fats, such as butter, margarine, or shortening, can be measured in several different ways. Two of the easiest are the stick method and the dry measuring cup method.

**Stick method.** Butter and margarine are sold by the stick. One stick weighs ¼ pound (125 g) and is equal to ½ cup (125 mL). The wrappers are usually marked off in tablespoons so you can cut off the amount you need.

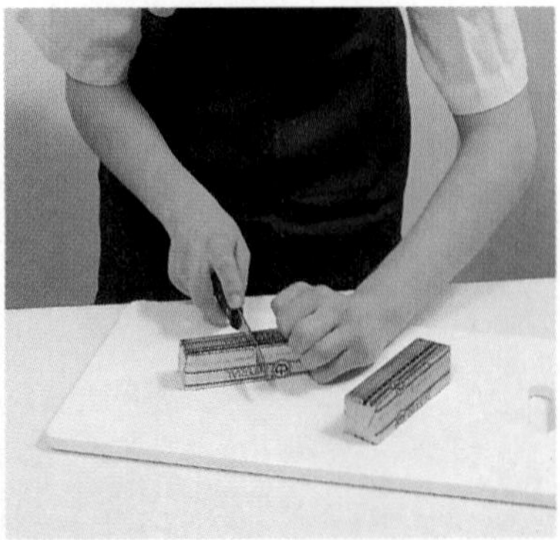

**You can use a table knife to cut a stick of margarine or butter while it is still in the wrapper.**

**Dry measuring cup method.** Spoon shortening into a dry measuring cup. Pack it down firmly. Be sure to work out all air bubbles so the measurement is accurate. Pack the cup slightly more than full, then level it off. To get the shortening out of the cup, use a rubber scraper.

## Chapter 13 Review

### Check the Facts

1. Describe three steps to follow when measuring dry ingredients.
2. How is measuring brown sugar different from measuring white sugar?
3. Why should you use a liquid measuring cup to measure liquids? A dry measuring cup to measure dry ingredients?
4. Describe three steps to follow when measuring liquids.
5. Describe two methods for measuring solid fats.

### Ideas in Action

1. Discuss what equipment you would use to measure the following ingredients: 2¾ cup flour, 1⅔ cup brown sugar, 1⅛ tsp. black pepper, ½ Tbsp. honey, ½ cup margarine.
2. With a partner, measure one cup of flour without sifting. Then put the same flour through a sifter and measure it again. What is the difference in volume after sifting? Why should flour be measured after sifting instead of before (unless otherwise directed in the recipe)? How does the flour change in appearance when it is sifted?

CHAPTER 14

# Basic Cooking Methods

**OBJECTIVES**

**Discover . . .**
- **three general types of cooking methods.**
- **the characteristics of different cooking methods.**
- **how to save nutrients when you cook.**

It was Josh's turn to make dinner. In the refrigerator he found a package of meat and some fresh green beans. Neither one came with cooking directions, and Josh didn't have time to look around for a recipe. "Oh well," he thought. "I know how to bake potatoes or a frozen pizza, so maybe I can cook these the same way." Josh put the meat on a pizza pan, dumped the beans in a dish, and put them both in the oven.

Josh didn't know that different foods need to be cooked in different ways. If he had, his family could have enjoyed a home-cooked meal instead of another night of fast-food burgers.

## Types of Cooking Methods

When you look through cookbooks, you can find hundreds of different ways to prepare food. However, most recipes use one or more of three basic cooking methods: dry heat, moist heat, and frying.

### Dry Heat Methods

*Dry heat methods* are those in which you cook the food uncovered without adding any liquid or fat. Broiling, roasting, and baking are examples of dry heat methods.

Cooking in dry heat improves the flavor, texture, and appearance of many foods. The food usually turns brown and develops a crisp or tender crust.

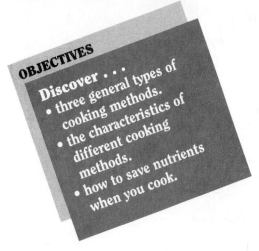

**Food cooked in dry heat develops a browned, flavorful crust.**

## Broiling

In broiling, the food is placed under the heating unit of an appliance such as a range, countertop broiler, or toaster oven. The food is cooked by direct heat from above.

A broiler pan has two parts: a bottom pan about 1 inch (2.5 cm) deep and a grid, or tray with holes, that fits on the pan. Food is placed on the grid. As the food broils, fat drains into the bottom pan.

Foods that can be broiled include tender cuts of meat, young poultry, fish, and some fruits and vegetables. When you broil food:

- Place the food on a cold broiler pan.
- Do not line the grid with foil—the fat will not be able to drain away. The food will fry and the fat could catch fire.
- Check the recipe for the proper distance between the broiler pan and the heat. You cannot choose a temperature for the broiler. Instead, you control how fast the food cooks by how far you place it from the heat. Thicker foods should be placed farther from the heat than thin foods.
- Follow the directions in the owner's manual for the broiler or oven. When broiling in an electric oven, the door is usually left slightly open. If you are using a gas range, the broiler door should be closed.

## Panbroiling

Panbroiling is a rangetop method of broiling food. It can be used for thin, tender cuts of meat, such as pork chops, bacon, or hamburgers.

To panbroil, place the food in an ungreased hot skillet. Cook, uncovered, until browned on one side. Turn and continue cooking to desired doneness. Pour off any fat that accumulates during cooking.

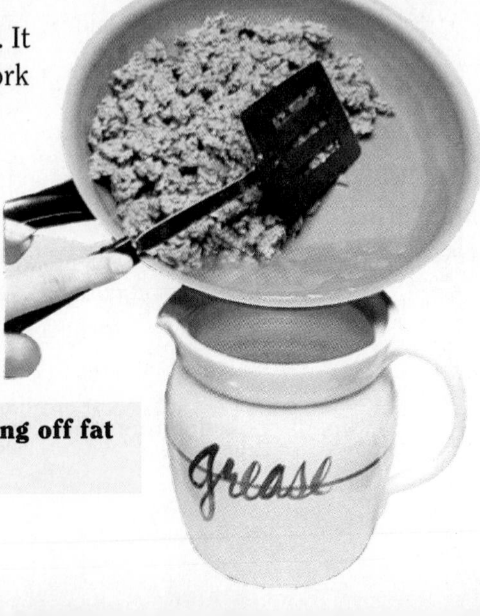


**Be careful when pouring off fat from cooked meat.**

**When you want to bake or roast food, leave the food uncovered. If you add liquid or cover the food, you will cook it in moist heat, not dry heat.**

## Baking and Roasting

"Baking" and "roasting" are two terms that mean the same thing—to cook food in dry heat in an oven. Foods that can be baked or roasted include fish, tender meats and poultry, and some fruits and vegetables. Breads, cakes, pies, cookies, and similar foods are also baked.

Baking and roasting can be done in a conventional oven or a convection oven. You can also use a toaster oven or a similar small appliance.

What about microwaving? Foods are also "baked" or "roasted" in the microwave oven. However, the microwave does not give the same results as a conventional or convection oven. That's because a microwave oven cooks differently. It does not cook with hot, dry air. For this reason, microwaving is not considered a dry heat method.

# Moist Heat Methods

*Moist heat methods* are those in which food is cooked using a hot liquid, steam, or a combination of both. You are using moist heat cooking whenever:

- The food being cooked is a liquid, such as a sauce or hot cocoa.

- The food is covered in liquid. For example, meat and vegetables could be cooked together in water to make a soup or stew.

- The pan or container is covered so that steam and moisture stay inside.

Foods cooked in moist heat do not brown. They also do not develop a crisp or tender crust.

Moist heat methods have many uses. For example, they may be used to tenderize foods, such as vegetables and some cuts of meat. Moist heat can also help keep food from drying out as it cooks. It is used to cook foods that must absorb liquid, such as noodles or dry beans. Sometimes foods are cooked together in a sauce or broth to blend their flavors.

Many different appliances can be used for moist heat cooking:

**Conventional oven.** Moist heat can be created by cooking food in a covered dish, sealing food in foil, or using a special plastic cooking bag.

**Microwave oven.** Microwaving is usually considered a moist heat method. You will learn more about microwave cooking techniques in the next chapter.

**Small appliances.** For example, you can use a slow cooker or a covered electric skillet.

**Rangetop.** When cooking on the rangetop, the most common moist heat methods are boiling, simmering, and steaming.

**Foil can be used to seal in steam so that food cooks in moist heat.**

**Can you explain why using a slow cooker is a moist heat method?**

## Boiling

The boiling point of a liquid is the temperature at which it turns to steam. The boiling point of water is 212°F (100°C). When liquid boils, bubbles rise up continuously and break the surface of the liquid.

There are only a few times when food should be cooked at a boil. For example, noodles must be cooked in a large amount of boiling water. Usually, however, it is better to simmer foods than to boil them. Why? Foods lose more nutrients, flavor, and texture when boiled. Boiling also toughens protein foods.

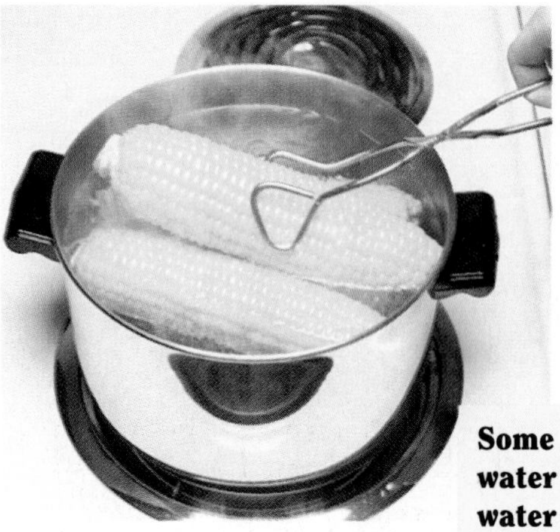

### Simmering

Simmering lets foods cook gently until they are done. The temperature of the liquid is just slightly below boiling. Bubbles rise slowly but do not break the surface.

Food may be simmered whole or cut into pieces. To make sure the food or liquid is at the right temperature for simmering, first bring it to a boil. Then lower the heat immediately so the bubbles do not break the surface.

**Some foods, such as corn on the cob, are simmered in enough water to cover them. Others are simmered in just a little water in a covered pan.**

### Steaming

Many foods, such as vegetables, can be cooked in steam. The most common method is to place a steamer basket inside a pan with a small amount of boiling water. The basket holds the food above the water, but has holes to let steam flow through and cook the food. After putting the food in the basket, cover the pan at once to keep the steam inside.

## Frying

Frying means cooking in fat. This cooking method makes food brown, crisp, and flavorful. However, frying is not as healthful as other methods because the food soaks up fat. Choose other cooking methods, such as broiling or panbroiling, most often.

**What are the advantages and disadvantages of frying food?**

When you do fry:

- Use as little fat or oil as possible.
- Avoid using hard fats such as butter or lard for frying. Liquid vegetable oil is lower in saturated fat. Another good choice is a vegetable-oil cooking spray, which will give just a light coating of oil.
- Follow the tips for safe frying in the box on the next page.

There are two basic kinds of frying. The main difference is in the amount of fat used.

## Deep-Fat Frying

This method is also called french frying. The food is completely covered in a large amount of fat heated to a specific temperature. A deep-fat thermometer is used to show the temperature of the fat. Of the two frying methods, deep-fat frying adds the most fat to food.

## Panfrying

Some foods can be fried in a skillet in a small amount of fat. This is called panfrying. You can use this method for tender or quick-cooking foods, such as eggs.

Panfrying is often used to precook foods such as onions, mushrooms, and green peppers before they are used in a recipe. Then it is usually called *sautéing* (saw-TAY-ing). The foods are chopped or sliced so that they cook quickly. Cook, stirring occasionally, just until the vegetables soften.

**Tips for Safe Frying**

Safety is of special concern when frying. Hot fat can catch fire or spatter and cause burns.

- Follow recipe directions carefully.
- Do not overheat the fat or oil.
- Be sure food is dry before frying it. Moisture can cause the hot fat to spatter.
- Know what to do if a grease fire starts. (See page 111.)

## Combination Methods

Braising and stir-frying are two methods that combine frying with moist heat.

**Braising** means to brown food in a small amount of fat, then finish with long, slow cooking in moist heat. Pot roast, chicken pieces, or vegetables such as carrots, potatoes, and parsnips may be braised.

**Stir-frying** is a method of frying food quickly in a small amount of oil at a high temperature. The food is stirred constantly to keep it from sticking to the pan. During the last few minutes of cooking, the pan may be covered so the food can steam. Stir-frying, which began in Asia, is most often used for cooking mixtures of vegetables and other foods. You will learn how to stir-fry in Chapter 35.

# Saving Nutrients When You Cook

Preparing food can cause it to lose nutrients. How? Some nutrients can be destroyed by heat or by the oxygen in the air. Water-soluble nutrients—the B vitamins and vitamin C—are most easily destroyed. Other times the nutrients are thrown away. For example, if you discard the skin of a potato, you are throwing away the vitamins and minerals found there.

When you prepare food, one of your most important goals will be to save nutrients. Here are some general guidelines. You will learn more when you study other chapters.

**Pare or trim as little as possible.** Many of the nutrients in fruits and vegetables are found in the outer portions, such as skins.

**Keep food whole or in large pieces when possible.** If food is cut into small pieces, more surface is exposed to air, water, or heat. That often means more nutrients are lost.

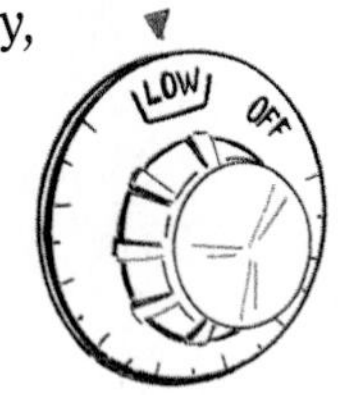


**Cook food at the right temperature.** Most protein foods, including meat, poultry, fish, eggs, milk, and cheese, are very sensitive to heat. They must be cooked at low temperatures. Otherwise they lose nutrients and may also become too tough or dry to eat.

**Cook food the right amount of time.** Overcooking can destroy vitamins or make the food inedible. To be safe, begin to test the food about 5 to 10 minutes before the cooking time is up.

**Save cooking liquids.** Water-soluble vitamins may move from food into the water in which it is cooked. If the cooking water is thrown away, the nutrients are lost. Instead, serve the liquid with the food or save it for another use, such as making soup.

## Chapter 14 Review

### Check the Facts

1. What are three basic types of cooking methods?
2. List four guidelines for broiling food.
3. Identify three reasons for using moist heat to cook food.
4. Why is simmering usually a better choice than boiling?
5. Name at least three safety guidelines for frying food.
6. What is the difference between braising and stir-frying?
7. Name five guidelines for saving nutrients when preparing food.

### Ideas in Action

1. In small groups, compare and contrast broiling and frying. What are the advantages and disadvantages of each? What reasons can be given for broiling foods rather than frying them?
2. Select a method for preparing food. Draw cartoons to illustrate it.
3. Select three recipes for cooked foods. What cooking method is used in each recipe? How could nutrients be saved when preparing these foods?
4. Create a bulletin board describing the three basic methods for cooking food.

CHAPTER 15

# Microwave Techniques

**OBJECTIVES**

**Discover . . .**
- how the microwave oven works.
- how to choose cookware for microwaving.
- basic techniques for microwaving.
- safety guidelines for microwaving.

Just a few years ago, microwave ovens were a new and unfamiliar appliance. Today, many people consider the microwave oven to be an essential part of the kitchen.

Using the microwave oven requires different cooking methods and techniques than conventional cooking. This chapter will help you learn these skills. Even if you have used a microwave oven before, you will find ways to be a more successful microwave cook.

## The Microwave Oven

Microwave ovens can be great time-savers. They can be used for:

**Heating convenience foods.** Many canned, packaged, and frozen foods include microwave directions. Some are made just for the microwave oven.

**Reheating leftovers.** Many foods can be reheated in a microwave oven in just seconds. They keep much of their original flavor and texture.

**Defrosting frozen foods.** Many microwave ovens have a defrost setting. You can thaw frozen meat, poultry, or fish in minutes.

**Cooking fresh foods.** Many foods can be cooked two to four times faster than with a conventional range. However, not all foods can be microwaved with good results. As you study other chapters in this book, you will learn more about which foods can be microwaved successfully.

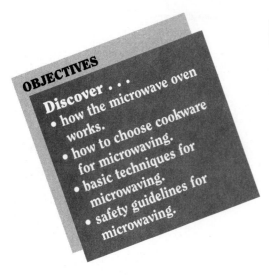

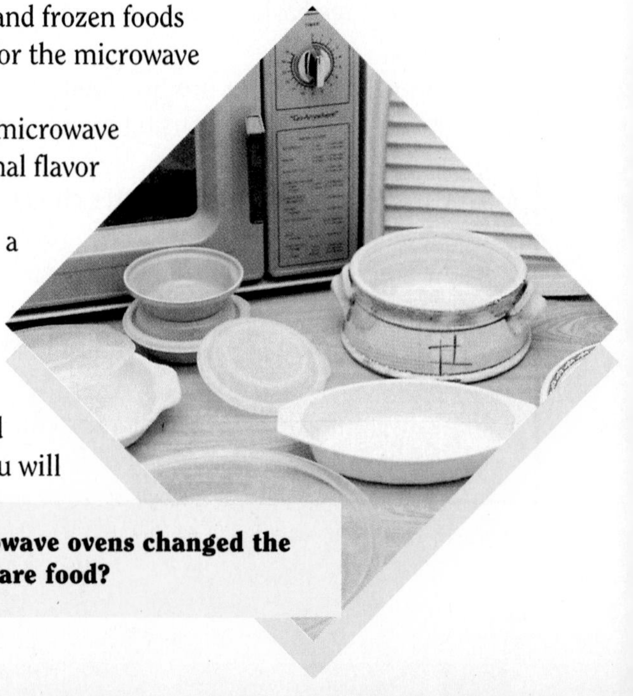

**How have microwave ovens changed the way people prepare food?**

## How Microwaves Work

Rub your hands together quickly for about 10 seconds. What do you feel? The heat in your hands is caused by friction. Microwave ovens also use friction to produce heat.

A microwave oven produces tiny waves of energy called *microwaves*. These bounce off the oven walls and into the food. As they penetrate the food, they cause molecules (tiny particles) within the food to vibrate very fast. The vibration causes friction between the molecules. The friction produces heat and cooks the food.

The amount of electricity the oven uses to create microwaves is known as the *cooking power*. Cooking power is measured in watts of electricity. Most ovens have a cooking power of about 500 to 700 watts. The higher the wattage, the faster the oven cooks.

With microwave cooking, you do not set a certain temperature as you would on a conventional oven. Instead, you have power settings that control the amount of cooking power. Most microwave ovens have several power settings. Others may have only one or two.

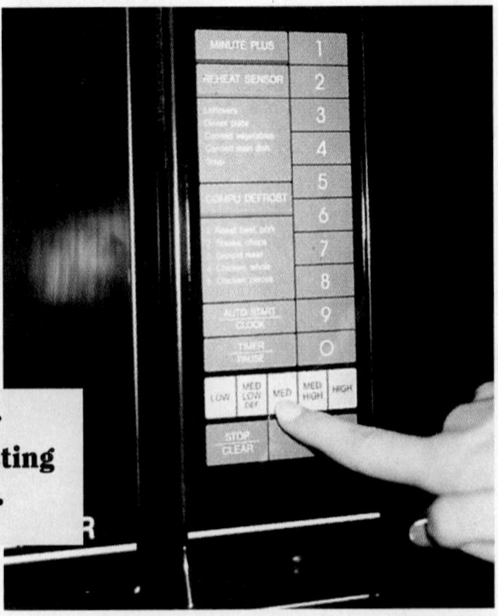


**Many microwave ovens let you set the power level. Lower power levels are used for defrosting and for foods that need to cook more slowly.**

# Materials for Microwaving

You can use some of the same cookware you use with a conventional range for microwaving. However, some materials cannot be used in the microwave oven.

Microwaves pass right through materials such as glass, paper, and many plastics to cook the food inside. However, always check paper and plastics to make sure they are labeled "microwave-safe." If not, they could start a fire.

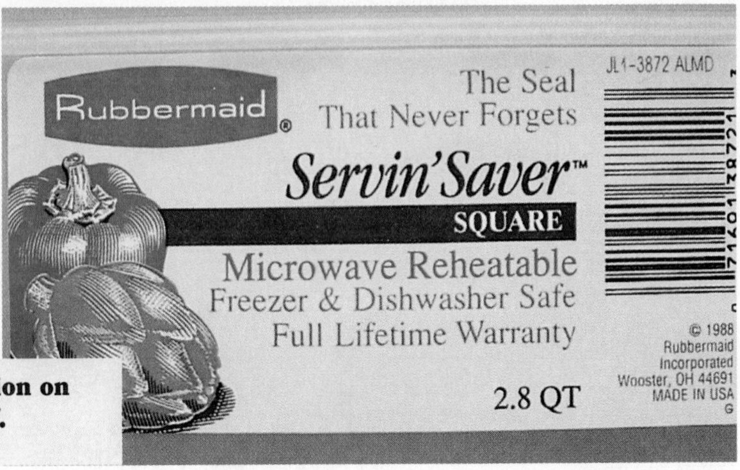

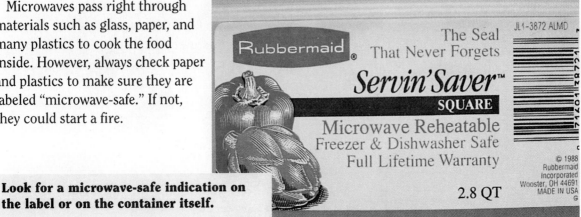

**Look for a microwave-safe indication on the label or on the container itself.**

## Safe Materials

In general, it is safe to use:

- Heatproof glass containers, such as casseroles, baking dishes, and liquid measuring cups.
- Plastic containers that are labeled "microwave-safe."
- Special microwave cookware. Follow the instructions in the owner's manual.
- Paper plates that are labeled "microwave-safe."
- Paper towels that do not contain plastic fibers or recycled paper.
- Wooden skewers for kabobs.

## Do Not Use These Materials

Some materials can cause problems in the microwave oven. Do not use:

- Metal cookware. Microwaves bounce off metal and can cause arcing (ARK-ing), which creates sparks in the oven. Arcing can damage the oven or start a fire.
- Aluminum foil, except for small amounts used as recommended in the owner's manual.
- Plastic containers from dairy foods, margarine, or take-out foods. These plastics are not microwave-safe.
- Brown paper bags or any products made of recycled paper. They may contain chemicals that will burn when heated.
- Paper towels made with plastic fibers, such as nylon. They may flame up.
- Straw or synthetic fibers, such as polyester. They may flame up.
- Wooden containers. They will dry out if microwaved over a period of time. Eventually, they may be damaged.

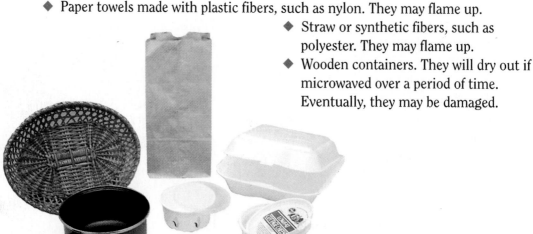

# Basic Steps in Microwaving

Most microwave recipes include a number of basic steps. Following these steps correctly will help you make sure the food cooks evenly without overcooking.

**For best results, follow microwave recipes exactly. This microwave cookbook is written in Braille, a system of writing for the blind.**

## Choosing a Container

The instructions should tell you what size container to use. Be sure it is made of microwave-safe material.

Microwave recipes often tell you to use a round, oval, or ring-shaped pan. Why? These shapes allow microwave energy to strike the food from all angles. If you use square or rectangular pans, the energy concentrates in the corners. Food in those areas overcooks.

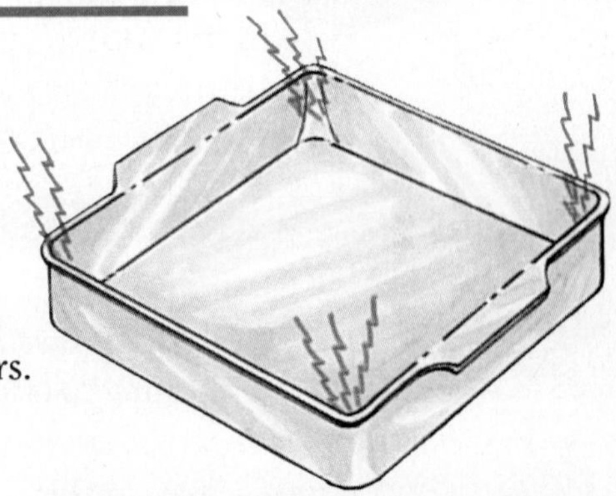

**Microwaves tend to concentrate in the corners of a square pan. Food in the corners overcooks.**

## Arranging the Food

For even cooking, it's important to arrange food as specified in the recipe. Individual items are often arranged in a ring or like the spokes on a wheel.

Make foods as uniform as possible. For example, cut carrots into pieces that are all about the same size and shape. Foods such as casseroles should be an even thickness.

Some foods, such as a chicken leg, are not uniform throughout. The parts that are thicker, more moist, or more dense will take longer to cook. Place these parts toward the outside of the container.

**Broccoli stems should be placed toward the outside of the dish because they are tougher.**

## Covering the Food

The recipe or cooking instructions may tell you to cover the food. A cover helps control the amount of moisture in the food. It also keeps food from spattering in the oven.

The container you're using may come with a microwave-safe cover. If not, use one of the following:

**Plastic wrap.** Use when you want to retain as much moisture as possible in the dish. Make sure the wrap's label says "microwave-safe." Fit the plastic on the dish loosely. If it's too tight, it may split during cooking. Vent the plastic to allow excess steam to escape. Do this by rolling back one edge of the plastic slightly, leaving a narrow opening.

**Waxed paper.** Use when you want most of the moisture to evaporate. Cover the dish loosely with the waxed paper.

**Paper towel.** Towels absorb moisture. They are generally used for heating rolls and sandwiches so the bread does not get soggy.

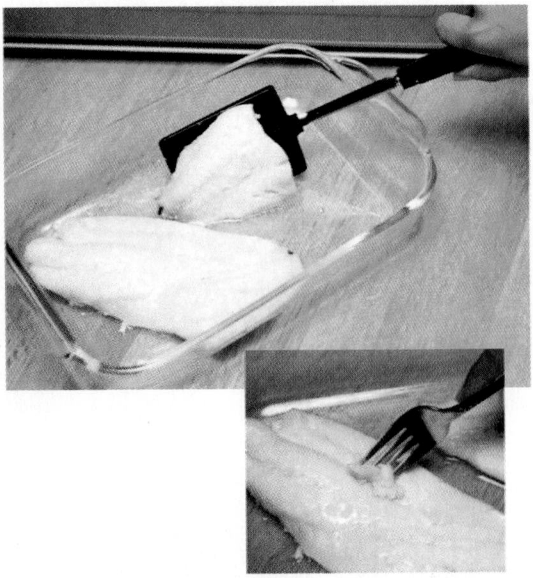

**Why should you check the food before the cooking time is up?**

## Cooking the Food

Set the oven for the correct power level and cooking time. Timing is especially important when microwaving. Overcooked foods become hard, tough, and chewy. Often, they cannot be eaten.

Most recipes give an approximate time for microwaving food. To avoid overcooking, turn off the oven a few minutes before the time is up. Check the food. Then add short cooking periods, if necessary. Once food is overcooked, there's nothing you can do to save it.

The cooking time depends on the number of servings you are making. If you heat two frozen dinners at the same time, for example, they will take longer to cook than one dinner alone. Check the instructions carefully.

## Rotating, Stirring, Turning, and Rearranging

To make sure the heat is evenly distributed, the instructions may tell you to rotate the food, stir it, turn it over, or rearrange it. Usually this is done after half the cooking time. Here's how:

**Stir.** Liquids should be stirred thoroughly. For a more solid food, stir from the center of the dish to the outside. Let the food that was on the outside of the dish move to the center.

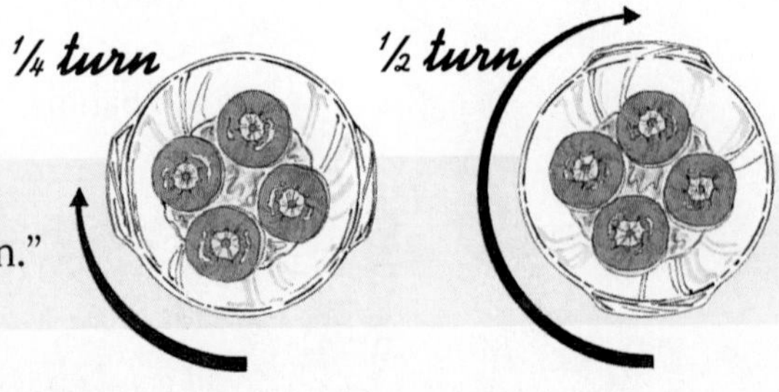


**Rotate.** Turn the plate or dish. The instructions may say "rotate one-quarter turn" or "rotate one-half turn."

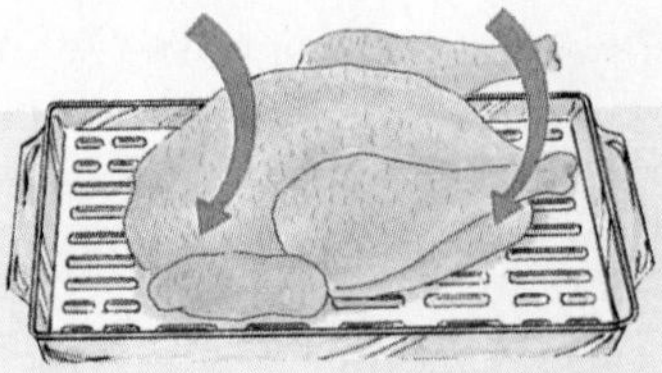

**Turn over.** Flip the food so the bottom becomes the top. The instructions may say "invert."

**Rearrange.** Move outside pieces toward the center and inside pieces toward the outside.

## Standing Time

When the oven shuts off after cooking, the molecules in the food continue to vibrate. The food keeps on cooking until it cools slightly. The period when the food continues to cook after microwaving is called *standing time*. Standing time also allows heat to penetrate all areas of the food.

If the instructions say "let stand," leave the food covered for the time specified. If the food needs more cooking after the standing time, return it to the oven.

**Standing time lets the food finish cooking.**

# Safety Tips for Microwave Use

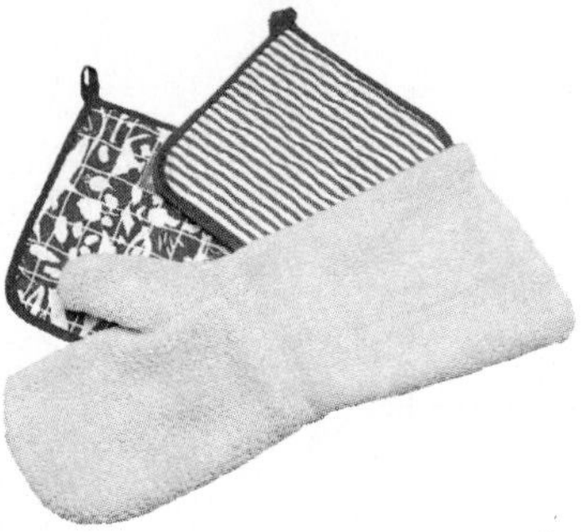

You don't see an open flame or a reddened heating element with a microwave oven, but you can still get burned or start a fire if you aren't careful. Follow these guidelines for safe microwave use:

- Always use potholders when handling food during or after microwaving. As the food cooks, the heat from the food passes into the cooking container and can make it extremely hot.
- If a food contains a concentration of fat or sugar, like cheese or a jelly filling, do not eat it as soon as it comes out of the oven. The fat or sugar will be extremely hot and could burn your mouth. Let the food cool first.
- Cook in small batches. Large amounts of hot food are difficult to handle. Smaller amounts will cook faster and can be handled more easily.

- Be careful when removing covers, especially plastic wrap. Escaping steam can severely burn your fingers, face, and eyes. Lift the cover so the steam flows away from your body. Keep your fingers out of the way. When opening a microwavable bag of popcorn, hold the bag away from your face and follow directions carefully.
- Never microwave whole eggs. They may explode, and you could be severely burned.
- Do not use containers with tight-fitting covers. Loosen the cover first. Otherwise the container could explode from the pressure of built-up steam.

- Foods with skins, such as potatoes, may explode if microwaved. Before putting them in the oven, pierce them several times with a fork so the steam can escape.

Also be careful in how you use and handle the microwave oven itself. Follow these guidelines:

- Don't turn the microwave oven on if the door doesn't close properly.
- Don't lean on the oven door or close it with something between it and the oven cavity, like a potholder. You could damage the door.
- Do not attach magnets to the oven. They can damage the electronics.
- Wipe up any spills or spatters after each use. Not only does this help keep food from becoming dried onto the surface, it can help prevent a grease fire.

**Don't do this to your microwave oven! Magnets can damage it. Put them on the refrigerator instead.**

## Chapter 15 Review

### Check the Facts

1. Identify at least three ways microwave ovens may be used in food preparation.
2. How does microwave energy cook food?
3. What is cooking power? How is it measured?
4. Name five cookware materials that are considered microwave-safe.
5. Name five cookware materials not recommended for use in microwave ovens.
6. Why are round, oval, or ring-shaped pans often used in microwave cooking?
7. Name four ways to make sure that heat is evenly distributed in microwaved foods.
8. What is standing time? Why is it needed?
9. List six safety guidelines to follow when using the microwave oven.

### Ideas in Action

1. Discuss the ways microwave cooking differs from cooking in a conventional oven.
2. Design a bulletin board that shows how to safely use a microwave oven. Use magazines and classroom resources for ideas.
3. Select a non-plastic cookware item from the foods lab that you think would be safe to use in a microwave oven. Test it using the following method: Fill a glass measuring cup with cold water. Place the cup of water in the microwave along with the cookware item. Microwave at 100 percent power for one minute. Does the cookware feel warm to the touch? If so, it is absorbing microwaves and may not be safe for microwave cooking. Share your results with the class.

CHAPTER 16

# Safety in the Kitchen

**OBJECTIVES**

**Discover . . .**
- how to identify safety hazards in the kitchen.
- how to prevent kitchen accidents.

Accidents don't "just happen." They are caused by not knowing the safe way to work.

You can reduce the chance of accidents. Learn about hazards and practice safe work habits. Keep the kitchen clean. Also be sure to keep appliances and equipment in good working condition and use them correctly.

What are the most common accidents in the kitchen? They include cuts, falls, electrical shock, burns, and poisoning. This chapter shows what you can do to help prevent these accidents.

## Preventing Cuts

Many cuts happen in the kitchen. Here are some ways to avoid them.

- When you use a knife, cut away from your body, not toward yourself. If the knife slips, you will not cut yourself. Do not cut toward other people. Do not point a knife or other sharp instruments toward others, even in fun. You could injure them.
- Use a knife only for cutting food. Don't use it for opening a can or tightening a screw on a handle. The knife could break and you could injure yourself.
- Wash knives separately from dishes. If you let them soak in soapy water, you can't see them and could cut yourself.
- To open cans, use a can opener that makes a smooth cut, not a jagged edge. Cut off the can top completely and throw it in the trash.
- Sweep up broken glass with a broom or a brush. Never pick it up with your bare fingers. To pick up tiny pieces, use a wet paper towel.

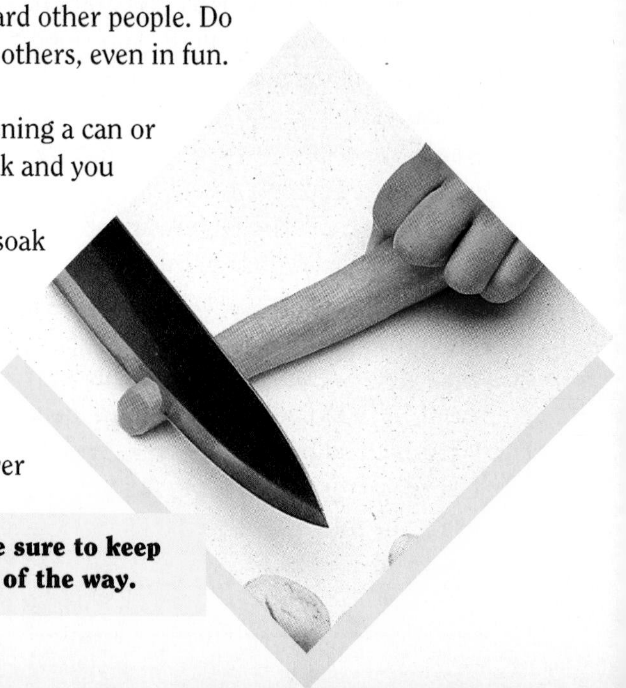

**When cutting, be sure to keep your fingers out of the way.**

# Preventing Falls

- Spills cause falls. If you spill something on the floor, wipe it up right away.
- Use a ladder or stepstool to reach high shelves. A chair or box can tip over easily.
- If you have a rug in the kitchen, be sure it has a nonskid back. This keeps it from sliding easily.
- If the floor is wet, do not walk on it. Wait until it is dry.

# Using Electricity Wisely

Many kitchen appliances run on electricity. Electricity, used wisely, can save time and work. If you misuse it, it can give you a severe shock or burn or even kill you. Remember, water and electricity do not mix.

- Never use an electrical appliance if your hands are wet or if you are standing on a wet floor.
- Keep electrical cords away from the sink and range.
- Keep appliances in good condition. Never use an appliance with a damaged cord. It could cause a shock or start a fire.
- Hold the plug, not the cord, when you disconnect an appliance. If you tug on the cord, you may damage it.
- Don't run electrical cords under a rug. They could get damaged.
- If you cannot get food out of an appliance, such as a toaster, disconnect it. Try turning the appliance upside down. If the food doesn't shake loose, take the appliance to a repair person. Never insert a fork or other object into the appliance. You could get a shock. Even if the appliance is disconnected, you could damage it.
- Don't plug too many appliances into one outlet. You could get a shock or start a fire.

**Water and electricity do not mix!**

**Why is this "electrical octopus" dangerous?**

# Preventing Burns and Fires

**Make sure your apron is tied. Tie back long hair. Hair will burn if it touches a flame or hot electric coil.**

Burns in the kitchen can come from many sources. Hot food, hot equipment, and steam are the most common. Fires can also start quickly in a kitchen. Here are some ways to prevent burns and fires.

- Wear close-fitting clothes. Roll up long sleeves when you cook.

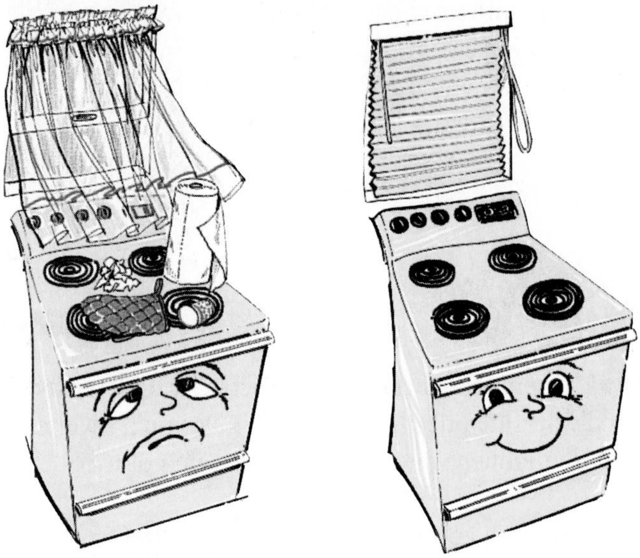

- Keep *flammable* materials (those that burn easily) away from the range. This includes kitchen curtains, towels, paper, potholders, and plastic items. Some plastics burn very fast and give off thick, black smoke and poisonous gases.
- Always use a potholder to handle hot pans. Be sure the potholder is dry. A damp potholder on a hot pan can cause a steam burn.

- Turn the handles of pans toward the center of the range. If handles are turned outward, someone may bump against them and knock the hot pan off the range.

- When you lift the cover from a hot pan, tilt the cover at an angle so the opening is away from you. Uncover the back of the pan first. The steam will flow away from you and cannot burn you.
- Wait until the range cools before you try to clean it.

- Use the oven safely. When you open a hot oven, stand to one side as you open the door.
- To put pans in the oven or remove them, use a potholder and pull out the oven rack. Put the pan on the rack or remove it. Gently slide the rack back into the oven.

- Aerosol sprays may be flammable. They can also explode if heated. Keep the cans and the spray away from heat sources, such as flames or radiators.
- Learn how to use a fire extinguisher. Every kitchen, at school or at home, should have one.

## Grease Fires

Fats and oils are very flammable. Keep equipment clean so grease doesn't build up. Watch cooking foods carefully. You must react quickly and correctly to stop a grease fire.

**DON'T . . .**

- Never pour water on a grease fire. It will cause the grease to spatter and burn you.
- Don't try to carry the burning pan to the sink. You could spill burning grease on yourself or cause the fire to spread.

**DO . . .**

- Turn off the heat immediately.
- Pour salt or baking soda over the flames. This will smother them.
- If salt or baking soda isn't nearby, put a cover on the pan. This will cut off the oxygen and smother the fire. You can also use a fire extinguisher.
- If the fire seems out of control, leave immediately. Alert others in the building to get out. Call the fire department.

**Use baking soda, salt, or a cover to smother grease fire flames.**

# Preventing Poisoning

Poisons can enter the body through . . .

◆ Drinking. ◆ Breathing. ◆ The skin.

Many household chemicals are poisonous. These include some products used for cleaning, pest control, personal care, medicine, gardening, and arts and crafts. Be alert for dangerous chemicals. Many times you can accomplish the same task with safer products.

**Choose household chemicals carefully. Are the directions easy to follow? Will you follow them?**

**Read labels carefully before using any household chemical.**

- ◆ When you shop for household chemicals, read the label directions carefully before you buy. Will you follow the directions? If not, choose a safer product.
- ◆ Don't buy more than you need. Some chemicals change as they age and may become dangerous to use. Disposing of leftover hazardous household chemicals can be a problem.
- ◆ Follow label directions exactly. You may be told to wear rubber gloves or a mask to prevent skin contact.
- ◆ If directions call for a well-ventilated area, open windows and use a fan. Otherwise, harmful fumes may build up.
- ◆ Never mix household cleaners together. Mixtures may release poisonous gases that could cause illness or death.
- ◆ Spray containers can contain poisonous chemicals. Be sure to point the nozzle in the right direction when you spray. Never spray toward another person or inhale the spray yourself.
- ◆ It may be necessary to use a *pesticide*—a poison which kills insects and other pests. Follow the directions carefully. You may have to cover food, dishes, and cookware or move them to another room.

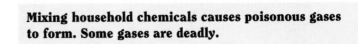

**Mixing household chemicals causes poisonous gases to form. Some gases are deadly.**

- Keep all household chemicals in their original containers. The labels give you information on use, storage, and what to do in case of an accident.
- Store chemicals carefully. Never store them in the same cabinet with food. The chemicals could spill into the food or someone could pick up the wrong container.
- If there are children in the household, buy products in childproof containers. Keep them in a locked cabinet.
- Get medical help immediately if somone is poisoned. Do you know the telephone number of the nearest poison control center? A *poison control center* has a staff specially trained to deal with poison emergencies. Be sure you know exactly what the poison is and about how much was taken or used. Have the container with you when you call.

**Store chemicals away from food to avoid contamination and poisoning.**

## Chapter 16 Review

### Check the Facts

1. Identify five common kitchen safety hazards.
2. Name two ways to prevent cuts.
3. What are two ways to prevent falls?
4. Name at least three general rules for using electrical appliances safely.
5. Describe how to safely remove pans from a hot oven.
6. What should you do in case of a grease fire?
7. Why is it important to read labels on household chemicals? Give at least three reasons.
8. Why is it harmful to mix household chemicals?
9. What is a poison control center?

### Ideas in Action

1. Develop a checklist for identifying kitchen hazards. Use your checklist at school and at home.
2. As a class, develop a list of ten safety rules to post in the foods lab. Make a poster for each lab unit.
3. In groups, select several common household chemicals used in the foods lab. Read the labels carefully. What warnings are given on the labels? Are first-aid instructions given? How could the labels be improved to make them more helpful to consumers?
4. Write a public service announcement concerning home safety for a local radio station. Focus on a specific safety topic.

CHAPTER 17

# Keeping Food Safe to Eat

**OBJECTIVES**

**Discover . . .**
- how harmful bacteria make food unsafe.
- how to keep food safe by practicing sanitation.
- how to keep food safe by storing it properly.

Cooking and eating food can be fun. You can keep it that way by learning how to keep food safe.

Have you ever heard someone say, "It must have been something I ate"? If food is not stored and handled properly, it can cause people to become ill. By following the guidelines in this chapter, you can make sure that the food you prepare and serve is safe to eat.

## Bacteria and Food

Illness caused by food that is not safe to eat is often called food poisoning. One type of food poisoning is called *salmonella* (sal-muh-NELL-uh). It can make you so sick you may have to go to the hospital.

Food poisoning is caused by certain types of bacteria. *Bacteria* (bak-TEER-ee-uh) are tiny living things that can only be seen with a microscope. Some bacteria are helpful. They are used to make food such as cheese and yogurt or to make medicine. Harmful bacteria, such as the ones that cause food poisoning, are sometimes called "germs."

Bacteria are everywhere. They are carried on people, animals, objects, raw food, and in the air.

Bacteria multiply very rapidly. In five hours, one bacteria can create 33,000! In order to multiply, bacteria need food and moisture. They also need warm temperatures. The chart on the next page shows how different temperatures affect bacteria.

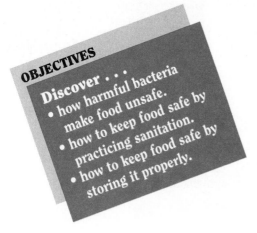

**Sanitation and proper storage are two ways to keep food safe to eat.**

## *Temperature Guide to Food Safety*

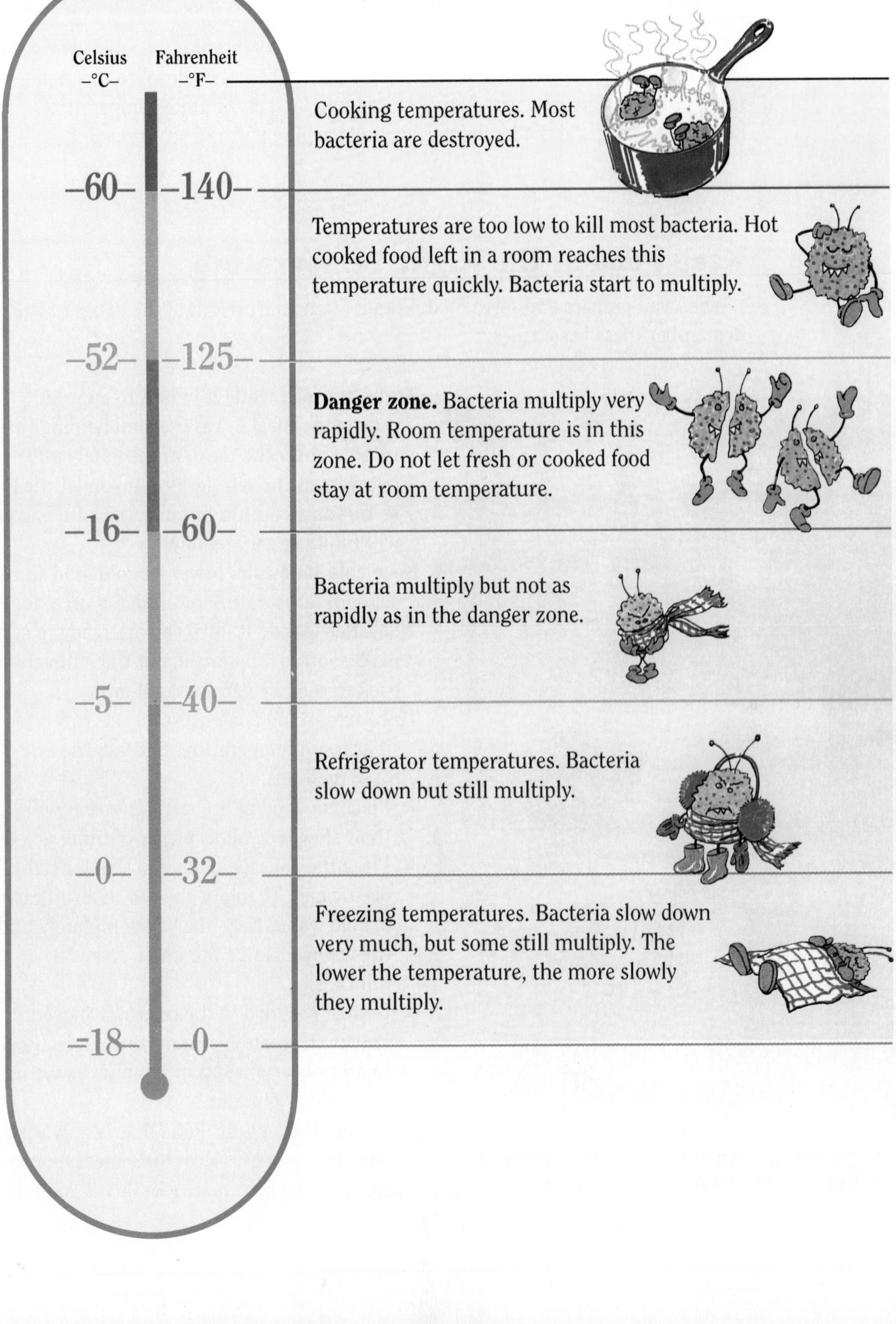

Celsius
–°C–
Fahrenheit
–°F–
Cooking temperatures. Most bacteria are destroyed.
–60– –140–
Temperatures are too low to kill most bacteria. Hot cooked food left in a room reaches this temperature quickly. Bacteria start to multiply.
–52– –125–
**Danger zone.** Bacteria multiply very rapidly. Room temperature is in this zone. Do not let fresh or cooked food stay at room temperature.
–16– –60–
Bacteria multiply but not as rapidly as in the danger zone.
–5– –40–
Refrigerator temperatures. Bacteria slow down but still multiply.
–0– –32–
Freezing temperatures. Bacteria slow down very much, but some still multiply. The lower the temperature, the more slowly they multiply.
–18– –0–

# Sanitation

One way to prevent food poisoning is to practice good sanitation whenever you work with food. *Sanitation* means keeping harmful bacteria down to as small a number as possible. You can do this by keeping food at the right temperature, keeping yourself and the kitchen clean, and keeping germs from spreading.

## Keep Food at the Right Temperature

When you prepare and serve food, keep its temperature out of the danger zone. Remember these basic rules:

**Serve hot food while it is hot. Keep the rest hot in case second helpings are needed.**

**Serve hot food while it is hot.** Keep it hot during the meal in case second helpings are wanted. After the meal, immediately put leftovers in the refrigerator. If you let the food sit out on a counter or table, harmful bacteria will multiply very rapidly.

**Keep cold food cold.** Never let cold food sit out at room temperature or outdoors on a hot day. Refrigerate it until you are ready to serve it. As soon as it is served, put the leftovers back in the refrigerator right away.

**Thaw frozen food safely.** Never let frozen food sit at room temperature. Instead, use one of these methods:

- Place the food in the refrigerator. It will thaw slowly, so allow plenty of time.
- Place the package of food in a water-tight plastic bag. Then put the bag in a container of cold water. Keep the bag completely under the water. Change the water every 30 minutes.
- Defrost the food in the microwave oven. Follow the manufacturer's directions. Food that has been thawed in the microwave must be cooked right away.

**Cook food thoroughly.** Food that is only partly cooked is not safe. Never taste meat, poultry, eggs, or fish when raw or while it's cooking.

## Keep the Kitchen Clean

Cleanliness is another very important rule when you work with food. Begin by making sure the kitchen is a clean place to work.

- Clean the kitchen and storage areas regularly. Then they will be less likely to attract insects and mice. These pests leave harmful bacteria wherever they go.
- Keep pets out of the kitchen, especially off the counters and table. Pet hairs carry harmful bacteria and can get into food easily.
- Keep your work area clean. Wash the countertop before you begin preparing food and after you are finished. Wipe up spills and spots immediately.
- Keep dirty dishes, pots, and pans away from the area where you prepare food.
- Have separate towels for wiping dishes and for wiping your hands. Never use the hand towel for wiping dishes—it may be loaded with harmful bacteria.
- In the kitchen, keep garbage in a can with a tight cover. Empty the garbage can daily—more often if needed.
- Rinse cans, bottles, and other food containers before recycling or throwing them out. Food left in containers breeds germs, creates odors, and attracts pests.

**Wipe up spills right away. If you let them sit, they can breed germs. They will become harder to wipe up, too.**

## Keep Yourself Clean

You wouldn't want to transfer dirt and harmful bacteria from yourself or your clothing to the food. Before you begin preparing food, give yourself a cleanliness inspection:

- Are you wearing clean clothes and a clean apron?
- If your hair is long, is it tied back to keep it out of food?
- Have you scrubbed your hands and fingernails with soap and hot water? If you have a cut or sore on your hands, wear rubber or plastic gloves. The wound contains harmful bacteria.

**Keep long hair tied back. Then you won't be tempted to touch it while preparing food.**

## Avoid Spreading Germs

**Why shouldn't you touch the rim of a glass when setting the table?**

After you start to work, be sure to prevent the spread of harmful bacteria from yourself to the food.

- After using the toilet, scrub your hands again. Body wastes are loaded with bacteria.
- Do not cough or sneeze into the food. Turn away and cover your nose and mouth with a disposable tissue or handkerchief. Wash your hands immediately.
- If you taste food during cooking, use the tasting spoon only once. Then wash it before using it again.
- When you set a table, avoid touching surfaces that come in contact with food or beverages, such as the rim or inside of a glass, the tines of a fork, or the center of a plate.

## Avoid Cross-Contamination

Raw meat, poultry, fish, and eggs can contain harmful bacteria. Cooking kills the bacteria in the food itself. But while you prepare these foods, the harmful bacteria gets on your hands, utensils, and work surface. Take steps to prevent *cross-contamination*—letting harmful bacteria spread from raw foods to other foods.

When you work with raw meat, poultry, or fish, always use a plastic cutting board, not a wooden one. Wooden boards are difficult to clean thoroughly. They can trap food particles and germs.

After working with raw meat, poultry, fish, or eggs:

- Wash equipment used for the raw food before it is used again.
- Wash the counter and your hands with hot, soapy water before handling other foods.
- Never put the cooked food back on the same plate that held the raw food. Instead, use a clean plate.

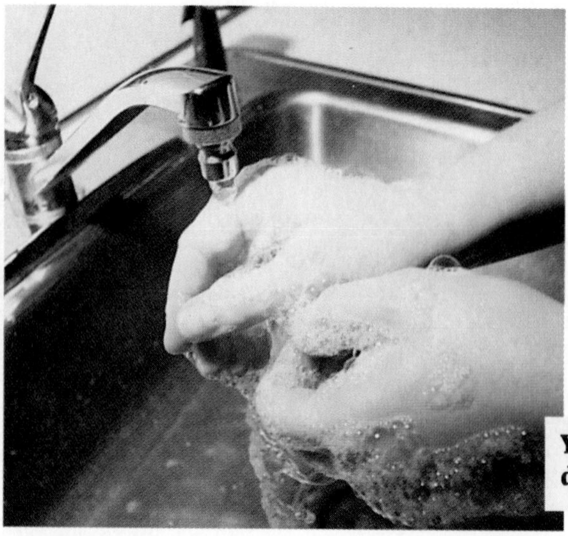

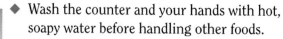

**You may need to wash your hands several times during food preparation. Can you explain why?**

# Storing Food

Another way to prevent food poisoning is to store food at the right temperatures. Proper storage also preserves the food's flavor and nutrients. It keeps food from becoming too moist or too dry and keeps dirt, dust, and insects away. Properly stored food stays fresh and usable for a longer time so you don't waste it.

There are three types of food storage areas: the refrigerator, freezer, and dry storage.

## Refrigerator Storage

The refrigerator provides short-term storage for foods that are *perishable,* which means they spoil easily. Perishable foods include meat, poultry, fish, milk, eggs, butter, and leftovers. Many fresh fruits and vegetables are also stored in the refrigerator to keep them fresh and crisp.

The temperature inside the refrigerator should be between 32°F and 40°F (0°C and 5°C). This degree of coldness helps prevent the growth of bacteria and preserves the flavor and texture of the food. Check the temperature regularly to be sure it stays in this range.

Some parts of the refrigerator may be colder than others. You can check with a thermometer. Shelves on the door are not as cold as the inside shelves.

Cover refrigerated food so it does not dry out. Perishable foods will keep in the refrigerator from a day to a few weeks, depending on the food. For longer storage, many foods can be frozen.

**It's a good idea to keep a thermometer in the refrigerator. Check it often to be sure the temperature stays at 32°F to 40°F (0°C to 5°C).**

## Freezer Storage

Freezing allows many foods to be stored for a longer time. However, keeping food safe and its quality high depends on proper freezing. Check the temperature of the freezer. It should be 0°F (-18°C) or below.

Foods you buy already frozen should be stored in their original packages. To freeze other foods, wrap in airtight wrapping such as freezer paper, heavy-duty aluminum foil, or freezer-quality plastic bags. You can also use plastic freezer containers. Avoid lightweight plastic tubs from foods such as cottage cheese, margarine, and yogurt. They do not provide enough protection in the freezer.

Not all foods freeze well. Avoid freezing cooked egg whites, foods made with mayonnaise or salad dressing, gelatin, and raw vegetables you don't plan to cook.

## Dry Storage

Foods that do not need refrigeration or freezing, such as unopened cans and many packaged foods, are stored in a dry storage area. This area can be a cabinet or shelves. It should be cool, dry, and clean.

Don't store food in cabinets above the refrigerator or range or near a radiator or furnace outlet. The temperatures will be too warm.

Once packages are opened, close them tightly before storing to keep out insects. You may also put the food in containers with tight-fitting covers.

## Storing Groceries

When you return from grocery shopping, store food right away. First put frozen foods in the freezer so they will not thaw. Next, refrigerate perishables such as milk, eggs, cheese, meat, poultry, and fish. Then store fruits and vegetables. (Refer to the guidelines in Chapters 26 and 27.) Finally, store foods that belong in the dry storage area.

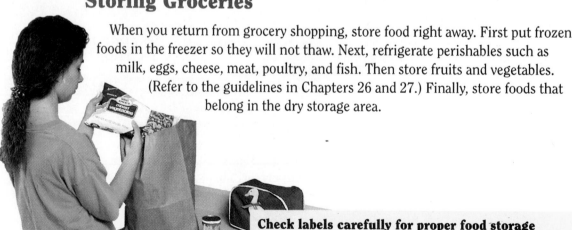

**Check labels carefully for proper food storage instructions. Food stays fresh longer when stored properly.**

When you put away your groceries, put new packages behind older ones of the same kind. By using up the older packages first, you will save food and money.

**Remember to use up older packages before you open new ones.**

## If Food Spoils

When food is not stored properly, or when it has been kept too long, it may spoil. Spoilage is caused by certain kinds of bacteria and by other organisms, such as mold. They can make the food unsafe or unpleasant to eat.

Food that has spoiled often has an unusual color, odor, texture, or flavor. If food shows any of these signs, discard it.

However, spoiled foods do not always show those signs. Don't take a chance. If leftovers are old, or you suspect they have not been stored properly, discard them. Remember this rule: "When in doubt, throw it out."

## Chapter 17 Review

### Check the Facts

1. What is food poisoning? What causes it?
2. What is the danger zone for food? Why is it dangerous?
3. Name four rules for keeping food at safe temperatures.
4. Name three safe ways to thaw frozen food.
5. Identify five important sanitation practices for keeping the kitchen clean.
6. What are five ways you can prevent spreading bacteria from yourself to food?
7. What is cross-contamination? List two ways to prevent it.
8. List three types of food storage areas. Give an example of food to be stored in each.
9. What should you do if stored food has an unusual color, odor, texture, or flavor? Why?

### Ideas in Action

1. Assume you are the local health inspector. Your job is to check sanitation practices at restaurants and cafeterias in your community. Make a list of items to look for as you are making the inspections. You may want to divide your list into categories such as food handling practices, kitchen cleanliness, and worker cleanliness.
2. Jeremy was babysitting for his neighbors. As he began preparing lunch for the children, he noticed that the refrigerator had stopped working. It had been working when he arrived at the house an hour earlier. Discuss what you think Jeremy should do.
3. Write a list of rules to promote sanitation in the foods lab.

CHAPTER 18

# Getting Organized

OBJECTIVES

Discover . . .
- how to plan for preparing food.
- how to work efficiently in the kitchen.
- the basic steps in cleaning up.
- how to be a member of the foods lab team.

Have you ever watched a cooking show on television? Perhaps you wondered how the chef could make such a complicated dish look so easy.

Successful food preparation calls for good management skills. Chefs on television have everything at hand. They know exactly what they are going to do and when they will do it. They are also practiced at working quickly and smoothly. Take a tip from them—learn to be organized when you work in the kitchen.

## Planning Ahead

When you think ahead and get ready before you start to work, food preparation is more successful and enjoyable. The first step is deciding what to prepare.

### Choosing a Recipe

Where can you find recipes? Good sources include cookbooks, magazines, newspapers, and food labels. Family and friends may also have favorite recipes to share.

Before you decide on a recipe, read through it carefully. Consider your resources:

**Time and energy.** How long will the recipe take to prepare? If time and energy are short, choose a simple recipe. Think about using some convenience foods or preparing some things ahead of time.

**Skills.** If you choose a recipe that calls for skills you have mastered, you can prepare it with confidence.

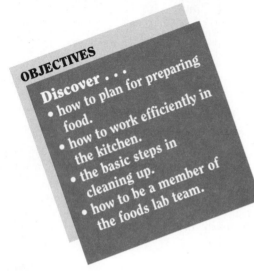

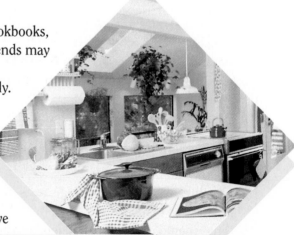

**By planning ahead, you can have your recipe and equipment ready when you begin to work.**

**Food.** Check to see if you have all the ingredients on hand. If not, add them to your shopping list.

**Money.** Will the recipe fit into your food budget? Perhaps you can find a recipe using foods that are on sale.

**Equipment.** Do you have the equipment you will need? Be sure you have the right size pan called for in the recipe.

**Always read through the recipe before deciding whether to use it. What should you look for as you read?**

If you are preparing an entire meal, you will probably need to choose more than one recipe. Chapter 20 will show you how to select foods that go together well for a meal. It also gives special tips for organizing meal preparation.

## Making a Work Plan

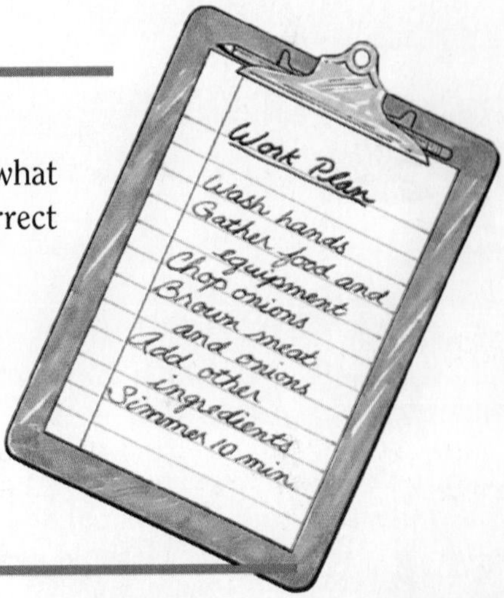


Another way to plan ahead is to make a *work plan*—a list of what you have to do to prepare the food. Each activity is listed in correct order so you do not miss a step.

When you make a work plan, be sure to include tasks that aren't in the recipe directions. For example, you might have to clean and chop vegetables, cook noodles, grease baking pans, or brown meat. This is called *pre-preparation*—getting the food or equipment ready to use in the recipe.

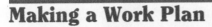

## Making a Schedule

Once you have a work plan, you can use it to make a time schedule. Estimate how long each step will take you. Subtract the total preparation time from the time you want the food to be ready. That tells you what time to start. For example, if you want the food ready at 6:00 and the preparation will take 45 minutes, you should start by 5:15.

When you are just learning to prepare food, it's a good idea to make a work plan and a schedule. As you gain more experience, you may not need to do so every time. But even experienced cooks use a work plan when they prepare a new dish or a special meal.

**If some steps in your work plan must be done ahead of time, use a note to remind yourself.**

# Working Efficiently

Now it's time to prepare the recipe. Before you begin, make sure you and your work area are clean. Review the cleanliness guidelines in Chapter 17.

As you work, think about whether there is a faster or better way to do the job. However, be sure to follow the rules of safety and cleanliness. Do not take shortcuts that may endanger you or the people who eat the food.

Here are some suggestions for working efficiently:

**Gather equipment and ingredients first.** By having everything you need at hand, you will be able to work without interruption. Arrange the items on the counter or table where you will work.

**Learn to use equipment properly.** Choose the right tool for the job and use it in the correct way. Otherwise, you will waste time and might damage the equipment.

**Set a timer.** If food must cook for a certain amount of time, don't rely on your memory.

**Use your work plan and time schedule.** Check off each task as you complete it.

**Dovetail tasks.** You may be able to work ahead on some steps while others are still going on. This is called *dovetailing*. For example, while waiting for water to boil, you can be measuring ingredients.

**Clean up as you work.** Have a clean, wet dishcloth handy to wipe up spills. Keep hot, sudsy water in the sink or a dishpan. When you have a few moments between tasks, wash any equipment you have finished using.

# Finishing the Job

After the food has been prepared and enjoyed, there is one more job left to do. The kitchen and eating area should be left clean and ready to use again.

When you serve the food, scrape it out of the pan thoroughly. Then rinse the pan. If food is stuck in the bottom, soak the pan in hot water.

After the meal, store leftovers properly. Then scrape all food off dishes into the garbage pail or the disposer.

If the kitchen has an automatic dishwasher, follow the directions in the owner's manual. Some items cannot be put in the dishwasher because it may damage them.

To wash dishes by hand, follow these guidelines:

- Use hot, sudsy water and a clean dishcloth.
- For hard-to-clean spots on pots and pans, use a scouring pad. Abrasive scouring pads should not be used on some cookware. There are nonabrasive pads for these materials.
- Wash glassware first, then other dishes used for eating. Save greasy or heavily soiled items for last.
- Rinse thoroughly in hot water. One way is to put the dishes in a rack in the sink and pour hot water over them.
- You can keep the dishes in the rack until they dry by themselves, or you can dry them with a clean dish towel.
- Put all dishes and equipment away as soon as they are dry. Otherwise, they may gather dust and bacteria.

**Line up dishes in the order they will be washed. Why are more heavily soiled items washed last?**

**Working together makes cleanup go faster.**

After the dishes have been washed, wipe up any crumbs or spills from the table and counters. Sweep the floor. If the kitchen is clean, the job is done!

# Teamwork in the Foods Lab

When you prepare food in the school foods lab, you work in a group with other class members. You use a work plan and time schedule, just as you have already learned. The difference is that the work is divided among the group members. For example, as one person preheats the oven and greases baking pans, another may measure ingredients, while a third sets the table.

**Learning to cooperate and work as a team is important to the success of any foods lab.**

Teamwork is the key to success in the foods lab. Everyone in the group must cooperate if you are to reach your goal. That means all team members must do their share of the work to the best of their ability.

Suppose your job is to measure the ingredients. If you don't have them ready when the others need them, your group may not finish on time. If you are careless, the recipe may not turn out right.

Teamwork also requires good planning. The different tasks must be timed so that the work flows smoothly.

Here are some suggestions to help your lab group work well together:

- Prepare your work plan together. Be sure you all understand and agree on it.
- As you plan, look for ways to work efficiently. Remember that your time in the lab is limited.
- Be sure the work is divided equally. Making one person do most of the work is not only unfair, it slows the whole group down.
- Try to stick to the plan as you work. However, be prepared to make changes if an unexpected problem comes up.
- Take responsibility for your share of the work. Remember, the whole team is depending on you.
- When you finish your part of the job, ask your partners how you can help them.

## Evaluating the Lab

As part of the foods lab, you will evaluate the food you prepared. Rate it according to its appearance, texture, and flavor. You may be given a scorecard which will help you with your evaluation.

**Evaluation is an important part of the lab experience. Why is it important to evaluate both the finished product and the group's performance as a team?**

It's just as important to evaluate how well you worked together. Evaluating the lab will help you be even more successful in the future. Get together with the other members of the team. Ask yourselves:

- Did the work go smoothly?
- Was the project completed on time?
- Did we leave the kitchen clean?
- Did any unexpected problems arise? How well did we handle them?
- How might we change the plan next time? Why?

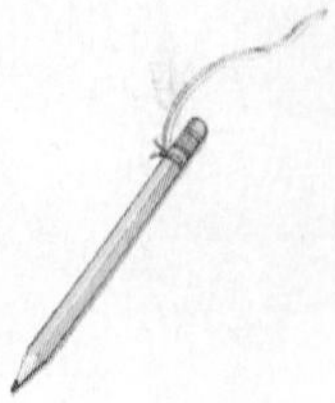

## Chapter 18 Review

### Check the Facts

1. Name five resources you should think about when choosing a recipe.
2. What is a work plan? Give two examples of tasks that might be included in a work plan.
3. Identify six suggestions for working efficiently in the kitchen.
4. In what order should dishes be washed by hand?
5. Give five general tips for washing dishes.
6. Why is teamwork important in the foods lab?
7. Give at least three suggestions that can help lab group members work well as a team.
8. After completing a foods lab work plan, how can you evaluate how well the plan worked? Name at least three specific ways.

### Ideas in Action

1. Discuss why it is helpful to clean up as you work.
2. Use the information in the chapter to prepare a demonstration on kitchen cleanup and dishwashing for a group of young children.
3. In small groups, select a simple recipe that could be prepared in the foods lab. Develop a work plan and time schedule that your group could use when preparing this recipe. Include the specific tasks that will be completed by each group member and the time you think each will take. If possible, use your plan and evaluate how well it worked.

CHAPTER 19

# Conserving and Recycling

**OBJECTIVES**

**Discover . . .**
- how to conserve fuel and water in the kitchen.
- how to cut down on food waste.
- what you can do to reduce, reuse, and recycle.

As you read in Chapter 2, most natural resources are scarce. This chapter will help you learn how to conserve resources when working in the kitchen. There are many other ways for you to conserve resources at home and in the community. Find out what else you can do to help.

Saving the environment begins with every person on this planet doing his or her share. You can make a difference by doing your part. Encourage others to do theirs by setting an example.

## Conserve Fuel

By using less fuel, you insure a supply for the future. You also help prevent pollution. Here are some guidelines to help you conserve fuel in the kitchen.

- When using appliances, carefully follow the directions in the owner's manual. Keep appliances clean and in good condition. Appliances that are dirty or not working properly use more fuel than normal.
- Use small appliances, such as a toaster oven or electric skillet, when you can. They are often more efficient than either the rangetop or a large oven.
- If you can't use a small appliance, remember that the oven is usually more efficient than the rangetop. In the oven, the heat comes on only when it must in order to keep the proper temperature. When you cook on top of the range, the heat flows constantly.
- Cook an entire meal in the oven at the same time so you get the most use of the fuel. For instance, you could bake meat loaf, potatoes, and a green bean casserole together.

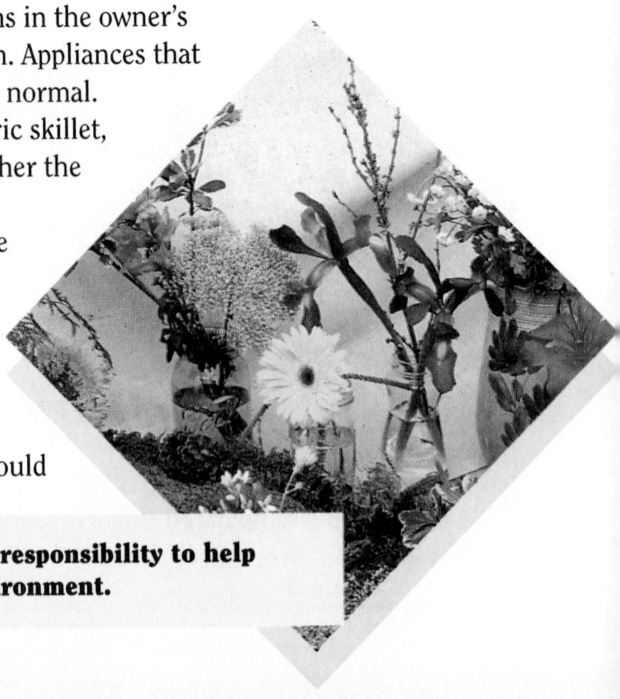

**Everyone has a responsibility to help protect the environment.**

- Keep the oven door closed. If you open the oven door frequently to see how the food is cooking, heat escapes, fuel is wasted, and the food takes longer to cook.

# Conserve Water

Communities depend on having a source of clean, fresh water. In some areas there is not enough water to go around. Droughts—unusually long periods with no rain or snow—can create a water shortage. In addition, pollution is ruining the water supply in some communities.

Even though your community may not be experiencing a shortage now, learn to conserve water. That way, you will help ensure a supply of good drinking water for the future. Here are some guidelines:

- Have dripping faucets repaired.

**One drop a second can waste 700 gallons (2800 L) of water a year.**

- Do not run a dishwasher unless you have a full load. If you have just a few dishes, wash them by hand.
- Don't let water run while you're doing something else.
- Use detergents and other cleaning compounds only as directed. If you use more than needed, you can pollute the water supply.
- Use detergents and other cleaners that do not contain phosphates. Phosphates are chemicals that pollute water.
- Dyed paper pollutes water. Buy plain white paper towels, napkins, and toilet paper.
- Use household chemicals completely before you throw out the container. Leftover chemicals in landfills can leak into the water supply.
- Do not pour household chemicals down the drain. Contact your sanitation department and ask how to dispose of them.

# Conserve Food

Sadly, food is not plentiful for everyone. The less food you waste, the more there will be to go around.

Food is a precious resource. It is scarce in many parts of the world. Yet a surprisingly large amount of edible food in the United States is thrown away as garbage. You can help prevent this needless waste.

When shopping, don't buy more food than you can use up before it spoils. Buy food that is in good condition and store it properly. Use it before it begins to lose quality.

Use correct cooking procedures. Food that is poorly cooked may end up in the garbage can.

When you help yourself to food, take only as much as you're sure you will eat. When serving food to others, keep portions small. Let people ask for seconds if they want them.

Store leftovers properly so that they stay safe and in good condition. Plan how you will use them.

# Conserve Other Resources

Every American produces about 4 lb. (2 kg) of trash every day! Why is this a problem? Throwing items away costs resources. For example, most plastics are made from petroleum (oil), a resource that is limited. The more plastic products that are made and thrown away, the faster petroleum is used up.

The way people get rid of trash also affects the environment. Trash is normally buried in landfills or dumps. Many communities are running out of space for landfills and are looking for solutions.

What can you do to help? Practice the environmental 3 Rs:

**Reduce. . . . . . . . . .Reuse. . . . . . . . . .Recycle**

Trash—and what to do with it—is a growing problem. How can you be part of the solution?

## Reduce

**It's easy to cut down on disposable items and packaging, once you get in the habit.**

First, look for ways to reduce the amount of paper, plastics, and other products you use. The less you use, the less you have to get rid of.

*Disposables* are products that are used once or perhaps a few times and then thrown away. Many people are in the habit of using them, but habits can be changed.

Try making the switch yourself. Instead of wiping up a spill with a paper towel, use a washcloth. Use cloth napkins instead of paper ones. Wash a glass instead of using a paper cup. Can you think of other ways to use fewer disposables?

Consumer packaging is another source of waste. It makes up about 50 percent of the trash. When you shop, look for items without a lot of packaging. When you buy something small that's easy to carry, tell the clerk not to put it in a bag. Be sure to get a receipt so you can prove you bought it when you leave the store.

## Reuse

Many items that you would normally throw away can be reused in the home. For example, you can use the colorful Sunday comics to wrap gifts. Even if your homemade wrap does eventually get thrown away, reusing kept you from having to buy paper just for wrapping. That saves money as well as natural resources.

Here are a few suggestions:

- Use large paper bags for trash. Smaller bags can be used to line wastepaper baskets, carry a lunch, or ripen fruit.
- Reuse foil containers from frozen foods for baking.
- Use plastic plates from frozen foods as saucers under potted plants.
- Save glass jars and covers. After washing, use them to store food in a cabinet or refrigerator. They're handy for bulk food items.
- Community centers, schools, and senior citizens centers always need materials for arts and crafts projects. Donate reusable items such as margarine tubs, juice cans, and cardboard rolls from paper towels.

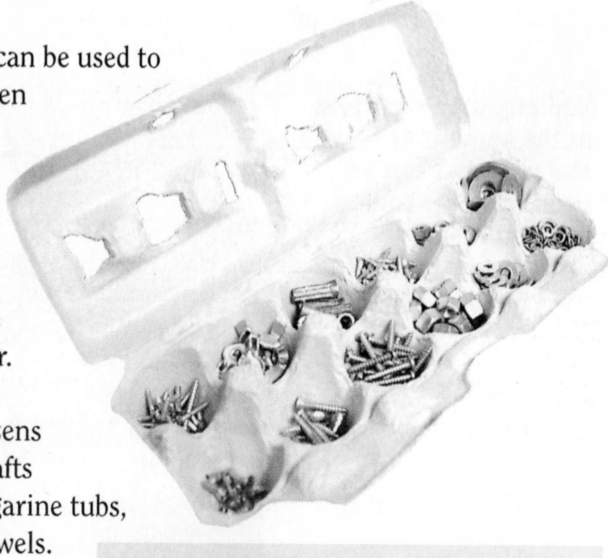

**Can you think of other creative uses for common household items?**

## Recycle

When items are recycled, they are put through a special process. The materials from these products are used to manufacture other items. It usually takes less fuel to make a product from recycled materials than from new ones.

If an item is recyclable or is made from recycled materials, it carries this recycling emblem...

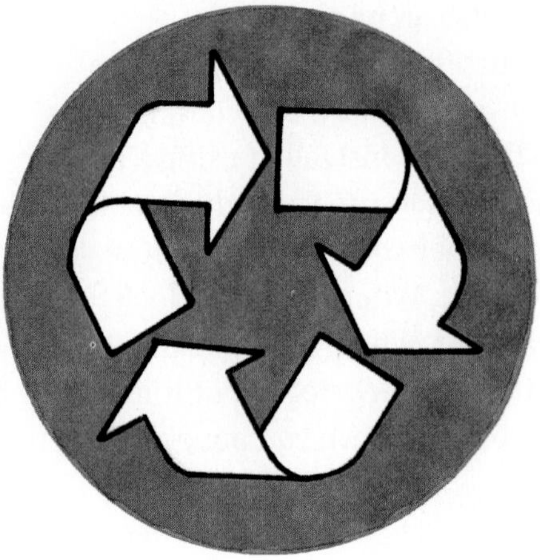

Look for the emblem whenever you shop. Try to buy recycled or recyclable items as much as possible. Fewer products will end up in the trash.

How do items get recycled? Instead of throwing away recyclable products, consumers save them. They give them to their community's recycling program. Newspapers, other paper, cardboard, aluminum and other metals, glass, and some plastics can be recycled.

**You might be surprised at the amount of material that can be recycled. Does your community have a recycling program?**

**When you recycle...**

- Follow the rules established by your community's recycling program. Be sure you know what types of items are accepted.
- Rinse containers thoroughly so there is no food left to attract mice, insects, and other pests.
- Prepare the items as directed. For example, you may have to remove labels from cans or sort glass by color.
- Save space by flattening cans, crushing plastic containers, and breaking cardboard boxes down.
- Find out what to do with the items you've saved. In some communities, recycled items are picked up as part of the regular trash collection or on special days. In others, consumers take the items to a collection station.

What if there is no recycling program in your community? Find out why. Perhaps you could volunteer to help start one.

## Chapter 19 Review

### Check the Facts

1. List three ways to conserve fuel in the kitchen.
2. Why is water conservation important?
3. Give at least four examples showing how to protect the water supply.
4. Identify four ways to conserve food.
5. Why is it important to cut down on the amount of trash produced?
6. Name two ways you can reduce your use of disposable items.
7. Make four suggestions for reusing household items.
8. How does recycling conserve resources?
9. Identify four guidelines for recycling.

### Ideas in Action

1. In small groups, brainstorm ideas for a recycling program for your school. Consider the kinds of items to be recycled, how to collect them, how the project will be managed, and how it can fit into a community program.
2. Draw cartoons to illustrate different ways to conserve natural resources.
3. Write a message about conservation to place in a time capsule. What are people doing now to conserve resources? How can they do more? What are your hopes and concerns for the future?
4. Create a 30-second radio commercial promoting recycling.

CHAPTER 20

# Meal Management

**OBJECTIVES**

**Discover. . .**
- how to plan the menu for a meal.
- how to make meals appealing.
- how to time meal preparation.

Have you ever prepared an entire meal for your family or friends? If you haven't yet, you will one day. How can you make the meal a success?

Successful meals don't just happen. They depend on a well-planned menu and a well-organized cook.

The key is *meal management*—using basic management skills, such as planning, making decisions, and using time wisely, to help you prepare good meals.

## Planning a Menu

Menu planning is the first step in meal management. A *menu* is a list of the foods that you plan to serve at a meal. The best meals are made up of nutritious foods that not only look and taste good, but go well together.

Where do you begin? It's often easiest to start by choosing a main dish. Then you can select other foods that will complement, or work well with, the main dish. As you make your choices, keep these points in mind:

**Meal patterns.** People often prefer different foods for breakfast than they would for lunch. Will this be a light meal or the main meal of the day?

**Nutrition.** Include foods from the five main groups in the Daily Food Guide. Choose foods that are nutritious without extra amounts of fat, sugar, and sodium.

**Individual needs.** Who will be eating the meal? What do they like and dislike? Does anyone have special nutritional needs?

**Your own resources.** Consider time, energy, food, money, skills, and equipment.

**A well-planned menu makes any meal more appetizing and nutritious.**

## Menus with Appeal

Another important consideration is meal appeal. You want the food you serve to be appetizing. It should look and taste good so that everyone will enjoy eating it.

When you plan a menu, think about:

**Flavor.** Have a variety of flavors in the meal. Balance strong, spicy flavors with milder ones.

**Color.** Try to include at least one brightly colored food in each meal, or a pleasing variety of colors. You can add color with a garnish such as parsley, a wedge of lemon, radish slices, carrot curls, or a sprinkling of paprika.

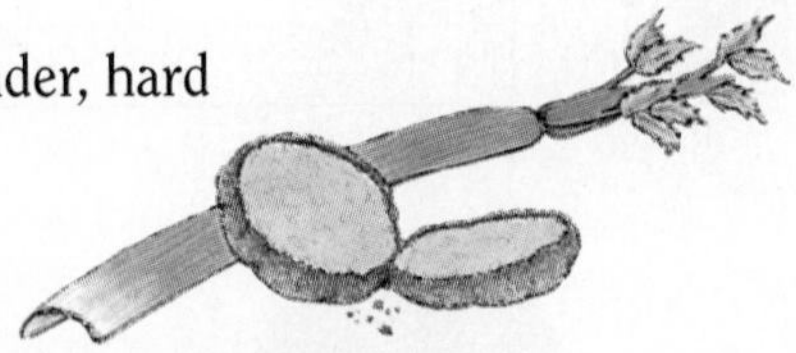

**Texture.** Texture means whether the food is crunchy or tender, hard or soft. A meal should have a mixture of textures.

**Temperature.** On a very hot day, a chilled salad would be more appealing than steaming soup. However, a variety of temperatures can make a meal interesting.

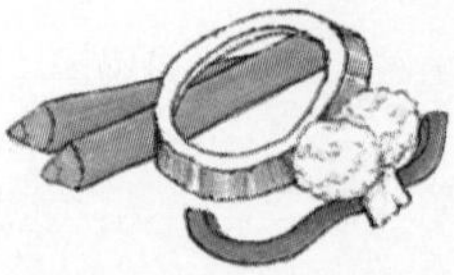

**Size and shape.** What's wrong with a meal of meatballs, peas, rolls, and melon balls? Use a variety of sizes and shapes in meals. Many foods can be cut into slices, strips, or cubes to add interest.

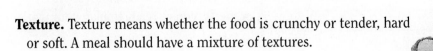

**Which of these two meals is more attractive? Why?**

# Timing a Meal

Once you've planned what to serve, you need to plan how you will prepare it. Your goal is to have all the foods for the meal ready at the right time.

A work plan makes it easier to coordinate meal preparation. In Chapter 18, you learned how to make a work plan by listing all the steps in preparing a recipe from start to finish. You also learned that once you have a work plan, you can make a schedule. Now you will learn how to make a work plan and schedule for an entire meal.

Suppose you will be preparing this menu:

Broiled Fish
Broccoli
Brown Rice
Fresh Spinach and Tomato Salad
Whole Wheat Rolls
Baked Apple
Skim Milk

Begin by thinking about your choices for each food—what to buy and how you will prepare it. For example, do you want to save time by using instant brown rice?

Use your menu to make out your shopping list, as you learned in Chapter 8. After you buy the food and store it properly, you're ready to plan your work.

## List Steps and Estimate Times

First, make a list with three columns. Write down:

- The foods on your menu.
- The basic steps you will use to prepare each food.
- How much time each step will take. Cooking times are usually given in the recipe or package directions. Estimate how much time you'll need for other steps.

The example on the next page shows how the beginning of your list might look.

Also list basic tasks like washing your hands, gathering food and equipment, setting the table, and putting food into serving dishes. Estimate how long they will take.

**Reading the package directions can help you estimate how much time you'll need to prepare the food.**

| Food | Basic steps | Time needed |
|---|---|---|
| Broiled Fish | • Thaw fillets in refrigerator | Overnight |
| | • Rinse thawed fillets; put on broiler grid | 10 min. |
| | • Broil in oven | 15 min. |
| Frozen Broccoli | • Remove from package; put in container | 5 min. |
| | • Microwave | 10 min. |
| | • Let stand | 1-2 min. |

## Decide on the Best Sequence

Next, think about the best order in which to complete all the steps. Why not just prepare the fish first, then the broccoli, and so on right down your list? If you did, the foods would not all be ready to serve at the same time. Also, the meal would take longer to prepare.

It's usually more efficient to have several foods "in the works" at the same time. You can complete some of the steps for one food and set it aside or let it start cooking. Then you can begin working on another food.

How can you plan the most efficient sequence?

- Look for tasks that can be done ahead of time. For example, you can make the salad early, then put it in the refrigerator until it's time to eat.
- Look for ways to dovetail tasks. Can you prepare another food while the salad vegetables are draining? Can the dessert microwave while you eat the rest of the dinner?
- Don't try to dovetail two tasks that require your full attention. Look for another solution. Perhaps one food could be prepared first, then reheated at the last minute.
- If someone will be helping you prepare the meal, divide the work so you each have specific jobs to do.

**A few extra minutes of planning can help you save time and effort in preparing the meal.**

## Plan What Time to Start

Once you have all the steps for preparing the meal written down in order, you have a work plan. To turn the work plan into a schedule, you just need to write down the time for starting each task. Remember, when you make a schedule, you work backward from the time you want to serve the meal.

Here is how your finished plan might turn out:

**WORK PLAN AND SCHEDULE**

| | |
|---|---|
| Night before | Put fish in refrigerator to thaw. |
| 4:25 | Wash hands, get ready to cook. |
| 4:30 | Set table. |
| 4:45 | Gather food and equipment. |
| 4:55 | Rinse apples and salad vegetables; let vegetables drain. |
| 5:00 | Prepare apples for microwaving; set aside. |
| 5:10 | Assemble salad; refrigerate. |
| 5:20 | Prepare fish for broiling. |
| 5:30 | Start water heating in saucepan; measure rice. |
| 5:35 | Prepare broccoli for microwaving. |
| 5:40 | Add rice to pan; cover and let stand. Put pan of fish in broiler; set timer. Put broccoli in microwave. |
| 5:50 | Set rolls on table. Remove salad from refrigerator. Pour milk. |
| 5:55 | Check fish for doneness. Put food in serving dishes. Put apples in microwave. |
| 6:00 | The meal is ready! |

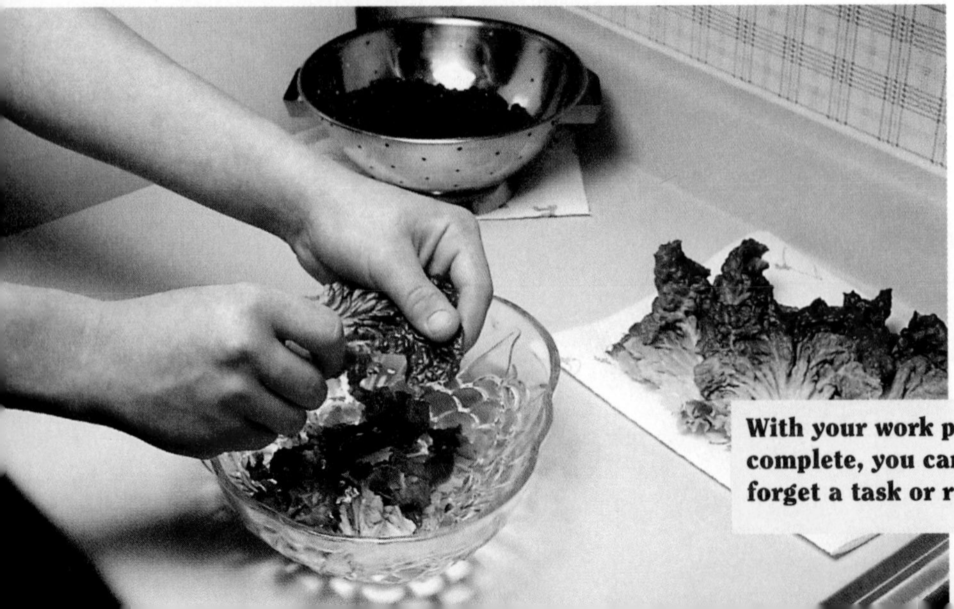

**With your work plan and schedule complete, you can be sure that you won't forget a task or run out of time.**

# Evaluating the Meal

Planning a menu, writing out a work plan, and making a schedule require some thought. But the few extra minutes you spend ahead of time can make the meal preparation go much more smoothly.

After the meal, evaluate how successful it was. Did your plan work as you expected? Did everyone enjoy the food? If so, save your menu and schedule to use again. If not, think about what you might change next time. Then try again. With practice, you will soon be skilled at making appealing, nutritious, well-managed meals.

**Preparing meals is a skill you can be proud of. It will help you now and in the future.**

## Chapter 20 Review

### Check the Facts

1. Name four points, other than meal appeal, to consider in planning a menu.
2. Identify five factors that make meals appealing. Give one example of how each may be used in meal planning.
3. Why is timing important when planning a meal?
4. Briefly describe how to make a work plan for a meal.
5. When preparing a meal, is it usually best to finish preparing one food before starting on another? Why or why not?
6. Describe how to develop a schedule for meal preparation.

### Ideas in Action

1. Make a poster showing different ways to create meal appeal. Find pictures showing different combinations of flavor, color, texture, temperature, size, and shape of foods.
2. Write a news bulletin offering busy people creative ideas for improving meal plans. Be sure to include ideas on using a work plan and schedule.
3. With a partner, plan a meal menu including at least three different foods. Develop a work plan for the menu according to the guidelines suggested in the chapter. Then develop a schedule for preparing the meal.

CHAPTER 21

# Serving A Meal

**OBJECTIVES**

**Discover . . .**
- basic methods for serving a meal.
- how to set a table.
- guidelines for table behavior.

Mealtime should be relaxing and enjoyable. This is true whether the meal is an informal one with family or friends or a more formal meal with guests or in a fancy restaurant. In this chapter, you will learn how to serve food and set the table in ways that help make any meal more pleasant. You will also find that good conversation and simple courtesy add to a meal's enjoyment.

## Types of Meal Service

Every family has its own customs about who sits where and how most meals are served. A well-planned routine can help mealtime be an orderly, relaxed, and comfortable time.

There are two basic styles that most people use to serve meals:

**Family style** means the food is placed in serving dishes on the table. People help themselves, passing serving dishes to each other.

**Plate service** means the food is already on each person's plate when it is brought to the table.

Families often use a combination of family style and plate service. Some foods, such as meat and dessert, may be brought to the table on plates. Others, such as salad and vegetables, are in serving dishes on the table.

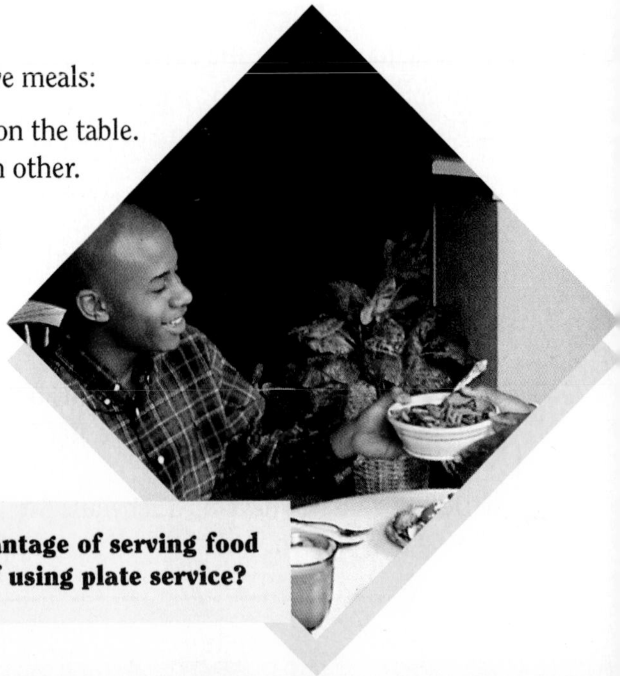

**What is an advantage of serving food family style? Of using plate service?**

# Setting the Table

Certain items, called tableware, are needed to serve and eat food. The tableware you need for a meal depends on the food you serve and the way you serve it. Tableware includes:

**Plates.** Large plates are usually used for the main course. Salads, desserts, and bread are often served on separate, smaller plates. Why? If these foods were placed on the large plate next to hot foods, they might wilt, melt, or get soggy.

**Other dishes.** Bowls are needed for foods such as cereal, soup, and some salads and desserts. Hot beverages are served in a mug or in a cup with a saucer. If you serve the meal family style, you will also need serving dishes, such as large bowls and platters.

**Glasses.** These can include a glass for water and a glass for another beverage, such as milk. Glasses come in two basic shapes. *Stemware* has a stem between the base and the bowl. It is fragile because the stem breaks easily. Hold stemware by the base of the bowl, not by the stem. *Tumblers* are glasses without stems. They come in many shapes and sizes.

**Flatware.** Items such as forks and spoons are called *flatware*. The basic items include a dinner knife to cut meat and spread butter, a dinner fork, and a teaspoon for beverages and some desserts. You might add another fork, slightly smaller than the dinner fork, for salad or dessert. A larger-bowled soup spoon is used for soups.

**Table linens.** These include napkins, placemats, and tablecloths.

# The Place Setting

Each piece of tableware has a specific place where it should be put on the table. The arrangement of tableware for each individual is called a *place setting*. It is designed for the convenience of the person eating.

**To set the table . . .**

1. Put a tablecloth or placemats on the table.
2. Decide what tableware will be needed for each person to eat the meal.
3. Arrange the items in each place setting. Use the picture and guidelines on these pages to help you place items correctly. Start by putting the plate in the center. Arrange the flatware next. Finally, add other items around the outside of the setting.

- The salad plate goes above the forks.
- Place the dinner plate in the center of each place setting. The edge of the plate should be about 1 inch (2.5 cm) from the edge of the table. If the food is being served on plates from the kitchen, allow enough space for the plate.
- Put the napkin to the left of the forks. The folded edge should be the farthest from the forks. The napkin can then be picked up by the corner edge and unfolded easily.
- Place the forks to the left of the dinner plate.
- What if you need both a salad fork and a dinner fork? A basic rule is to arrange flatware so that the piece you use first is farthest from the plate. If the salad is to be eaten before the main course, you would place the salad fork on the outside.

## Table Decorations

A table decoration in the center of the table, no matter how simple, can make a meal more pleasant. Ordinary items in your home can be the beginning of a table centerpiece. Here are some ideas:

- An arrangement of fruit in a bowl or basket or on a cutting board. You might serve the fruit as dessert.
- Flowers in an attractive container, such as a teapot, a pitcher, or an old, unusual coffee pot.
- A grouping of several different candles on a placemat.

- Put the water glass just above the tip of the knife. If there is another beverage glass, place it to the right and slightly in front of the water glass.

- Put the cup and saucer to the right of the spoons.

- Place the knife to the right of the plate with the blade facing the plate.
- Put the spoon to the right of the knife. If there is more than one, place the spoon that will be used first (such as a soup spoon) farthest from the plate.
- Be sure the handle end of each flatware piece lines up with the lower edge of the plate.

# Making Meals Pleasant

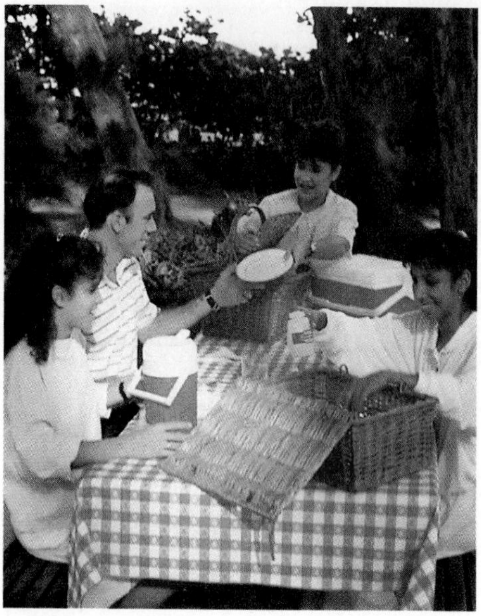

Mealtime can be a pleasant time of sharing.

Mealtime is time for those gathered about the table to talk about their day, share ideas, and enjoy each other's company. Good conversation can make the whole meal more enjoyable—and easier to digest, too. Help keep the conversation cheerful and positive. Save any disputes or problems for after the meal.

## Basic Table Manners

Table manners are really a matter of courtesy. They make everyone more comfortable so the meal is more enjoyable. Remember to use good table manners every day, not just on special occasions. Soon they will become a habit.

Here are some guidelines for good table manners:

- Place your napkin in your lap.
- If you are in a small group, be sure everyone has been served before you begin to eat. In a large group, you may start to eat as soon as three or four people have been served. Otherwise your food might get cold.
- If you don't know which piece of flatware to use, watch the host or hostess. Remember, flatware is placed so that the piece you use first is farthest from the plate. Start with the piece on the outside and work your way in.
- Don't talk with food in your mouth.
- Reach for food only if you do not have to lean too far across the table or reach in front of anyone. Otherwise, ask your neighbor to pass it to you. Be sure to say "please" and "thank you."
- Avoid putting your elbows on the table as you eat. However, you may rest your elbows on the table between courses if you like.
- Cut off as much meat as you can from foods like chicken, steak, and chops. At home or in informal restaurants, you may then pick up the bone with your fingers and chew off the remaining meat.
- At a formal meal, only foods such as olives and celery may be eaten with the fingers.

- Some foods, such as corn or peas, may be difficult to get onto a fork. Push them on the fork with a piece of bread or a knife.
- If you cough or sneeze, turn your head away from the table. If you have a coughing or sneezing spell or must blow your nose, excuse yourself and leave the table.
- When you are not eating, rest your fork and knife on the plate. When you are through eating, put them in the center of the plate.

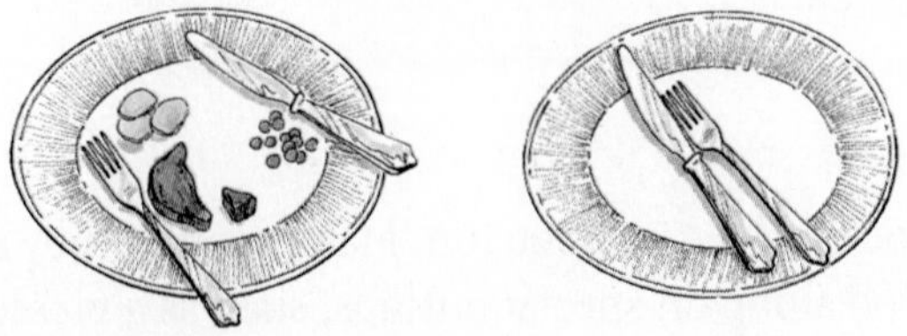

## Clearing the Table

After everyone is finished eating, it's time to clear the table. Stand to the side of each person as you pick up dishes from the place setting. Then carry the dishes to the cleanup area. Do not scrape or stack dishes at the table.

## Chapter 21 Review

### Check the Facts

1. Name and describe the two basic styles for serving most meals.
2. What is tableware? Give at least two examples of each type of tableware.
3. Draw a place setting using the following items: placemat, dinner plate, salad plate, napkin, salad fork, dinner fork, knife, teaspoon, water glass, and a glass for milk.
4. Why should good table manners be practiced daily? List two reasons.
5. What should you do if you are unsure about which piece of flatware to use?
6. List at least six guidelines for good table manners.

### Ideas in Action

1. Brainstorm a list of possible conversation topics for mealtime. What kinds of questions can you ask to get a conversation going? How may planning some topics of conversation benefit mealtime?
2. In small groups, design a flyer giving teens helpful guidelines on table behavior.
3. Assume you are going to entertain five of your friends for an evening meal. Write the menu for the food to be served. Using the guidelines in the chapter, list what tableware you will need to serve this meal. Plan the table linens and decorations.

CHAPTER 22

# Packing A Lunch

**OBJECTIVES**

**Discover . . .**
- how to plan a nutritious packed lunch.
- how to keep a packed lunch safe to eat.
- ideas for adding variety to your lunch.
- how to prepare and pack your lunch.

Food on the go can be fun. Many people enjoy taking food along on special outings, such as a picnic or football game. Perhaps you bring your lunch to school every day.

What is your goal when making a packed lunch or any other portable meal? You want the meal to be safe and in good condition when you eat it. You also want a lunch that is nutritious, interesting, and tasty.

## Nutrition for Packed Lunches

To plan a nutritious packed lunch, use the Daily Food Guide (pages 42-43). Be sure to include plenty of fruits, vegetables, and whole grains. Add a high-protein food, such as lean meat, cooked dry beans, or peanut butter. A dairy food, such as skim milk, yogurt, or cottage cheese, can round out the meal.

## Food Safety for Packed Lunches

As you learned in Chapter 17, food must be kept either cold or very hot. Otherwise harmful bacteria soon begin to multiply and could cause serious illness.

Your lunch container may have to sit at room temperature for several hours. How can you keep the food inside safe? Read on to find out.

**Foods brought from home can make up all or part of a nutritious lunch.**

## Using a Vacuum Bottle

A *vacuum bottle* is an insulated bottle that keeps foods at their original temperature. Narrow-mouth vacuum bottles are used for beverages. Wide-mouth vacuum bottles are used for hot foods such as soups, casseroles, and chili. Bottles with a glass or stainless steel lining do a better job of keeping foods hot than those with plastic interiors.

Vacuum bottles need to be prechilled or preheated to help keep food and beverages at the right temperature. For cold foods and beverages, you can fill the bottle the night before and refrigerate. For hot foods and beverages, pour hot water into the bottle in the morning. Let it stand a few minutes while you heat the food to be packed. Pour out the hot water and fill with the heated food or beverage.

**If you can't buy a nutritious beverage at lunchtime, take one along in a prechilled vacuum bottle.**

## Tips for Keeping Food Cold

A vacuum bottle will work for a cold beverage, but not your sandwich or carrot sticks. Here are some other ways to keep food cold:

- Keep cold foods in the refrigerator or freezer until you are ready to pack your lunch in the morning.
- Pack a tightly-sealed container of frozen water or juice with your lunch. You can also buy small, reusable packs of frozen gel to use instead.
- Include a frozen sandwich in your lunch. It will stay cold longer and help keep the other foods cold, too. By lunchtime, the sandwich will be thawed and ready to eat.
- Pack your lunch in an insulated bag.
- Store your lunch in as cool a place as possible. Keep it out of sunny areas and away from heat sources, such as a radiator.

**A freezable gel container can help keep your lunch cold.**

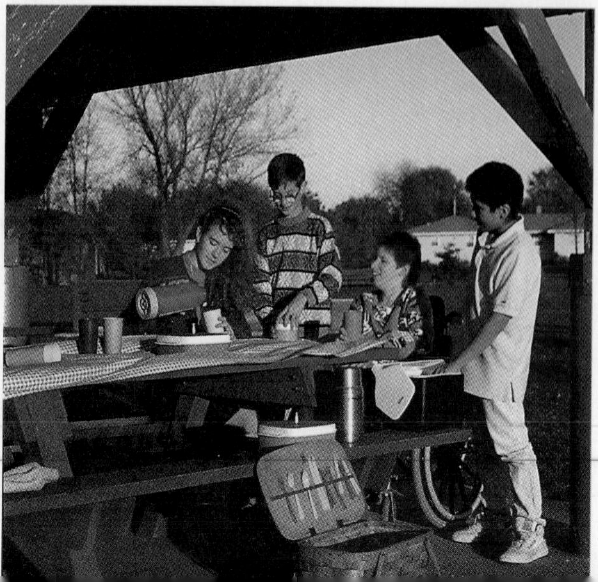

**When you go on a picnic, be sure you keep hot foods hot and cold foods cold. Use vacuum bottles, gel packs, or insulated containers.**

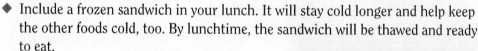

# Ideas for Packed Lunches

How can you keep your packed lunches interesting from day to day? Use your creativity to come up with ideas that are nutritious, quick to fix, low-cost, and tasty.

- Try packing leftover pizza or chicken pieces and eating them cold.
- If you have a wide-mouth vacuum bottle, you can pack hot, hearty dishes such as chili or pasta with sauce.
- Sandwiches are popular. You can vary the bread and fillings to make almost endless combinations.

## Sandwich Ideas

**Breads:** Whole wheat ◆ Multi-grain ◆ Rye ◆ Bagel ◆ Tortillas ◆ English muffin ◆ Pita ("pocket") bread ◆ Roll ◆ Biscuit

**Main fillings:** Leftover cooked poultry, fish, or meat ◆ Mashed cooked dry beans ◆ Low-fat cheese ◆ Peanut butter

**Additions:** Lettuce or other salad greens ◆ Sliced or chopped tomatoes, cucumbers, onions ◆ Shredded carrots ◆ Bean or alfalfa sprouts ◆ Green pepper rings or pieces ◆ Well-drained sauerkraut ◆ Sliced or chopped fruit

# Preparing and Packing Your Lunch

You will need airtight wrapping or containers to help keep your packed food fresh. Many foods can be wrapped tightly in plastic bags, plastic wrap, or waxed paper. However, all of these are throwaways. Instead, you might want to put foods in reusable plastic containers.

If you use a lunchbox or lunch tote, wash it in warm, soapy water, rinse, and dry after every use. Do the same with plastic containers. Let them air dry to get rid of previous food odors.

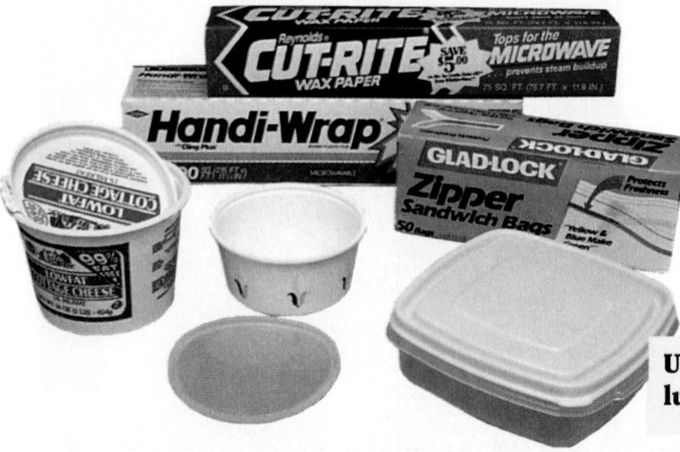


**Use containers or wrappings to keep your lunch foods fresh and in good shape.**

## Tips for Packing a Lunch

- With a little planning, you can prepare much of your lunch the evening before. For example, you can wash, pare, and slice carrots, put them in a container, and refrigerate them. In the morning they'll be ready to pop into your lunch bag.
- If you want a sandwich with fresh vegetables, such as lettuce, tomato slices, or sprouts, pack the vegetables separately. Add them to the sandwich just before you eat it. Otherwise, they may wilt or make the bread soggy.
- Pack salad and dressing in separate containers. Add the dressing just before you eat.
- To freeze sandwiches ahead of time, wrap them individually in freezer wrap. Sandwiches made with eggs, jelly, mayonnaise, or raw vegetables do not freeze well.
- Don't forget to pack a napkin and a fork or spoon, if needed.

**Try taking a salad in your lunch. Pack vegetables and dressing separately.**

## Chapter 22 Review

### Check the Facts

1. How can you be sure a packed lunch is nutritious?
2. Why is food safety especially important when packing a lunch?
3. Describe how to use a vacuum bottle for cold foods and hot foods.
4. Identify four ways to keep food cold other than using a vacuum bottle.
5. Give three creative packed lunch ideas.
6. What is a disadvantage of using plastic wrap when packing a lunch? How can you avoid this problem?
7. How can planning ahead make it easier to pack a lunch?

### Ideas in Action

1. In small groups, plan healthful, creative lunches for one week. Be sure to consider the Dietary Guidelines, the Daily Food Guide, and food safety.
2. Make a poster showing examples of how to safely pack foods for a lunch.
3. Plan a demonstration showing how to creatively prepare and pack a lunch in ten minutes or less. Consider good nutrition and safe food handling practices.

# CHAPTER 23

# Milk

**OBJECTIVES**

**Discover . . .**
- how milk fits into a healthful eating plan.
- how to select and store milk.
- how to cook with milk.

What's so special about milk? Milk is one of the most nutritious beverages you can drink. You can find it in many different forms when you shop and use it in many different ways for meals and snacks.

## Nutrition Notes

Milk and other dairy products are an important part of healthful food choices. Remember that you need two to three servings from the Milk, Yogurt, and Cheese group each day.

Milk is a good source of nutrients such as:

- Protein for growth and repair of the body.
- Calcium, phosphorus, and vitamin D for strong bones and teeth.
- Vitamin A and B vitamins for growth and health.

The fat content of milk varies, depending on the type of milk.

**Whole milk** is highest in fat. Over half its calories come from fat.

**Low-fat milk** has had some of the fat removed. From 6 to 35 percent of its calories come from fat.

**Skim milk** has had almost all of the fat removed. Less than 6 percent of its calories come from fat.

To include milk in a healthy diet, choose skim or low-fat milk. However, children under age two need whole milk for proper growth.

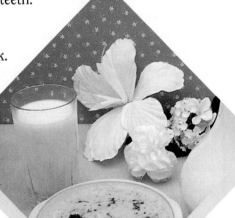

**What do these foods have in common?**

# Consumer Power

You can choose from many different kinds of milk in fresh, canned, or dry form. They are all convenient in their own way. Most types of milk are ready to use. Some can be stored for a long time.

## Kinds and Forms of Milk

**Fresh milk** is found in the refrigerated case at the store. It comes in glass bottles, paper cartons, or plastic jugs. You can choose from skim, low-fat, or whole milk. There are also flavored milks, such as chocolate milk. Buttermilk has a thick texture and tangy flavor.

**UHT milk** can be stored at room temperature. *UHT (ultra-high temperature)* means the milk is processed using extra-high heat to kill all bacteria. Then it is packaged in sterile (bacteria-free) cartons. UHT milk is similar in taste and nutrition to fresh milk.

**Evaporated milk** comes in cans. It is whole or skim milk with half of the water removed. You can use it full strength in place of cream or mix it with water to use as fresh milk.

**Sweetened condensed milk** is also canned. It is concentrated milk with at least 40 percent sugar added. You can use it in candy and dessert recipes.

**Nonfat dry milk** is a powder. It is made by removing most of the fat and water from milk. Mix it with water to use as fresh skim milk or use it dry in cooking.

The type of milk you choose depends on how you plan to use the product. If several types would suit your purpose, compare the price and advantages of each before you decide.

## Buying Fresh Milk

When buying fresh milk, you may see the following on the label:

**Grade A.** This means the milk meets quality standards set by the U.S. Public Health Service.

**Pasteurized.** *Pasteurized* (PASS-tyoor-ized) milk has been heat treated to kill harmful bacteria.

**Homogenized.** *Homogenized* (huh-MAH-jen-ized) means the fat is broken into tiny drops and mixed permanently with the milk. Otherwise, the fat would rise to the top as cream.

The label will also tell you what nutrients have been added. Most milk is fortified with vitamin D. Vitamin A is always added to skim and low-fat milk. It replaces the vitamin A that was removed along with the fat. Sometimes extra protein is added.

When you buy fresh milk:

- Read the label to be sure you are getting the type of milk you want.
- Check the date on the package. It tells you the last day the milk should be sold.
- Buy milk that is pasteurized and fortified with vitamin D.
- Be sure the container does not leak.

## Storing Fresh Milk

Refrigerate fresh milk in its original container. Why? If you pour milk into another storage container, it might pick up harmful bacteria. Then it will spoil more quickly. Close the container tightly.

To keep milk fresher longer, keep it cold. As soon as you have poured the amount of milk you need, close the container. Return it to the refrigerator at once.

## Buying and Storing Other Forms of Milk

Canned, dry, and UHT milk are convenient to keep on hand. UHT milk usually costs more than fresh milk. However, canned and dry milk are low in cost. When buying, follow the general guidelines in Chapter 8.

- UHT milk can be stored unopened up to 3 months. Refrigerate after opening.
- Store canned milk in a dry, cool area. Opened cans should be covered and refrigerated.
- Store nonfat dry milk in a dry, cool area. Once the package is opened, put the dry milk in an airtight container. After dry milk is mixed with water, store it in the refrigerator.

# Food Skills

How many uses for milk can you think of? As a beverage, milk goes well with meals and snacks. It can even be a snack in itself. You can make refreshing, nutritious blender drinks with milk. (See Chapter 37 for some ideas.)

Milk has many uses in cooking. You can make hot milk beverages, such as cocoa. You can thicken and flavor milk to make sauces and puddings. Milk is often an ingredient in soups, casseroles, and baked goods.

## Principles of Cooking with Milk

Milk is a protein food, so it must be cooked slowly at low temperatures. When milk is cooked properly, the product should have a smooth, creamy texture. It should have a rich, mild, pleasant flavor.

What happens if you cook milk at too high a temperature or for too long a time? The solids in milk will brown and then *scorch,* or burn. This gives the milk a burnt flavor and robs it of nutrients. To prevent scorching, use low heat and watch carefully.

How can you prevent this from happening?

### Keeping a Skin from Forming

When milk is heated, a skin sometimes forms on the surface. The skin is made up of milk solids and fat. Because the skin prevents steam from escaping, the milk may boil over. To keep a skin from forming, cover the pan or stir the milk frequently as it cooks.

What if a skin forms? Some people throw the skin away because it is tough and chewy. Many prefer to stir it back into the milk because it contains valuable nutrients.

## Keeping Milk from Curdling

Milk sometimes *curdles,* or separates into many small lumps and a watery liquid. Milk will usually curdle if you add it too quickly to a mixture that is hot or acid, such as tomato soup.

**To keep milk from curdling . . .**

1. Measure out the amount of milk and pour it into a bowl.

2. Slowly pour some of the hot or acid mixture into the milk, stirring constantly.
   ▲ This warms the milk or makes it more acid so it will not curdle easily.

3. Slowly add the milk to the remaining mixture, stirring constantly.

## Making White Sauce

White sauce, or cream sauce, is milk thickened with flour. When flour is cooked with a liquid, the grains of flour swell up and thicken the liquid.

White sauce can be used to make casseroles and other main dishes. It is also used for creamy gravies, creamed vegetables, cream soups, and as a base for other sauces.

**To make white sauce . . .**

1. Melt 2 Tbsp. (30 mL) butter or margarine in a saucepan over low heat.

2. Blend in 2 Tbsp. (30 mL) flour and a dash of pepper. Use a wooden spoon.

3. Cook over low heat, stirring constantly, until the mixture is thick and bubbly.

4. Remove the pan from the heat.

5. Pour 1 cup (250 mL) skim milk into the flour mixture, a little at a time. Stir constantly to make a smooth mixture.

6. Return the pan to the heat. Cook and stir until the mixture bubbles and thickens. Yield: about 1 cup (250 mL) white sauce.

Here are some ideas for varying the basic white sauce recipe:

- For a thinner sauce, use less butter or margarine and less flour. For a thicker sauce, use more. Just be sure to use equal amounts of each.
- For cheese sauce, stir 1 cup (250 mL) grated cheddar cheese into the hot white sauce. Season with paprika and a dash of cayenne pepper.

## Microwaving Milk

Many recipes made with milk, such as beverages, sauces, soups, and casseroles, can be heated in the microwave oven. Unless it is overcooked, milk is less likely to scorch in the microwave than cn the rangetop.

Remember, microwaves cook quickly and milk is sensitive to heat. Follow power level and temperature directions in recipes.

Milk boils over easily when microwaved. Use a container large enough to keep the milk from foaming over into the oven. Watch closely during cooking. Turn the power off as soon as the milk begins to foam.

Be sure to stir milk beverages before heating. Stirring breaks up a thin film on the surface of the liquid. If not stirred, the film holds heat in. It could cause the milk to splatter as it heats. Stir again after microwaving to distribute the heat evenly. Otherwise, if one part is hotter than the rest, you could burn your mouth.

White sauce should be microwaved long enough to cook the flour. Otherwise the mixture will have a raw flour flavor. Stir the sauce several times during heating to keep it from getting lumpy.

### Microwave Hints

- A temperature probe is convenient to use when heating milk. Soups and beverages with milk should be heated to 140°F (60°C).
- If lumps form in white sauce, use a wooden spoon to press them against the side of the container until they disappear.

## Using Nonfat Dry Milk

To *reconstitute* means to replace water that has been removed from a food. To reconstitute dry milk, follow the directions on the package.Use as you would fresh skim milk.

For more nutrients, especially calcium, add nonfat dry milk to recipes. You can add it to either the dry or liquid ingredients. Mix well. Here are some suggestions:

- Ground meat, chicken, or turkey: Mix in ½ cup (125 mL) dry milk for every pound (500 g) of meat.
- Grain products: Mix equal amounts of dry milk and rice, cereal, or other grain products before cooking. Cook as directed on the package.
- Mashed vegetables: Add ⅓ cup (75 mL) dry milk to mashed vegetables, such as potatoes or squash. If necessary, add cooking water.

## Chapter 23 Review

### Check the Facts

1. List two reasons why milk is an important part of a healthful eating plan.
2. Identify three things to look for when buying fresh milk.
3. Name three things you can do to keep milk fresh and safe. How should other forms of milk be stored?
4. Name at least two general principles to follow when cooking with milk.
5. Why should milk be stirred before and after microwaving?
6. Name two ways nonfat dry milk can be used in cooking.

### Ideas in Action

1. Working in groups, develop a magazine advertisement promoting milk. Keep in mind that a good advertisement persuades people to buy a product based on its appeal and benefits.
2. Jenny was sent to the supermarket to buy milk for her family for dinner. When she arrived at the store, Jenny was surprised and a bit confused by all the types of milk available. What advice would you give Jenny that would help her decide what type of milk to buy for her family?
3. Develop an eating plan for the next three days. Include a variety of milk and milk products essential in maintaining health.

# Recipe Focus

Read the following recipe carefully.

1. What equipment would you need to complete this recipe? How would the equipment differ if you were to make eight servings?
2. You would like to make this cocoa recipe on a weekend camping trip. Fresh milk will not be available. What changes could you make in the recipe to make it more convenient to prepare while camping?

## Mocha Cocoa

| Customary | Ingredients | Metric |
|---|---|---|
| ¼ cup | Unsweetened cocoa powder | 50 mL |
| ¼ cup | Sugar | 50 mL |
| ¼ cup | Water | 50 mL |
| 4 cups | Skim milk | 1 L |
| 2 tsp. | Instant coffee (optional) | 10 mL |
| ½ tsp. | Vanilla | 2 mL |
| ½ tsp. | Ground cinnamon | 2 mL |
| Dash | Ground nutmeg | Dash |

**Yield:** 4 servings, approximately 1 cup (250 mL) each

### Conventional Directions

**Pan:** 2-qt. (2-L) saucepan

1. **Combine** cocoa powder, sugar, and water in saucepan. Stir until mixed.
2. **Cook** over low heat, stirring constantly, until cocoa and sugar dissolve.
3. **Stir in** milk, coffee, vanilla, cinnamon, and nutmeg.
4. **Cook** over medium heat, stirring occasionally, until hot but not boiling.

### Microwave Directions

**Pan:** 2-qt. (2-L) microwave-safe container
**Power Level:** 100%

1. **Combine** cocoa powder, sugar, and water in container. Stir until mixed.
2. **Cook** at 100% power, uncovered, for 30 seconds to 1 minute or until cocoa and sugar dissolve.
3. **Stir in** milk, coffee, vanilla, cinnamon, and nutmeg.
4. **Cook** at 100% power, uncovered, for 9 to 10 minutes or until thoroughly heated. Stir after 5 minutes and again at the end.

Nutrition Information

**Per serving (approximate): 134 calories, 8 g protein, 24 g carbohydrate, 1 g fat, 4 mg cholesterol, 150 mg sodium**

**Good source of: calcium**

CHAPTER 24

# Yogurt and Cheese

**OBJECTIVES**

**Discover . . .**
- how yogurt and cheese fit into a healthful eating plan.
- how to select and store yogurt and cheese.
- how to use yogurt and cheese.

Yogurt and cheese are milk products. Yogurt is made by adding a special bacteria to milk. This process gives it a smooth, thick texture and a tangy flavor.

There are many ways to make cheese, but all of them include the same basic steps. First, milk is thickened. Then the solid part, or *curd*, is separated from the liquid, or *whey*. The curd is made into cheese.

## Nutrition Notes

Yogurt and cheese offer another way to get servings from the Milk, Yogurt, and Cheese group. This is especially important for people who cannot drink milk or do not like to drink it.

Like milk, yogurt and cheese are an important source of nutrients such as:
- Protein for growth and repair of the body.
- Calcium and phosphorus for strong bones and teeth.
- Vitamin A and B vitamins for growth and health.

Yogurt is generally low in fat and sodium. Many cheeses, however, are not. High-fat cheese should be eaten in moderation. Often just a small amount of cheese is added to a dish for flavor and added nutrients.

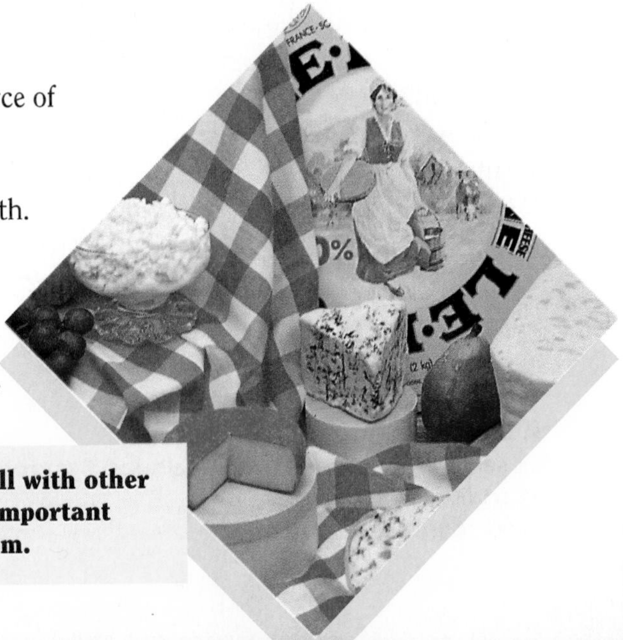

**Yogurt and cheese go well with other foods. They also supply important nutrients, such as calcium.**

# Consumer Power

You have many choices when it comes to yogurt and cheese. To get the most for your money, shop carefully and store products properly.

## Types of Yogurt and Cheese

Yogurt is available plain or with flavorings added, such as fruit and sugar. You can choose low-fat or nonfat yogurt.

Frozen yogurt is a popular dessert. It is made from yogurt with added flavorings and sweeteners. It is lower in fat than ice cream.

Hundreds of different cheeses are available. They vary in color, texture, and flavor. However, cheeses can be grouped into three general types:

**Unripened cheese.** Cottage cheese and cream cheese are examples. They are soft and stay fresh only a few days after purchase.

**Ripened cheese.** This type can be stored longer than unripened cheese. Some popular ripened cheeses are cheddar, brick, Swiss, and Parmesan.

Colby
Swiss
Grated Parmesan
Cheddar
Brick

**Ripened cheeses range from mild to sharp in flavor. Which of these have you tasted?**

**Process cheese and cold-pack cheese.** These products are made from ripened cheeses blended with other ingredients. They are smooth, melt quickly, and can be stored even longer than ripened cheese. Process American cheese is the most common example.

Cheese is sold in a variety of forms. For example, you can buy blocks or loaves, slices, shredded cheese, grated cheese, and containers of cheese spread.

## Buying Yogurt and Cheese

- Read labels carefully. Compare nutrients, fat content, and calories in different types and brands.
- Compare prices. Some ripened cheeses are very expensive. Process cheeses are usually lower in cost.
- Decide whether you are willing to pay more for cheese that is already sliced or shredded.
- Look for a freshness date on the package. Buy only as much as you can use within the storage life of the product.

## Storing Yogurt and Cheese

Most types of yogurt and cheese must be refrigerated. Keep them in the original package, or wrap ripened cheese in foil or plastic wrap. Use yogurt and soft unripened cheese within a few days. Use other cheeses within a few weeks.

# Food Skills

All kinds of yogurt and cheese are ready to eat. In addition, cheese can be used in cooking.

## Using Yogurt and Unripened Cheese

Yogurt and cottage cheese make delicious snacks, salads, or light desserts. Here are some ideas:

- Eat them as is. They taste good chilled.
- Mix plain yogurt or cottage cheese with fruit.
- Blend low-fat cottage cheese with a little lemon juice. Use as a topping for baked potatoes.

What other ideas can you think of?

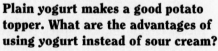

**Plain yogurt makes a good potato topper. What are the advantages of using yogurt instead of sour cream?**

**You can make a dip from plain yogurt or cottage cheese and seasonings. Serve with fresh fruits or vegetables.**

Cream cheese is sometimes used for dips and sandwiches. However, cream cheese is high in fat. You can make a delicious low-fat substitute from yogurt. Yogurt cheese can be used whenever cream cheese is called for, except in cooking.

**To make yogurt cheese . . .**

1. Line a colander with two layers of clean cheesecloth. Place the colander over a pan (such as a cake pan).

2. Place 1 pint (500 mL) *plain* nonfat or low-fat yogurt in the colander. Cover with waxed paper.

3. Refrigerate. Allow yogurt to drain for about 8 to 10 hours.

4. Remove yogurt cheese from cheesecloth. Pack it into a storage container. Cover tightly and refrigerate. Discard the liquid that dripped into the pan.

## Using Ripened and Process Cheese

Ripened cheese can be added to sandwiches or salads, served with fruit for dessert, or eaten by itself as a snack. The cheese will taste best if you remove it from the refrigerator about an hour ahead of time.

**A combination of cheese and other foods makes a tasty appetizer or salad. How many food groups are represented here?**

## Cooking with Cheese

Cheese adds special flavor to many cooked dishes. For example, it can be mixed with chili or melted into a sauce. You can use it to top casseroles, pizza, or burgers. For cooking, ripened or process cheese is usually used.

Because cheese is a protein food, it should be cooked at low temperatures. Cheese does not have to cook a long time—only long enough to melt.

Properly cooked cheese has a smooth, tender texture. It should be evenly melted with no hard pieces or brown spots.

**How would you rate the appearance of this melted cheese?**

If you overcook cheese, some of the protein is lost. The cheese becomes tough and rubbery. Here are some ways to keep cheese from overcooking:

- Use low heat.
- Add cheese near the end of cooking time.
- Grate or slice the cheese so it melts evenly.
- Layer the cheese between other ingredients to protect it from direct heat.

### Microwave Hints

- Process cheese is less likely to overcook in the microwave than ripened cheese.
- For an "ungrilled" cheese sandwich, put sliced cheese between toasted bread slices. Microwave at 50% power for about 20 seconds to melt the cheese.

## Microwaving Cheese

The principles of cooking cheese are similar for both conventional and microwave cooking. Cheese overcooks easily in the microwave. If it does, it will get tough and stringy. To keep this from happening:

- Use the power level specified in the recipe.
- If possible, grate the cheese, add it near the end of cooking time, or layer it between other ingredients.
- Check often for doneness. Stop cooking when the cheese starts to lose its shape.

**You can use the microwave to prepare a hot cheese sandwich without the added fat of grilling.**

## Chapter 24 Review

### Check the Facts

1. Name five important nutrients provided by yogurt and cheese.
2. Why should most cheeses be eaten in moderation?
3. What three general types of cheese are available? Name at least one example of each type.
4. How long can yogurt and cottage cheese be stored?
5. Give at least three examples of uses for yogurt.
6. Identify at least three ways to prevent cheese from becoming overcooked.

### Ideas in Action

1. You write a food and nutrition column in your local newspaper. A reader writes in and asks: "I don't like to drink milk, but am concerned about getting all the nutrients that milk supplies. What can I do to make up for the servings of milk that are part of a healthful eating plan?" Write a response that includes specific suggestions for the reader.
2. An 8-oz. package of shredded cheddar cheese costs $1.79. A 16-oz. block of cheddar cheese costs $2.98. Which cheese is the better buy per ounce? When choosing which to buy, what might you consider besides cost?

# Recipe Focus

1. You are having five friends over to your house after the football game on Friday night. You want to make enough Cheesy Mini-Pizzas for each friend and yourself to have two. How many servings do you need to make? How much would you need of each ingredient?
2. What could you substitute for English muffin halves in the Cheesy Mini-Pizza recipe?

## Cheesy Mini-Pizzas

| Customary | Ingredients | Metric |
|---|---|---|
| 4 | English muffin halves | 4 |
| ½ cup | Prepared pizza sauce | 125 mL |
| ½ cup | Shredded, low-fat mozzarella cheese | 125 mL |
| 1 Tbsp. (each topping) | Your choice of up to 3 vegetable toppings, such as:<br>• chopped onion<br>• chopped green pepper<br>• sliced mushrooms<br>• green or black olives | 15 mL (each topping) |

**Yield:** 4 servings, each ½ English muffin

### Conventional Directions

**Pan:** Broiler pan
**Temperature:** Broiler setting

1. **Place** English muffin halves on the broiler pan. Position the pan so the top of the muffins are about 3 inches (8 cm) from the heat. Broil until lightly browned.
2. **Spread** each muffin half with 2 Tbsp. (about 30 mL) prepared pizza sauce.
3. **Top** with your choice of vegetables.
4. **Sprinkle** each muffin half with 2 Tbsp. (about 30 mL) mozzarella cheese.
5. **Broil** until cheese melts. Remove from broiler immediately and serve hot.

### Microwave Directions

**Pan:** Microwave-safe plate
**Power Level:** 100%
**Follow** steps 2-4 of conventional directions. Then proceed as follows:

5. **Place** prepared pizzas on microwave-safe plate.
6. **Microwave** at 100% power for 1 minute or until cheese melts.

**Note:** Microwave pizzas will not have a crisp crust.

**Nutrition Information**

**Per serving (approximate): 128 calories, 8 g protein, 19 g carbohydrate, 3 g fat, 8 mg cholesterol, 310 mg sodium**

**Good source of: calcium**

CHAPTER 25

# Grain Products

**OBJECTIVES**

**Discover . . .**

- how grain products fit into a healthful eating plan.
- how to select and store grain products.
- how to prepare grain products.

How many different kinds of grain can you name? Did you think of wheat, corn, rice, barley, oats, rye?

Grains are the kernels, or seeds, of plants known as cereal grasses. They are the major food source on this planet. Grains are processed to make an endless variety of grain products, including breads, cereals, rice, and pasta.

## Nutrition Notes

Foods in the Bread, Cereal, Rice, and Pasta Group are an important source of carbohydrates. As explained in Chapter 5, carbohydrates are the best source of energy for your body.

Grain products also supply incomplete protein. How can you turn it into complete protein? Remember, you can combine incomplete proteins to make complete ones Just include dry beans and peas in your daily food choices.

In addition, grain products can be a good source of:

- B vitamins for growth and health.
- Iron for healthy red blood cells.
- Phosphorus for strong bones and teeth.

Foods in the Bread, Cereal, Rice, and Pasta Group are generally low in fat, sugar, and sodium. However, the way they are processed, prepared, and served can make a difference. For example, many breakfast cereals contain added sugar and sodium. If you spread bread with butter, margarine, or cream cheese, or serve pasta with a rich sauce, you add fat and calories.

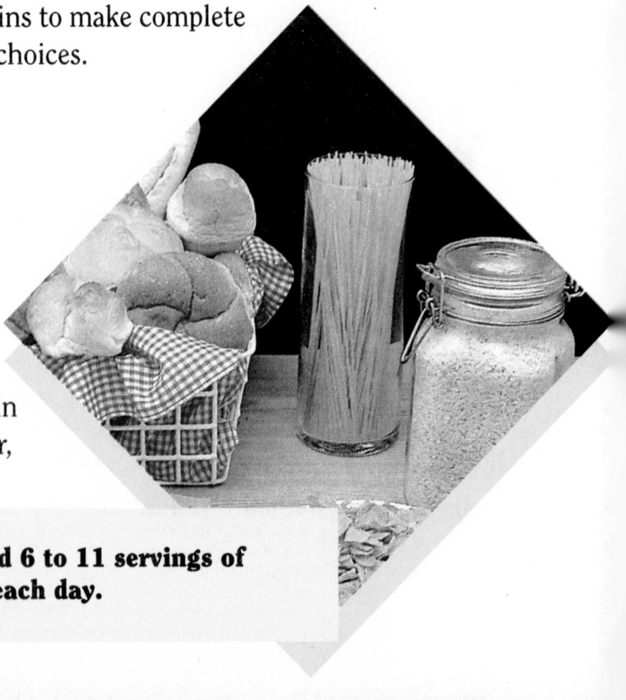

**Most people need 6 to 11 servings of grain products each day.**

## Parts of the Grain Kernel

All grain kernels have three basic parts. Each part contains valuable nutrients.

*Bran*

The bran is the outer covering of the kernel. It contains fiber and B vitamins.

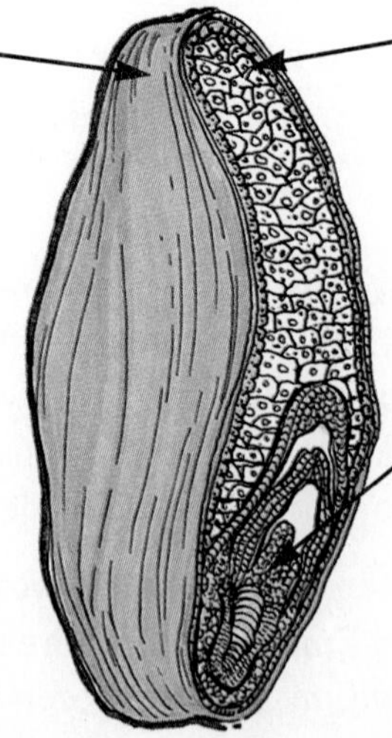

*Endosperm*

The endosperm is made up mostly of carbohydrates and protein.

*Germ*

The germ is the sprouting section from which a new plant can grow. It contains minerals, B vitamins, and fat.

Which parts of the grain kernel go into grain products? The answer depends on the particular grain products you buy.

*Whole-grain products* are made using all three parts of the kernel. Some examples of whole-grain products are brown rice, oatmeal, and bread made with whole wheat flour. Whole-grain products contain most of the grain's original nutrients. They are good sources of fiber.

Some other grain products are made from only the endosperm. For example, all-purpose white flour is the ground endosperm of wheat. When the bran and germ are removed, so are the nutrients they contain. To make up for some of these losses, the products are enriched with iron and B vitamins.

You can also find grain products that contain only the bran. (Have you ever had bran cereal for breakfast?) Still others are made from a mixture of different grains and grain parts. For example, a bread may include white flour, whole wheat flour, and oat bran.

**How can you tell whether products are whole-grain or enriched?**

When choosing grain products, remember:

- ◆ Both whole-grain and enriched products supply carbohydrates, protein, vitamins, and minerals.
- ◆ To add fiber to your diet, choose products made with whole grains or bran.

# Consumer Power

Dozens of different grain products fill the store shelves. Knowing about the choices that are available can help you decide what type of bread, cereal, rice, or pasta to buy.

## Breads

**How could this variety of breads be used in meals?**

There are many different types of bread. For example:

- Loaves, rolls, and buns come in different shapes and sizes.
- Bagels are doughnut-shaped rolls with a chewy texture.
- Pita is a thick, flat bread that forms a "pocket."
- Tortillas are a thin, flat bread made from cornmeal or wheat flour.

Breads can be bought in fresh loaves, either sliced or unsliced. Some bagels and English muffins are refrigerated to preserve their freshness. In addition, look for frozen breads and refrigerated or frozen dough.

## Breakfast Cereals

The shelves of breakfast cereals at the store offer many choices. Ready-to-eat cereals need no preparation. Some have fruits, nuts, sugar, or other flavorings added. Other cereals, such as oatmeal, require cooking and are eaten hot. They may come in regular, quick-cooking, and instant varieties. Some instant cereals have added sweeteners and flavorings.

**Cereals are a convenient breakfast food.**

## Rice

Three basic types of rice are available: long-grain, medium-grain, and short-grain. Long-grain rice cooks dry and fluffy. Short-grain and medium-grain rice have moister kernels and tend to stick together.

Rice is sold in boxes and bags. You can choose from rice processed in different ways. For example:

**Brown rice** is whole-grain rice. It has a rich, nutty flavor and a chewy texture.

**Enriched rice** is also called white rice. It has less fiber than brown rice.

**Instant rice** is precooked, rinsed, and dried. It takes only a short time to prepare. Both enriched and brown instant rice are available.

**Rice can be prepared in many flavorful ways, such as this Spanish-style dish.**

You can also buy rice packaged along with a seasoning mix or sauce mix. Other convenience forms include cooked rice in cans or frozen packages.

## Pasta

*Pasta* is a general term for spaghetti, macaroni, noodles, and similar products. In fact, pasta comes in about 200 different shapes. Some of them are shown below. Most pasta is simply a combination of enriched or whole-wheat flour and water. Noodles also contain eggs for added tenderness.

Corkscrew

Elbow

Egg noodles

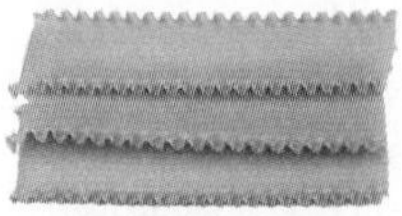

Lasagne

Manicotti

Shells

Spaghetti

Rigatoni

Dried pasta is sold in bags and boxes. You can also buy refrigerated fresh pasta, fresh-frozen pasta, and frozen cooked pasta. Some canned, frozen, or packaged main dishes and meals include pasta.

## Buying Grain Products

- ◆ Read labels carefully. For more fiber, look for whole grains or bran. Choose products that are low in fat, sugar, and sodium.
- ◆ Think about what the words on the label mean. "Wheat bread" doesn't mean the same as "whole wheat bread"—it may contain only a small amount of whole wheat flour.
- ◆ Don't be misled by cereals with added vitamins and minerals. Good nutrition comes from eating a balanced diet each day, not from one bowl of cereal.
- ◆ Compare prices. Grain products with many added ingredients usually cost more than simpler kinds.
- ◆ Follow the general guidelines for buying food in Chaper 8.

**Which of these two cereals do you think would cost less? Which would give you better nutrition?**

## Storing Grain Products

- Bread can usually be left in the store wrapper and kept in a cool, dry place. Most breads stay fresh longer at room temperature than in the refrigerator.
- If the kitchen is hot and humid, refrigerate bread to keep mold from growing.
- Freeze bread for longer storage.
- Store most other grain products in a cool, dry place. The package or container should be tightly sealed.

**Refrigerator or bread box? Where you store bread may depend on the weather.**

# Food Skills

Grain products play a versatile role in meal planning. Think about what you have eaten in the last day. How many main dishes, salads, side dishes, breakfast foods, and snacks contained grain products?

## Using Ready-to-Eat Grain Products

Ready-to-eat breads and cereals can be used right from the package. They do not require cooking. Still, they can be prepared in many different ways.

Bread can be warmed in the oven or toasted, if desired. All types of bread can be used to make sandwiches. (See Chapter 22 for creative sandwich ideas.)

For a nutritious breakfast, serve skim milk with whole-grain ready-to-eat cereal. If you like, add nuts and fresh, canned, or dried fruits.

Whole-grain cereals can also be used in other ways to add fiber to your diet. For example, you can add crunchy cereal to yogurt. Mix several cereals and add seasonings for a nutritious snack. Try using crushed cereal in place of bread crumbs in a recipe.

**A nutritious sandwich is easy to make.**

# Cooking Grain Products

Grain products such as rice, pasta, and oatmeal are cooked in water. As they cook, they absorb water and swell to double or triple their original size. For example, one cup of raw rice becomes three cups of cooked rice.

Different grain products require different cooking times and methods. Follow the instructions on the package.

When properly cooked, grain products are tender throughout. Undercooked grains are hard or chewy. If overcooked, grains become soft and sticky.

Do not rinse grain products before or after cooking. Rinsing washes away valuable nutrients.

When cooking rice, stir as little as possible. Stirring scrapes the starch off the grains and makes the rice sticky.

## Cooking Pasta

Properly cooked pasta is tender but still firm in the center. An Italian phrase for this is "*al dente*" (ahl-DEHN-tay), meaning "to the tooth." However, if the pasta is to be used in a recipe that will be cooked, shorten the boiling time slightly. Remove the pasta before it is completely cooked.

1. Bring water to a boil in a large pot.
   - ▲ Use 2 quarts (2 L) water for every 8 ounces (500 g) of pasta.
2. Add the pasta slowly so the boiling does not stop. Also add 1 teaspoon (5 mL) cooking oil.
   - ▲This helps keep the pasta from sticking together.
3. Cook until tender. Stir occasionally to keep pasta from sticking.
4. Drain pasta in a strainer or colander without rinsing.

**Microwave Hints**

- Remember that grain products double or triple in size as they cook. Be sure to use a microwave dish that is large enough to allow easy stirring and to prevent sticking.
- Use the microwave to reheat leftover cooked rice or pasta. Check a microwave cookbook for directions.

## Microwaving Grain Products

Cooking grain products such as pasta and rice in the microwave oven takes almost as long as conventional cooking. Why? The grains need time to absorb water so they can soften. This process cannot be speeded up.

New products are being developed to solve this problem. For example, special microwavable pasta is available.

Some cooked cereals can be prepared in the microwave. Follow directions on the package.

**Look for microwave directions on grain products that you buy. Read them carefully—they may not always save time.**

## Chapter 25 Review

### Check the Facts

1. List five nutrients commonly found in grain products.
2. Name and describe the three basic parts of a grain kernel.
3. What is the benefit in using whole-grain products instead of enriched grain products?
4. What should you think about when deciding what type of breakfast cereal to buy? Explain at least three guidelines.
5. How should grain products be stored to maintain freshness? Name at least two guidelines.
6. List at least four guidelines for cooking grain products.

### Ideas in Action

1. Saundra was preparing rice to serve with dinner. As she put the cooked rice into a serving bowl, she noticed that the grains were sticking together. What are three possible reasons for the rice being sticky? What could Saundra do to prevent this from happening again?
2. Imagine that you and your group members are menu and nutrition consultants for your school district. Plan the school lunch menus for the next week. Include at least five different types of grain products during the week. Be sure to include foods from every food group in each menu.

# Recipe Focus

Read the recipe on the next page.

1. Why aren't microwave directions given for the pasta?
2. What are the advantages of combining a convenience food, such as prepared spaghetti sauce, with added ingredients?

# Pasta with Pronto Sauce

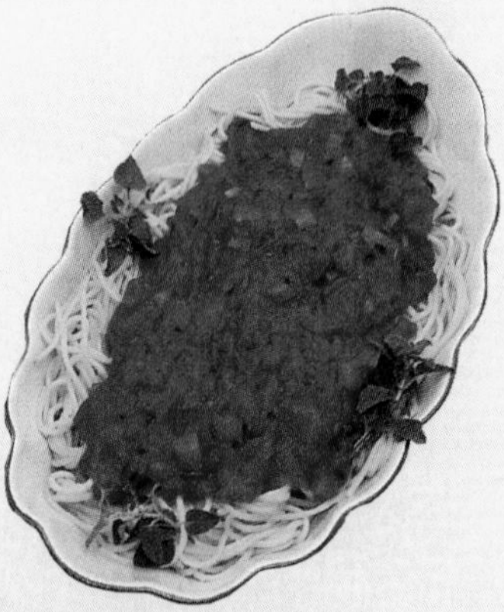

| Customary | Ingredients | Metric |
|---|---|---|
| 1 tsp. | Vegetable oil | 5 mL |
| 8 oz. (by weight) | Pasta | 250 g |
| 2 Tbsp. | Vegetable oil | 30 mL |
| ¼ cup | Chopped green pepper | 50 mL |
| ¼ cup | Chopped onion | 50 mL |
| ¼ cup | Diced carrots | 50 mL |
| 1 clove | Garlic, minced | 1 clove |
| 2 | Tomatoes, chopped | 2 |
| ½ tsp. | Dried basil, crushed | 2 mL |
| 1 cup | Prepared spaghetti sauce | 250 mL |

**Yield:** 4 servings

### Directions for Cooking Pasta

**Pan:** 4-qt. (4-L) pot

1. **Bring** 2 qt. (2 L) water to boil in pot.
2. **Add** 1 tsp. (5 mL) vegetable oil and pasta to boiling water. (Be sure the water does not stop boiling.) Cook, stirring occasionally, 8 to 10 minutes or until pasta reaches *al dente* stage. Drain.

**Note:** While pasta is cooking, prepare sauce following either conventional or microwave directions.

### Conventional Directions for Sauce

**Pan:** 1-qt. (1-L) saucepan

1. **Heat** 2 Tbsp. (30 mL) oil in saucepan. Add green pepper, onion, carrot, and garlic. Cook 5 to 7 minutes or until tender.
2. **Stir in** tomatoes and basil. Cook over medium-low heat 5 to 7 minutes or until tomatoes soften.
3. **Add** spaghetti sauce, mixing until well blended. Bring to boil; reduce heat. Cover; simmer 10 minutes.
4. **Serve** over hot cooked pasta.

### Microwave Directions for Sauce

**Pan:** 1½-qt. (1½-L) microwave-safe container
**Power Level:** 100%

1. **Combine** green pepper, onion, carrot, garlic, and 2 Tbsp. (30 mL) oil in microwave-safe container. Cook at 100% power 2 to 5 minutes or until vegetables are tender, stirring once.
2. **Stir in** tomatoes and basil. Cook at 100% power 3 to 5 minutes, stirring after 2 minutes.
3. **Stir in** spaghetti sauce. Cover with waxed paper. Continue cooking at 100% power 3 to 4 minutes.
4. **Let stand** 2 to 3 minutes before serving.
5. **Serve** over hot cooked pasta.

**Nutrition Information**

**Per serving (approximate): 372 calories, 9 g protein, 57 g carbohydrate, 12 g fat, 0 mg cholesterol, 320 mg sodium**

**Good source of: vitamin A, vitamin C, B vitamins, iron, other minerals**

CHAPTER 26

# Fruits

**OBJECTIVES**

**Discover . . .**
- how fruits fit into a healthful eating plan.
- how to select and store fruits.
- how to prepare fruits.

Fruits add color and flavor to meals and make delicious snacks. They are nutritious, easy to prepare, and can be low in cost.

## Nutrition Notes

Fruits are an important part of your daily food choices. Remember, you need two to four servings from the Fruits Group each day.

Fruits are a good source of carbohydrates and fiber. Do you remember why these are needed? Carbohydrates supply your body with energy. Fiber is needed for good digestion and good health.

Fruits also provide many of the vitamins and minerals you need for good health, such as:

- Vitamin C. Citrus fruits, such as oranges, grapefruits, and lemons, are especially good sources of this vitamin. So are melons, kiwis, and strawberries.
- Vitamin A. Good sources include deep yellow fruits, such as mangoes, cantaloupes, apricots, and peaches.
- Potassium. Bananas, cantaloupes, oranges, and nectarines are good sources.

Fruits are low in sodium and fat and have no cholesterol. Most are low in calories.

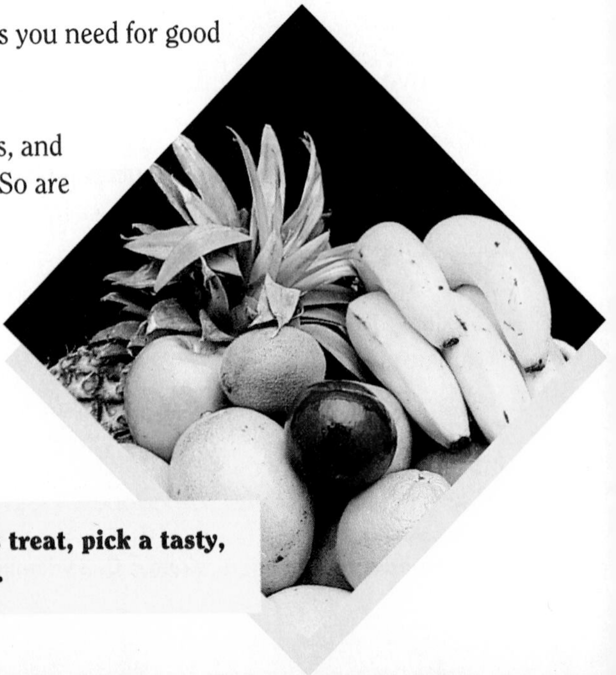

**For a nutritious treat, pick a tasty, refreshing fruit.**

# Consumer Power

There are dozens of different kinds of fruit. How many have you tried? How many others can you think of?

**How might you use these forms of fruit?**

## Forms of Fruit

Fruits are sold in several forms: fresh, canned, frozen, and dried. Fresh fruits in good condition have the most nutrients, but other forms of fruit are still nutritious.

Frozen fruits often cost more than fresh or canned fruits. However, prices will vary depending on the time of year and the kind of fruit.

Another form of fruit is fruit juice. It is discussed in Chapter 37.

## Buying Fresh Fruits

Fresh fruits are found in the produce section of the store. Sometimes they are sold loose so that you can choose the pieces of fruit you want. Other times a number of fruits are packaged together in a bag or wrapped tray. If a package of fruit is too large for you, ask the clerk to open the package so you can select the amount you want. Do not open the package yourself.

Fresh fruits are very perishable. Buy only the amount you will use in a few days. Handle fresh fruits gently—they are easily damaged.

### Buying in Season

Most fruits have a peak *season*—a certain time of year when the supply is greatest and the quality is highest. During these months, the fruit is said to be "in season." For example, peaches and cherries are in season during summer. Cranberries are in season during autumn.

Since the supply is greatest when fruits are in season, prices are usually lower then. Knowing when fruits are in season can help you find the best buys.

**For best quality and value, take advantage of times when particular fruits are in season.**

## Ripeness

Fruits that are *ripe* are ready to eat. They have developed their full flavor and sweetness. They are not too hard or too soft.

Fruits begin to ripen while they are still growing. Some fruits stop ripening when they are picked. Examples are apples, berries, and grapes. Buy these fruits fully ripe.

Some other fruits, such as bananas, peaches, and pears, continue to ripen after being picked. Choose these fruits according to when you will use them. For immediate use, buy ripe ones. Choose slightly underripe fruits to use several days later.

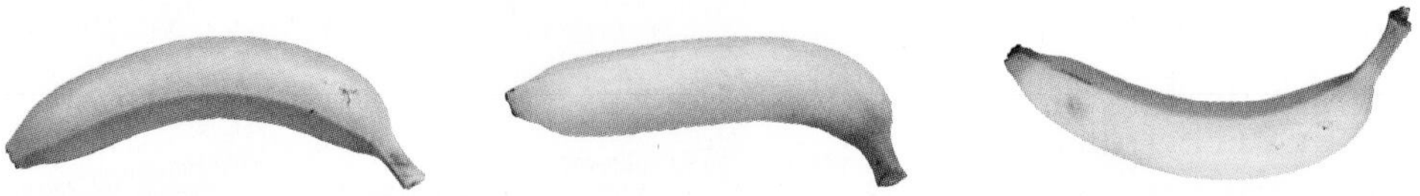

**Bananas change color from green to yellow as they ripen.**

## Signs of Quality

High-quality fresh fruits have the best flavor and nutrition. Low-quality fruits are no bargain. They have already lost nutrients and flavor. How can you judge quality and ripeness? Look for fruits that are:

**Full size.** Fruits that are smaller than normal were picked too soon and will not ripen properly.

**The right color.** Fruits should have good, full color.

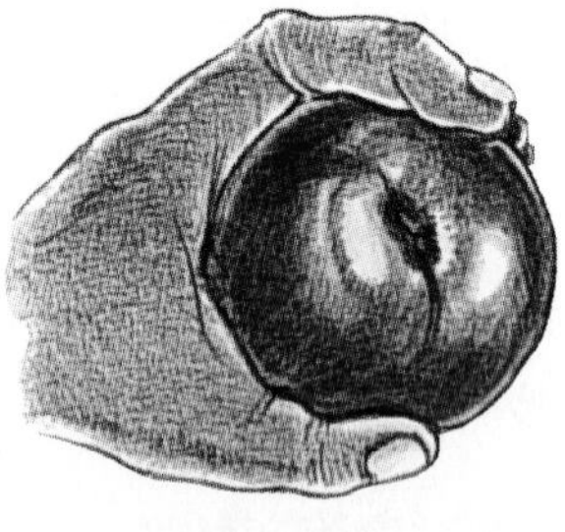

**Firm to the touch.** Press the fruit gently so you do not damage it. Very soft fruit may be overripe and lack flavor. Hard fruit may not ripen.

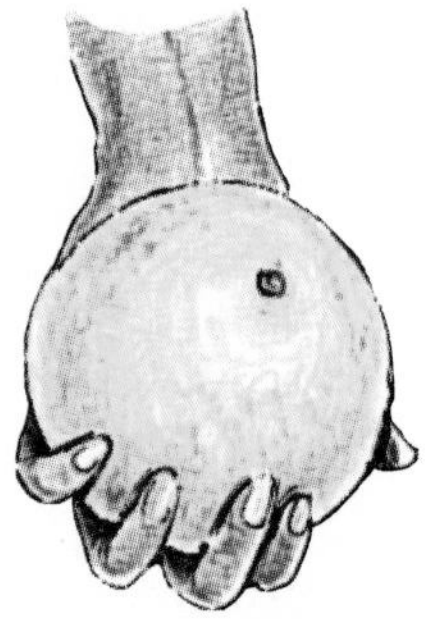

**Plump and heavy for their size.** This usually means they are juicy.

**Free of decay, damage, or mold.** Avoid fruits with mushy brown spots or powdery areas.

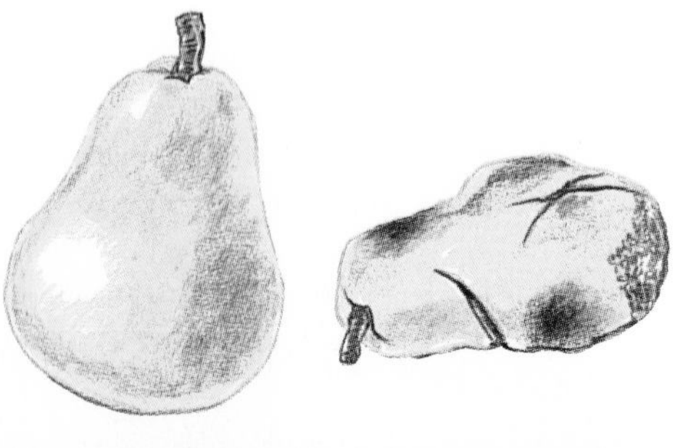

## Storing Fresh Fruit

- Do not wash fruits until you are ready to use them.
- Refrigerate ripe fruits as soon as you bring them home. Put them in a plastic bag or in the crisper section. Use within a day or two.
- Let slightly underripe fruits stand at room temperature in a paper bag. When fully ripe, use them at once or refrigerate them.
- Store cut fruits in an airtight container or wrap them in foil or plastic. Use as soon as possible.

**Fruits ripen faster in a paper bag.**

## Buying Frozen, Canned, and Dried Fruit

When buying these forms of fruit, follow the general guidelines in Chapter 8. Read labels carefully.

- Frozen fruits are sold in cartons or plastic bags. Some have sugar added.
- Canned fruits may be bought whole, halved, sliced, or in pieces. Whole fruits are usually the most expensive. Decide what form is best suited to your needs.
- Some fruits are canned in a sugar syrup. Look for fruits packed in water or juice instead.
- Dried fruits, such as raisins and dried apricots, are sold in packages or in the bulk food section. They should be fairly soft and moist, not hard.

**What form of pineapple would you buy to use in a bowl of mixed fruit?**

## Storing Frozen, Canned, and Dried Fruit

- Store frozen fruits in the freezer until needed. Thaw in the refrigerator.
- Store unopened cans of fruit in a cool, dry place.
- Refrigerate leftover canned fruit in an airtight container, not in the can.
- Store dried fruits in an airtight container in a cool, dry place.

**Because dried fruits are naturally high in sugar, they attract insects. Keep the fruit in an airtight container.**

# Food Skills

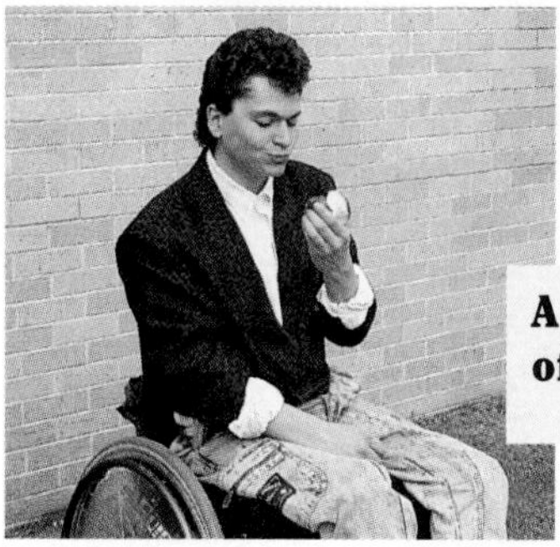

Fruits can be served plain or fancy for breakfast, lunch, or dinner. They can be used in salads and main dishes. They make flavorful, nutritious desserts and tasty snacks.

**A fruit snack can be as simple as a juicy apple eaten right out of your hand.**

## Preparing Fresh Raw Fruits

Most fresh fruits should be washed before they are eaten or cooked. Washing removes dirt and bacteria that could cause illness. To wash fruits, hold them under running water. Fruits with peels that are not eaten, such as bananas and oranges, do not have to be washed.

Fresh fruits may be cut into halves, wedges, or slices for serving. Use a sharp knife and a cutting board. Remember that when fruits are pared or cut, they quickly lose some of their vitamin C. Do not let them sit too long before they are eaten.

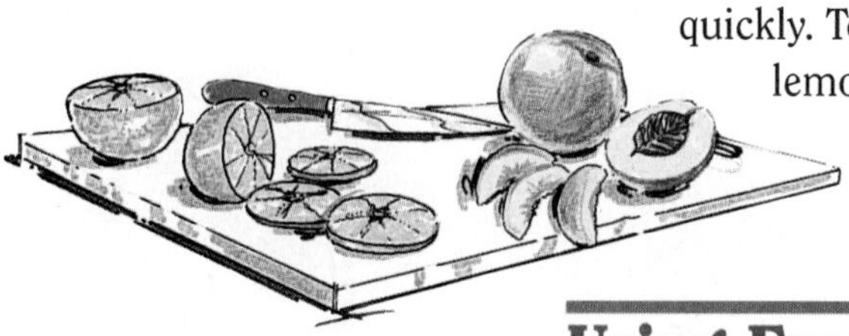

Most cut fruits, such as sliced apples or bananas, turn brown quickly. To keep them looking fresh, try coating them with lemon, grapefruit, or orange juice. You can also buy a powdered ascorbic (uh-SKORE-bik) acid mixture for the same purpose.

## Using Frozen, Canned, and Dried Fruits

Convenience forms of fruit can be used in most of the same ways as fresh fruit. Here are some tips:

**Add nuts or crunchy cereal to dried fruit for a tasty snack.**

- Frozen fruits are soft and lose their shape when completely thawed. Many people prefer to serve them before they thaw completely. Ice crystals help the fruits hold their shape.
- If canned fruits are packed in juice, serve the juice over the fruits or save it for another use.
- Dried fruits are as sweet as candy but more nutritious. Try mixing several kinds together.

# Cooking Fruits

Many fruits can be cooked to add variety to meals. Remember to wash fresh fruits before cooking.

Cooking affects fruits in several ways. It:

- Breaks down the fibers and softens the fruits.
- Makes the flavor more mellow and less acid-tasting.
- Changes the color.

When properly cooked, fruits should be soft and tender. They should retain as much of their natural color as possible and be pleasantly flavored. Overcooking causes fruits to lose nutrients, color, and flavor. They become mushy and unappetizing.

Fruits can be cooked in a variety of ways. Here are some ideas:

- Simmer dried apricots or prunes in water. Serve them with the cooking liquid.
- Bake sliced bananas and pears together in an orange juice sauce.
- Brush pineapple slices or grapefruit halves with melted butter or margarine. Sprinkle with brown sugar and broil.
- Make a fruit sauce, such as applesauce.

**For something different, try broiling sliced fruit or simmering whole fruit in a sauce.**

**To make a fruit sauce . . .**

1. Pare and slice fruit. Remove the core and seeds.

2. Put the fruit in a saucepan. Add just enough water or fruit juice to cover the bottom of the pan ¼ to ½ inch (3 to 13 mm) deep. Cover.

3. Simmer, stirring occasionally, until the fruit breaks down into a sauce.

4. Add sugar to taste. You can also add a spice such as cinnamon or nutmeg.
   ▲ Remember to use a clean spoon each time you taste.

5. If you prefer a smoother sauce, mash the cooked fruits by putting them through a food mill, a strainer, or a blender.

### Microwave Hints

- Pierce or slit the skin of whole fruit to allow steam to escape. Otherwise the skin may burst.
- Try this easy dessert: Pour canned fruit pie filling into a microwave-safe baking dish. Cook on full power until heated through. Top with granola or another crunchy cereal.

## Microwaving Fruits

Many popular fruit dishes can be prepared using the microwave oven. Fruits cook very quickly in a microwave oven because they are high in sugar and water. Quick cooking helps fruits keep their nutrients and flavor.

Unless the recipe tells you otherwise, cover fruits when microwaving them. Time cooking carefully. If overcooked, fruits will be hard and dry.

**How can you avoid overcooking fruit in a microwave?**

## Chapter 26 Review

### Check the Facts

1. Name at least three nutrients commonly found in fruits. Give one example of a fruit source for each nutrient.
2. What is the benefit of buying fresh fruit in season?
3. Describe five quality characteristics you should look for when buying fresh fruit.
4. How should fresh fruit be stored? Dried fruit?
5. What happens to fruit when it is cooked? Identify at least three changes.
6. Why should you slit the skin of a whole fruit that is being cooked in the microwave?

### Ideas in Action

1. Maria, a foreign exchange student from Mexico, is a new student in your school. One day she asks for your advice. She wants to pick up some fresh fruit at the store on her way home from school. However, Maria is unsure about how to buy fresh fruit and doesn't know what fruits are in season in your area. What advice would you give Maria?
2. Draw a cartoon that illustrates why it is important to include fruit in a healthful eating plan.
3. In small groups, brainstorm different ways you could serve fresh fruit. Share your ideas with the class.

# Recipe Focus

1. Look up the nutrition information for a slice of apple pie in a classroom reference book. Compare this information with the nutrition information for "Spiced Apples." How do these foods compare in calories and grams of fat? What conclusions can you draw about fat and calories in pies?
2. If you wanted to make two servings of "Spiced Apples," how much would you need of each ingredient?

## Spiced Apples

| Customary | Ingredients | Metric |
|---|---|---|
| ½ cup | Dark brown sugar | 125 mL |
| 2 Tbsp. | All-purpose flour | 30 mL |
| 1 tsp. | Ground cinnamon | 5 mL |
| ¼ tsp. | Ground nutmeg | 1 mL |
| Dash | Ground ginger | Dash |
| 1 tsp. | Grated lemon rind | 5 mL |
| 4 | Baking apples | 4 |
| 1 Tbsp. | Melted butter or margarine | 15 mL |
| 1 tsp. | Lemon juice | 5 mL |

**Yield:** 4 servings

### Conventional Directions

**Pan:** 2-qt. (2-L) baking dish with cover
**Temperature:** 400°F (200°C)

1. **Preheat** oven to 400°F (200°C).
2. **Grease** baking dish.
3. **Combine** brown sugar, flour, cinnamon, nutmeg, ginger, and grated lemon rind in a small bowl. Stir to mix.
4. **Core** the apples. Do not pare.
5. **Cut** each apple into quarters and each quarter into 3 slices.
6. **Place** apples in a large bowl. Sprinkle with sugar mixture. Mix until well coated.
7. **Spoon** the apples into the baking dish.
8. **Combine** the melted butter or margarine and lemon juice. Pour over the apples.
9. **Cover** the baking dish.
10. **Bake** for 30 minutes. Serve warm.

### Microwave Directions

**Pan:** 2-qt. (2-L) microwave-safe baking dish with cover
**Power Level:** 100%
**Follow** steps 3-9 of conventional directions. (Do not grease the baking dish.) Then continue with steps below.

10. **Microwave** 9 to 11 minutes at 100% power, stirring 3 or 4 times. Keep larger pieces farthest from the center of the dish.
11. **Let stand,** covered, for 5 minutes. Serve warm.

**Nutrition Information**
**Per serving (approximate): 225 calories, 1 g protein, 51 g carbohydrate, 3 g fat, 8 mg cholesterol, 38 mg sodium**
**Good source of: vitamin C**

CHAPTER 27

# Vegetables

**OBJECTIVES**

**Discover . . .**
- how vegetables fit into a healthful eating plan.
- how to select and store vegetables.
- how to prepare vegetables.

Vegetables are colorful, flavorful, and nutritious. Hundreds of different kinds are available, each with its own appeal. They can be prepared in many different ways.

Take advantage of these choices by eating a variety of vegetables. Your meals and snacks will be not only more healthful, but more interesting, too. How many different vegetables have you tried?

## Nutrition Notes

Vegetables are an important part of your daily food choices. Remember, you need three to five servings from the Vegetables Group each day. Why? Vegetables are an excellent source of the carbohydrates your body needs for energy. In addition, they are an excellent source of fiber. Vegetables are also among the best sources of vitamins and minerals, such as:

- Vitamin A. Deep yellow or orange vegetables (such as carrots) and deep green ones (such as spinach) are excellent sources of this nutrient.
- Vitamin C. Good sources include broccoli, raw cabbage, kale, sweet potatoes, tomatoes, and green peppers.
- Calcium. Broccoli, kale, and turnip greens can help supply the calcium you need for strong bones and teeth.

Fresh vegetables are low in fat, sodium, and calories. They have no cholesterol. As long as little or no fat, salt, or sugar is added to the vegetables, they will keep these advantages.

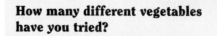

**How many different vegetables have you tried?**

# Consumer Power

Did you know that vegetables come from many different parts of plants? Vegetables can be:

- Fruits of a plant—such as tomatoes, eggplants, and peppers.
- Flowers of a plant—such as broccoli and cauliflower.
- Stems—such as asparagus and celery.
- Roots—such as potatoes, carrots, beets, and onions.
- Leaves—such as cabbage, greens, kale, and spinach.
- Seeds—such as beans, corn, and peas.

## Forms of Vegetables

Vegetables can be purchased fresh, frozen, or canned. High-quality fresh vegetables have the most nutrients, but frozen and canned vegetables are not far behind. Compare the prices of different forms when you shop.

You can also buy convenience products such as instant mashed potatoes, potato and sauce mixes, and vegetables in microwavable packages. What might be some advantages and disadvantages of these products?

**Fresh vegetables are processed into a variety of convenience forms. What should you consider when deciding which form to buy?**

## Buying Fresh Vegetables

Fresh vegetables are found in the produce section of the store. They are sold loose or in packages, just as fruits are. Sometimes several pieces are held together with a band or tape and sold as a unit.

Many fresh vegetables are available in supermarkets all year round. Because they are shipped from wherever they can be grown, there is a steady supply. Locally grown vegetables can be bought only during their growing season. These are usually fresher and lower in price than those shipped from other areas.

**Most supermarkets carry a wide selection of vegetables. Prices vary depending on the time of year.**

## Signs of Quality

When you buy fresh vegetables, buy only the amount you can use during their storage life. Look for these signs of quality:

*Solid — should feel heavy in relation to its size*

*Good color — not too pale or too dark*

*Crisp or firm*

*In good condition — no decay, soft spots, or damage*

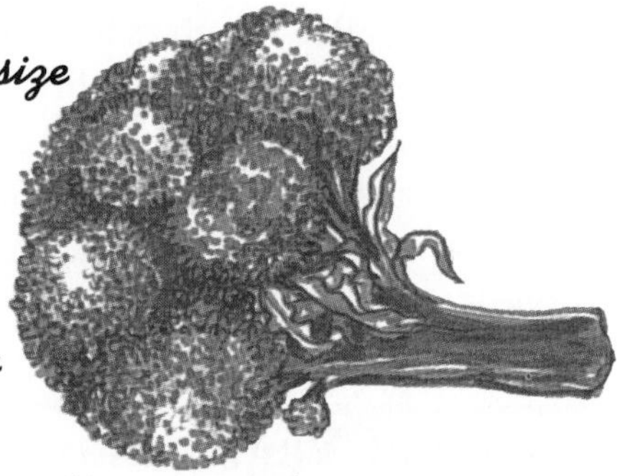

## Storing Fresh Vegetables

- Store potatoes and onions separately in a cool, dry, dark area. They will keep for several weeks.
- Other vegetables should be refrigerated as soon as you bring them home. If they are dirty, first rinse them briefly. Shake out excess water. Store in the crisper or in plastic bags or containers. For best quality, use within a few days.

## Buying and Storing Other Forms of Vegetables

Frozen vegetables are available in a wide range of choices. You can buy one kind of vegetable or packaged mixed vegetables. Some are frozen in a sauce.

Canned vegetables are available whole, sliced, or in pieces. Some are packed in special sauces. Canned vegetables are already cooked. They need only be heated. Follow directions on the label.

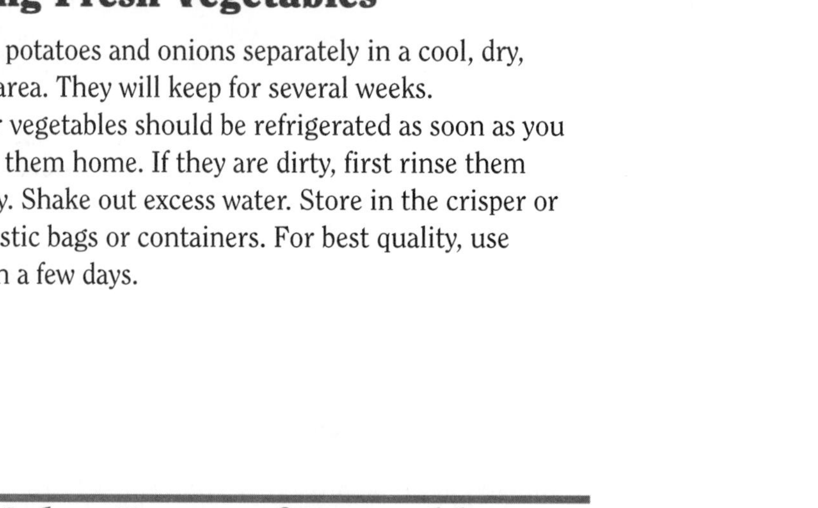

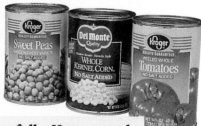

**Remember to read labels carefully. Many canned and frozen vegetables are high in sodium, but low-salt or no-salt products are available.**

# Food Skills

There are many ways to include vegetables in daily menus. For example, vegetables are popular as side dishes and in salads. They appear in many main dishes, such as stews, soups, and casseroles. Besides being an important part of a meal, vegetables make delicious snacks.

## Preparing Raw Fresh Vegetables

Many vegetables, such as carrots, cauliflower, broccoli, mushrooms, and peppers, can be eaten raw.

Before you prepare fresh vegetables, wash them thoroughly to remove dirt and harmful bacteria. Hold the vegetables under cold running water. Hard vegetables, such as carrots, should be scrubbed with a vegetable brush. To preserve nutrients, do not soak the vegetables.

**Raw fresh vegetables make appetizing, nutritious snacks and party foods.**

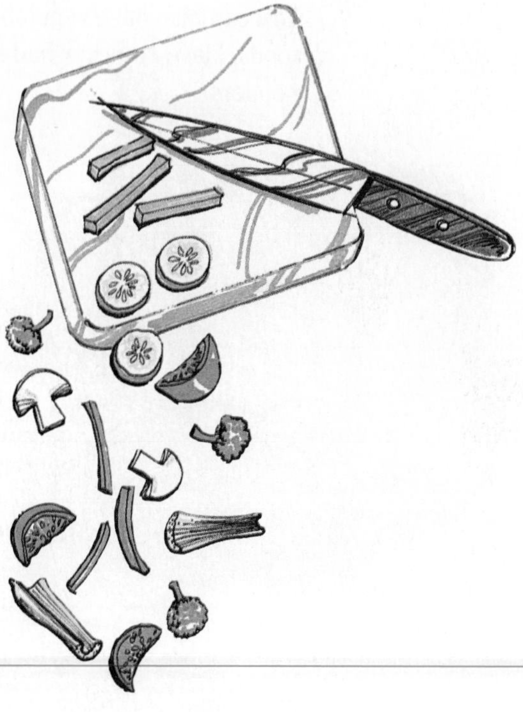

Cut off damaged spots and parts that cannot be eaten. Remember to trim or pare vegetables as little as possible. The most nutrients are often found in the outer portions.

To make the vegetables easier to pick up and eat, you can cut them into wedges, slices, strips, or chunks. Refrigerate the cut vegetables in a covered container until it's time to eat. Keeping them crispy fresh will preserve their appearance, flavor, and nutrients.

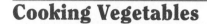

## Cooking Vegetables

Cooking makes vegetables easier to chew and digest. Many vegetables, such as green beans and potatoes, must be cooked before you can eat them. Remember to wash fresh vegetables before cooking.

When vegetables are cooked properly, they . . .

- Lose few nutrients.
- Stay a bright, attractive color.
- Are *tender-crisp*—tender but still firm.
- Have a mild, mellow flavor.

When vegetables are overcooked, many nutrients are lost. The vegetables become mushy and unappetizing. They may lack flavor or have a strong, unpleasant flavor.

**Which plate of broccoli shown above was overcooked? Which is more appetizing?**

When cooking fresh or frozen vegetables, avoid methods that are not healthful. For example, deep-fried vegetables soak up large amounts of fat. More healthful cooking methods preserve nutrients while adding little or no fat. Here are some ideas:

- Many fresh and frozen vegetables can be cooked using a steamer basket. Follow the general directions in Chapter 14. Let the vegetables steam until tender-crisp.
- Some vegetables, such as potatoes and squash, can be baked right in their skin. You can also bake vegetables in a dish along with a sauce, topping, or other foods. Have you ever had scalloped potatoes, green bean casserole, or stuffed peppers?

**Baking is a popular cooking method for many vegetables, such as stuffed green peppers or whole sweet potatoes.**

- Stir-frying is a quick and fun way to cook vegetables. Although few nutrients are lost, stir-frying does add a small amount of fat. You can combine different kinds of vegetables for color, flavor, and nutrition. You can also add fish, poultry, or meat to turn the stir-fry into a main dish. For more on stir-frying, see Chapter 35.

Two other healthful ways to cook vegetables are simmering and microwaving.

**Vegetables for stir-frying should be in small, even pieces. Use just a small amount of oil.**

## Simmering Vegetables

Fresh or frozen vegetables can be simmered in a small amount of water. The less water used, the fewer water-soluble nutrients will be lost. For most vegetables, there should be just enough water to cover the bottom of the pan.

Use a pan with a tight-fitting cover. This keeps steam in the pan. The vegetables that are not in the water cook in the steam.

Never add baking soda to vegetables. It destroys vitamins.

**To simmer vegetables . . .**

1. Bring a small amount of water to a boil.
2. Add the vegetables. Cover the pan and turn down the heat.
3. Simmer the vegetables just until they are tender-crisp.
4. Serve the cooking liquid along with the vegetables. It contains some of the nutrients that were lost from the vegetables. It will also help keep the vegetables warm.

## Microwaving Vegetables

Microwaving is an excellent cooking method for most vegetables. The short cooking time preserves flavor and nutrients.

Basic microwave methods for vegetables are simple. Fresh or frozen vegetables are usually placed in a covered microwave-safe dish with a small amount of water. Most microwave cookbooks include a chart that tells how to cook each type of vegetable.

You can also use the microwave oven to prepare vegetable casseroles and other dishes. Check a microwave cookbook for directions.

**Fresh vegetables can be microwaved with only a few tablespoons of water. Why is this an advantage?**

### Microwave Hints

- Never heat home-canned vegetables in the microwave oven. It is not safe.
- It's easy to "bake" a potato in the microwave oven. Scrub a whole potato and pierce it with a fork in several places. Place on a paper plate. Microwave at full power 4 to 6 minutes. Let stand a few minutes to finish cooking.

## Chapter 27 Review

### Check the Facts

1. List at least three nutrients found in vegetables. Give an example of a good vegetable source for each nutrient.
2. What four signs of quality should you look for when buying fresh vegetables?
3. How should fresh vegetables, other than potatoes and onions, be stored?
4. Why should vegetables be trimmed or pared as little as possible?
5. Name at least four methods of cooking vegetables.
6. Give at least three guidelines for simmering vegetables.

### Ideas in Action

1. Discuss what causes people to like or dislike certain vegetables. What can be done to make vegetables more appealing?
2. In small groups, develop a script for a "Consumer Tips" radio commercial emphasizing the best ways to cook vegetables to conserve nutrients. Present your commercial to the class.
3. Develop a simple recipe to use with your favorite vegetable. Write your idea on a recipe card for future use.

# Recipe Focus

1. Read the recipe below. What equipment would you need to gather? What would you need to do to get the ingredients ready to cook?
2. Write a menu for a family dinner using this recipe as the vegetable. The meal should be nutritious and appealing.

## Country-Style Zucchini

| Customary | Ingredients | Metric |
|---|---|---|
| 2 Tbsp. | Butter or margarine | 30 mL |
| ½ cup | Chopped onion | 125 mL |
| 4 | Medium zucchini (about 1 lb. or 500 g) | 4 |
| 2 | Tomatoes, chopped | 2 |
| Dash | Pepper | Dash |
| ¼ tsp. | Dried, crushed oregano | 1 mL |

**Yield:** 4 servings

### Conventional Directions

**Pan:** 10-inch (25-cm) skillet with cover

1. **Slice** zucchini into ¼-inch (6-mm) slices. (Do not pare zucchini.) Set aside.
2. **Melt** butter or margarine in skillet over medium heat.
3. **Add** chopped onion. Cook over medium heat until tender, about 5 minutes.
4. **Add** zucchini, tomatoes, pepper, and oregano. Mix well.
5. **Cover** and cook over medium-low heat for 15 to 20 minutes or until zucchini is tender-crisp. Stir occasionally.

### Microwave Directions

**Pan:** 2-qt. (2-L) microwave-safe container with cover

**Power Level:** 100%

**Ingredients:** Omit butter or margarine

1. **Slice** zucchini into ¼-inch (6-mm) slices. (Do not pare zucchini.) Set aside.
2. **Place** chopped onion in casserole. (No butter or margarine is needed.)
3. **Microwave**, uncovered, at 100% power for 1 to 1½ minutes or until onions become transparent. Stir every 30 seconds.
4. **Add** zucchini, tomatoes, pepper, and oregano. Stir to blend. Cover.
5. **Microwave**, covered, at 100% power for 6 to 7 minutes. Stir every 2 minutes.
6. **Let stand**, covered, for 3 to 5 minutes or until zucchini is tender-crisp.

### Nutrition Information

**Per serving (conventional method, approximate): 90 calories, 2 g protein, 8 g carbohydrate, 6 g fat, 16 mg cholesterol, 69 mg sodium**

**Good source of: vitamin A, vitamin C, B vitamins**

CHAPTER 28

# Legumes

**OBJECTIVES**

**Discover. . .**
- how legumes fit into a healthful eating plan.
- how to select and store legumes.
- how to prepare legumes.

*Legumes* (leh-GYOUMZ) are seeds that grow in a pod. They include dry peas and dry beans. As peas and beans mature, they dry out and turn into seeds. These seeds store food for the sprouting plant. As a result, dry peas and beans have more nutrients than the fresh, green ones.

## Nutrition Notes

Legumes fit into two of the food groups:

- Meat, Poultry, Fish, Dry Beans and Peas, Eggs, and Nuts Group. Like other foods in this group, legumes are an excellent source of protein. Your body needs protein for growth and repair. Remember, however, that plant protein is incomplete. To turn it into complete protein, include grain products, such as bread or rice, in your daily diet.
- Vegetables Group. Like other vegetables, legumes are high in complex carbohydrates and fiber. As you learned in Chapter 5, you need complex carbohydrates for energy. Fiber plays an important role in preventing health problems.

Legumes are also a good source of many vitamins and minerals, such as:

- Iron to strengthen the blood.
- Calcium and phosphorus for strong bones and teeth.
- B vitamins and vitamin E for growth and health.

Legumes have no cholesterol. Most are low in fat. They are easy to fit into a healthful diet.

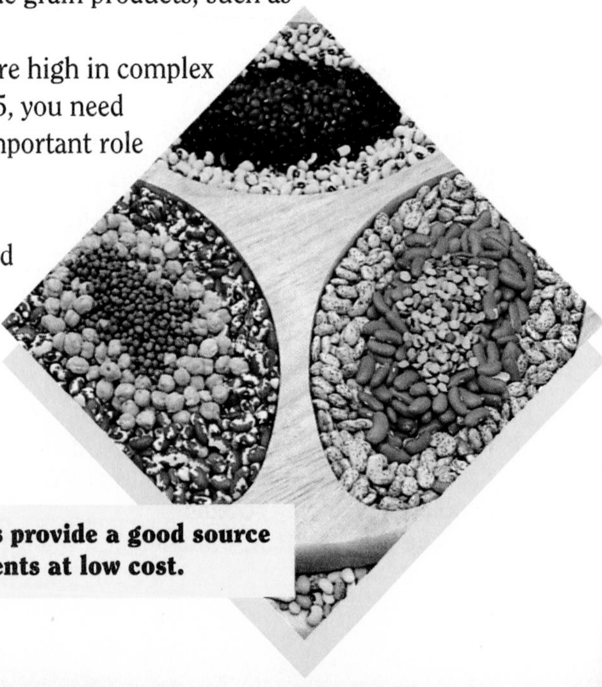

**Legumes provide a good source of nutrients at low cost.**

# Consumer Power

Even if the term "legumes" is new to you, you've probably eaten legumes before. Get to know the different types of legumes and how to buy and store them.

## Kinds of Legumes

Dry peas and beans come in a wide range of sizes, shapes, and colors. Some of the more popular ones are:

**Split peas.** Yellow or green. Mild flavor. Used mainly in soups.

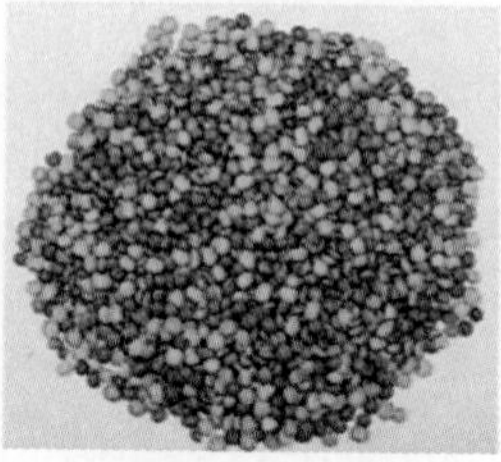

**Black-eyed peas.** Small, oval, white with black spots. Mild flavor. Many uses.

**Lima beans.** Small or large size. Mild, buttery flavor. Many uses.

**Navy beans.** Small, white beans. Mild flavor. Many uses, including baked beans and soups.

**Kidney beans.** Large beans. Light or dark red. Hearty flavor.

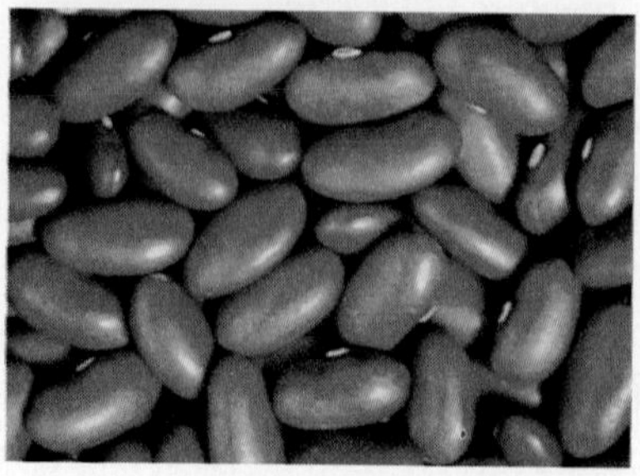

**Pinto beans.** Small, oval beans with pink dots. Mild flavor. Used for chili, refried beans, and other Mexican foods.

**Garbanzo beans.** Also known as chickpeas. Round with rough texture. Crunchy, nut-like flavor. Many uses, especially in Mexican foods.

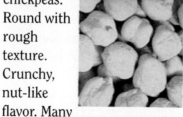

# Forms of Legumes

Both dry peas and dry beans are available in uncooked form. They are usually sold in plastic bags or in boxes.

You can also buy canned, cooked beans. Some are plain for use in recipes. Others have flavored sauces, such as pork and beans in tomato sauce.

**Several forms of dry beans and peas are available. Which form would you buy? Why?**

How can you decide whether to buy uncooked beans or canned ones? Here are some points to consider:

- ◆ Uncooked beans are easy to prepare, but the cooking may take several hours. Canned beans are ready to use.
- ◆ Both uncooked and canned beans are inexpensive—especially when compared to other protein sources, such as meat. However, uncooked ones are more economical.
- ◆ You will probably find more varieties of uncooked beans than canned ones.
- ◆ Uncooked beans take less storage space.
- ◆ Canned beans are often high in sodium.

You can also buy a variety of convenience products made with legumes, such as canned split pea soup or bean salad. Another product made from legumes is tofu. See the box on the next page.

# Buying and Storing Legumes

When buying legumes, follow the general guidelines in Chapter 8. Uncooked legumes should have good color and equal size.

Store uncooked legumes in a tightly covered container in a cool, dry place. Use one package completely before opening a new one. Why? Older peas and beans need a longer cooking time than newer ones. You will get better results when cooking legumes that come from the same package.

Leftover cooked legumes will keep for several days in the refrigerator. For longer storage, freeze them in serving-size portions.

## Tofu

Soybeans are members of the legume family. They are used to make *tofu* (TOE-foo), a custard-like product that is very high in protein. It is also high in calcium, but low in calories and sodium.

Tofu has a very mild flavor. It can be used in many different ways, such as in soups, stir-fried dishes, dips, and casseroles. It needs only enough cooking to heat through and absorb the flavors of the other foods in the dish.

Tofu comes in a choice of textures, soft or firm. When shopping, look for packages of tofu in the refrigerated section or on store shelves. Refrigerated tofu is perishable and must be used within a week. Special packaging allows some tofu to be stored longer. Read and follow package directions carefully. Leftover tofu can be frozen for longer storage.

**Tofu (right) can be used in many delicious dishes, such as vegetable lasagne (left).**

# Food Skills

Legumes can add flavor, texture, and variety to your daily food choices. They can be used for quick, nutritious meals or snacks.

## Using Canned Beans

Canned beans are cooked and ready to use. If you are concerned about too much sodium, rinse the beans first. Here are some ideas for using them:

- Add garbanzo beans to a salad.
- Mash beans into a paste to be used in spreads or dips.
- Use beans in soups, chili, and main-dish recipes, such as beans and rice.
- Serve beans as a side dish. Popular seasonings include tomato sauce, onions, molasses or brown sugar, and spices.

**Legumes can perk up the flavor of a salad. Serve with corn bread or a tasty muffin.**

## Using Dry Legumes

What can you do with uncooked legumes? Plenty! You can find many ideas in cookbooks. For example, dry peas are good in soups. They take just 30 to 45 minutes to cook.

Dry beans are very versatile. Follow basic directions to cook them. Then you can use them in any of the ways described for canned beans.

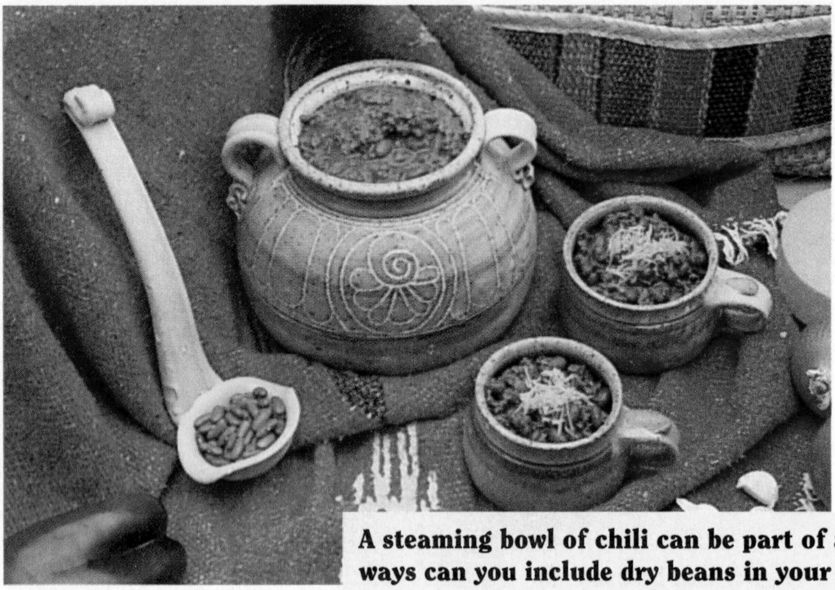

**A steaming bowl of chili can be part of a hearty meal. What other ways can you include dry beans in your eating plan?**

Keep in mind that legumes expand when cooked. One cup (250 mL) of dry beans makes about 2¼ to 3 cups (550 to 750 mL) when cooked.

Preparing dry beans involves three basic steps: sorting, soaking, and simmering.

### Sort the Beans

Before cooking beans, sort them carefully. Remove any foreign material, such as pebbles. Remove beans that are discolored, wrinkled, cracked, or that have holes.

Rinse beans several times to wash off dirt and dust. Swish them in a bowl of cool water or use a sprayer. Check to be sure the beans smell clean, not musty.

### Soak the Beans

If desired, soak beans overnight before cooking. Soaking will cut the cooking time by 15 to 30 minutes. It can also help prevent the beans from causing gas to form in the digestive system.

To soak, place beans in a large pot. Add about 5 cups (1250 mL) of water for every 1 cup (250 mL) of dry beans. Cover and let stand overnight. After soaking, pour off the water. Use fresh water for cooking.

Some beans do not require soaking because they are preprocessed. Check the label on the package.

## Simmer the Beans

Beans should be simmered until they are tender. This will take from 1 to 3 hours, depending on the type of beans. Check the package for guidelines. If not cooked long enough, the beans may feel gritty or hard. If overcooked, the beans get mushy and fall apart.

1. Combine water and beans in a large pot with a cover.
   ▲ As a general rule, use 3 cups (750 mL) cold water for each cup (250 mL) dry beans. If you have soaked the beans, you may be able to use less water.

2. Put the cover on, but leave it slightly ajar so that steam can escape. This keeps the beans from boiling over.

3. Simmer gently until done.
   ▲ If necessary, add enough hot water to keep the beans covered.

## Tips for Cooking Beans

- ◆ Time management skills can help you make more use of dry beans. Cook a large amount of beans at one time. Divide the beans into smaller portions and freeze for future use.
- ◆ Undercook beans if they will be cooked again later as part of a recipe.

- ◆ Overcook beans slightly if you plan to use them for dips or sandwich spreads. That way they will be easier to mash.
- ◆ Salt, sugar, and acid foods, like tomatoes and vinegar, toughen beans. If you want to use these seasonings, add them near the end of the cooking time.
- ◆ Do not add baking soda when cooking dry beans. The baking soda cuts down a little on the cooking time. However, it destroys thiamin, one of the B vitamins found in beans.

## Microwave Hints

- Cooked beans are easy to reheat in the microwave oven. Cook on full power for 15 seconds. Stir. Repeat until heated through.
- Thaw frozen beans in the microwave oven. Check a microwave cookbook or owner's guide for how to defrost food.

## Microwaving Legumes

Legumes need time to absorb water and soften. Therefore, they take about as long to cook in a microwave oven as they do on the range.

The procedure for cooking dry beans in the microwave is similar to the conventional method. The beans are soaked overnight, drained, then simmered in fresh water until tender. Check a microwave cookbook for complete directions.

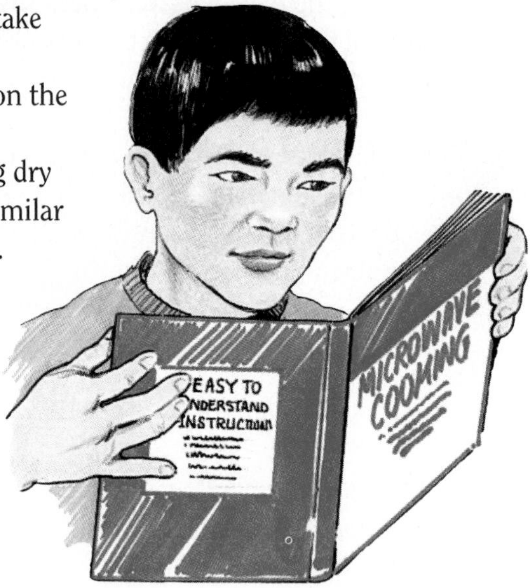


## Chapter 28 Review

### Check the Facts

1. Why are dry beans and peas high in nutrients?
2. Name at least four nutrients found in legumes. Identify one function of each nutrient.
3. When buying and storing uncooked legumes, what three guidelines should you follow?
4. What is tofu? How is it used?
5. Why should uncooked dry beans be sorted before cooking?
6. Briefly describe the process for cooking dry beans.

### Ideas in Action

1. Look through recipe books for recipes that combine legumes with a grain. In small groups, compare the recipes for flavor combinations, nutrition, and appeal.
2. Write a news bulletin describing the benefits of eating legumes as part of a healthful diet.
3. Have a brainstorming session to think of different ways tofu can be used in recipes.

# Recipe Focus

1. Read the "Tostada Melt" recipe that follows. What could you substitute for pinto beans if they were not available?
2. If you were to serve this recipe for a meal, what other foods would you serve with it?

# Tostada Melt

| Customary | Ingredients | Metric |
|---|---|---|
| 16-oz. can | Pinto beans | 453-g can |
| 1 tsp. | Dried, crushed oregano | 5 mL |
| 1 tsp. | Chili powder | 5 mL |
| ½ tsp. | Ground cumin | 2 mL |
| ¼ tsp. | Garlic powder | 1 mL |
| ¼ tsp. | Onion powder | 1 mL |
| Six 6-inch | Corn tostada shells* | Six 15-cm |
| ¾ cup | Shredded cheddar cheese | 175 mL |
| 1½ cups | Shredded lettuce | 375 mL |
| ¾ cup | Salsa | 175 mL |

**Yield:** 6 servings (1 tostada each)

### Conventional Directions

**Pan:** Broiler pan
**Temperature:** Broiler setting

1. **Mash** pinto beans in a medium bowl.
2. **Combine** oregano, chili powder, cumin, garlic powder, and onion powder with mashed beans. Mix until well blended.
3. **Spread** about ⅓ cup (75 mL) of bean mixture on each tostada shell.
4. **Top** each with 2 Tbsp. (about 30 mL) shredded cheddar cheese.
5. **Place** tostadas on broiler pan. Position the pan under the broiler so the tops of the tostadas are about 3 inches (8 cm) from the heat.
6. **Broil** just until cheese melts. Remove from broiler.
7. **Top** each tostada with ¼ cup (about 60 mL) shredded lettuce.
8. **Spoon** about 2 Tbsp. (30mL) salsa over lettuce.

***Note:** If you prefer crisp tostada shells, heat them in the oven according to the package directions to crisp them before spreading with bean mixture.

### Microwave Directions

**Pan:** Microwave-safe plate
**Power Level:** 100%
**Follow** steps 1-4 of conventional directions. Then proceed as follows:

5. **Place** tostadas on a microwave-safe plate one or two at a time.
6. **Microwave** at 100% power for about 45 seconds or just until the cheese melts.
7. **Top** each tostada with ¼ cup (about 60 mL) shredded lettuce. Spoon salsa over top.

**Nutrition Information**
**Per serving (approximate): 223 calories, 10 g protein, 30 g carbohydrate, 7 g fat, 15 mg cholesterol, 230 mg sodium**
**Good source of: B vitamins, calcium, iron, phosphorus**

CHAPTER 29

# Poultry

**OBJECTIVES**

**Discover . . .**
- how poultry fits into a healthful eating plan.
- how to select and store poultry.
- how to prepare poultry.

*Poultry* refers to birds raised for food, such as chickens and turkeys. Poultry is one of the most popular main-dish foods. It is nutritious, relatively low in cost, versatile, and flavorful.

## Nutrition Notes

Poultry is part of the Meat, Poultry, Fish, Dry Beans and Peas, Eggs, and Nuts Group. It provides important nutrients, such as:

- ◆ Protein for growth and repair of the body.
- ◆ Iron for healthy red blood cells.
- ◆ B vitamins for a healthy nervous system.
- ◆ Phosphorus for healthy bones and teeth.

Chicken and turkey contain less total fat and saturated fat than some meats. Most of the fat is located in and just under the skin. If you remove the skin before eating, you will eat less fat.

The amount of fat in poultry also depends on the cooking method. Frying, for example, adds considerable fat. Other methods of cooking, such as broiling and roasting, can give poultry a delicious flavor and crispy texture without extra fat.

Many people use chicken or turkey instead of beef or pork in recipes. For example, you could use ground turkey in chili instead of beef. Substituting poultry for meat can make favorite dishes lower in fat. However, the amount of cholesterol is about the same.

**Eating poultry is a popular way to meet your daily protein requirement. What ways do you like to eat poultry?**

# Consumer Power

Chicken and turkey are the most common kinds of poultry. Turkeys are much larger than chickens, and their meat has a stronger flavor.

Both chicken and turkey have white and dark meat. White meat, which comes from the breast, is more tender and milder in flavor than dark meat. It also has less fat.

## Forms of Poultry

Uncooked chicken and turkey are sold fresh or frozen. You can choose:

- A whole bird.
- A bird cut in halves, quarters, or individual pieces.
- Parts packaged separately, such as breasts, legs, or thighs.
- Boneless parts and ground poultry.

Chicken and turkey are also available in a wide variety of convenience forms. (See page 199.) Consider cost and nutrition before deciding what form of poultry to buy.

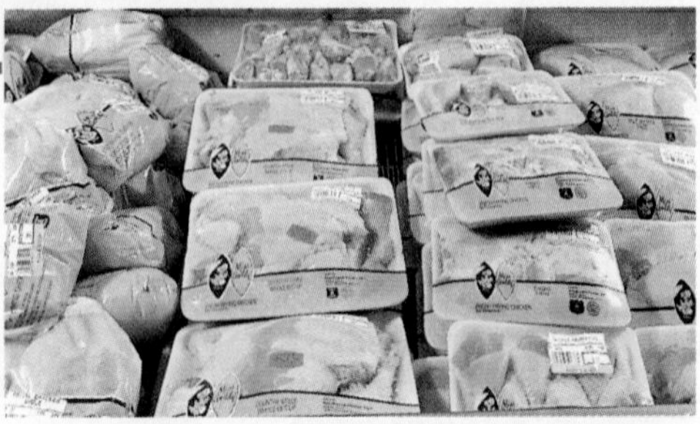

**The form of poultry you buy may depend on how you want to use it.**

## Buying Fresh and Frozen Poultry

Here are some tips to help you find quality and value in fresh or frozen poultry.

- Check the label for the type of bird. The most common type of chicken is usually called "broiler" or "fryer." It is tender and can be broiled, roasted, braised, or fried. A "stewing chicken" or "hen" is less tender and should be simmered in liquid.
- Look for a grade shield. Grade A poultry is meatier than Grade B poultry. Not all poultry is graded.
- Choose fresh poultry that has a clear, bright color and no bruises. Frozen poultry should be frozen hard.
- When buying ground poultry, read the label carefully. Some contains skin, which adds fat.

USDA
A
GRADE
INSPECTED FOR WHOLESOMENESS BY U.S. DEPARTMENT OF AGRICULTURE
ALL NATURAL
NO PRESERVATIVES
NO ARTIFICIAL INGREDIENTS
MINIMALLY PROCESSED
HOLLY'S® 9 PIECE
Whole Chicken Cut Up
KEEP REFRIGERATED


**What does the Grade A symbol tell you?**

## Reading Price Labels

Most packages of poultry, fish, and meat carry similar price labels. Understanding the information on the label is a basic shopping skill. For example, here is a package of chicken legs. The label shows:

***Unit price***
This is usually the cost per pound. It varies depending on the type of poultry, fish, or meat. For example, chicken legs may cost less per pound than chicken breasts.

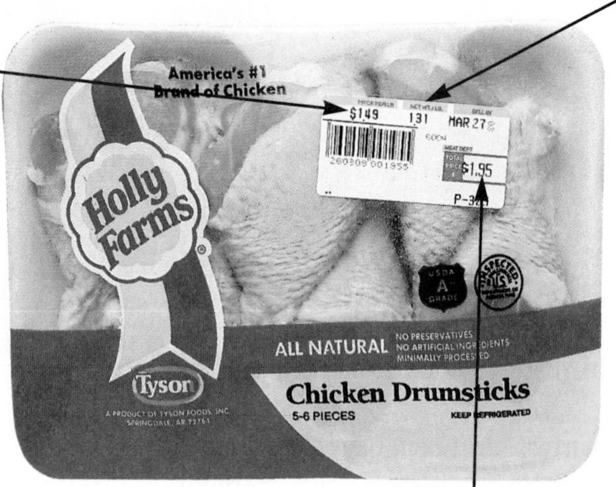


***Net weight***
This is the weight of the poultry itself. It includes parts that cannot be eaten, such as bones.

***Price for this package***
This is the net weight multiplied by the unit price.

## Finding the Cost per Serving

When buying poultry, fish, or meat, compare the cost per serving, not just the cost per pound. Why? Some packages include more bone and fat than others. You would have to buy more in order to get the same number of servings as you would from a package with less bone and fat.

To calculate the cost per serving, first find the unit price on the label. You also need to know about how many servings you can get from a pound (500 g) of the poultry, fish, or meat. Most poultry gives about two servings per pound. Boneless or ground poultry will give about four servings per pound. Servings per pound for fish and meat are shown on pages 208 and 219.

Now use the formula:

$$\text{cost per serving} = \text{cost per pound} \div \text{servings per pound}$$

Figure out the cost per serving for the different types of poultry, fish, or meat you might buy. Then compare to decide which is the best value.

## Storing Fresh and Frozen Poultry

Store fresh poultry in the coldest part of the refrigerator. (This is usually under the freezer compartment or in a special meat-keeper section.) Leave the poultry in the store wrapper. Place the package on a plate or in a plastic bag so that juices do not drip onto other foods. Use within one or two days. For longer storage, wrap the poultry in airtight wrapping and freeze it.

Poultry that was purchased frozen can be kept in its original wrapper. Store in the freezer up to 12 months.

Leftover cooked poultry should be stored in a covered container in the refrigerator. It will keep for three to four days. If you want to keep it longer, freeze it.

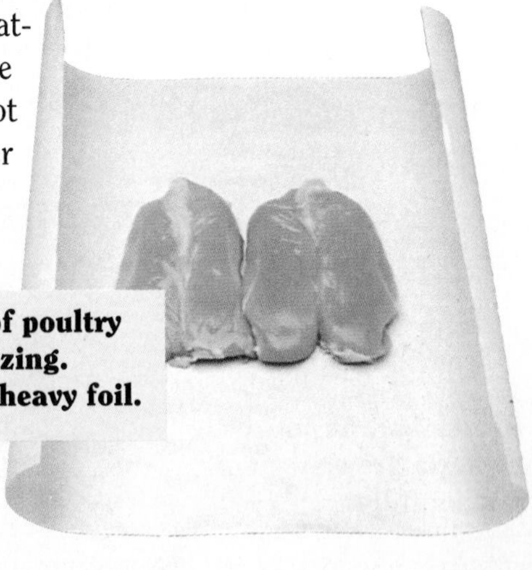

**You can divide a large package of poultry into smaller portions before freezing. Wrap tightly in freezer paper or heavy foil.**

## Convenience Poultry Products

Chicken and turkey are also used to make cured products, such as cold cuts, frankfurters, and bacon. *Cured* means the product has been treated with ingredients that slow spoilage and add a distinctive flavor. Curing ingredients include salt, sugar, and chemicals such as sodium nitrite. Many cured poultry products are ready to eat, while others need to be cooked.

Many other convenience forms of poultry are available. For example, you can find canned chicken meat and microwavable meals on store shelves. Frozen main dishes and dinners often include poultry. The deli department may have precooked chicken ready to heat and serve.

When buying convenience poultry products, read labels and compare the nutrition of different products. Follow package directions for storage and use.

**Many people like using cured poultry products for family meals. Some cured poultry products are lower in fat than many other types of cured meat products.**

**What might be the advantages and disadvantages of these products?**

# Food Skills

Poultry is a versatile part of meal planning. It can be a main dish in itself or part of a recipe for soup or a casserole. Cooked poultry can be sliced or cubed for use in salads and sandwiches.

## Keeping Poultry Safe to Eat

**Remember, harmful bacteria grow at room temperature.**

Proper food handling is especially important when you work with poultry. Raw poultry may contain salmonella, a harmful bacteria. Review the food safety guidelines in Chapter 17. Pay special attention to these points:

- Never let poultry sit at room temperature to thaw. Instead, thaw the poultry in the refrigerator, in cold water, or in the microwave oven. If you don't have time to thaw frozen poultry properly, you can cook it while still frozen. Frozen poultry takes about 1½ times longer to cook than thawed poultry.
- Don't remove poultry from the refrigerator until you are ready to cook it.
- Rinse poultry thoroughly under cold running water just before cooking. Pat dry with a paper towel.
- After working with raw poultry, thoroughly wash your hands, tools, work surfaces, and anything else that touches uncooked poultry.
- To store leftovers from a whole turkey, first remove the bones. (If you wish, you can use them as the base for turkey soup.) Divide the meat into several small portions for faster chilling. Do the same with the stuffing. Refrigerate or freeze.

## Principles of Cooking Poultry

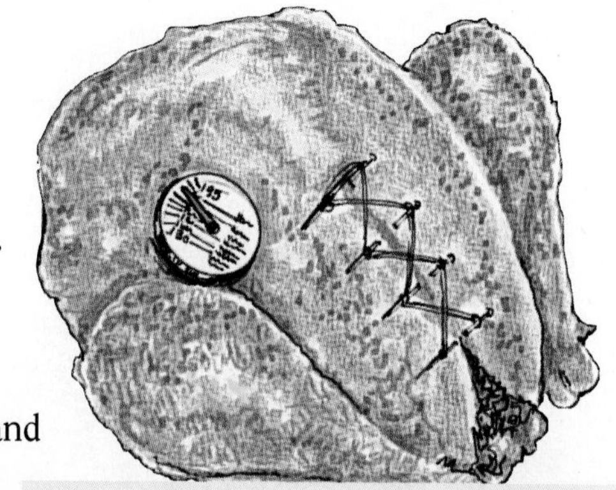


**When inserting a meat thermometer, be sure it does not touch bone.**

Poultry is a protein food. Remember, protein foods are delicate. When overcooked, they become tough and dry.

Properly cooked poultry is tender, moist, and flavorful. If roasted or broiled, the crust should be brown and crisp.

Undercooked poultry looks pale and the inside is still pink and firm. It is not safe to eat because it has not been cooked long enough to kill harmful bacteria.

How can you tell if poultry is done? For whole poultry and large pieces, such as turkey breasts, use a meat thermometer. Cook to an internal temperature of 185°F (85°C).

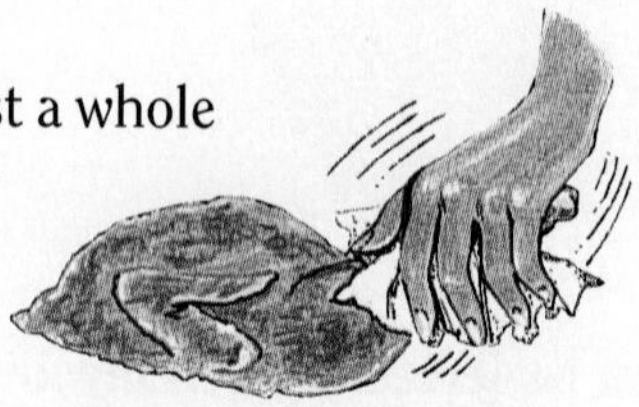

What if you don't have a meat thermometer? To test a whole bird or a half, hold the drumstick with a folded paper towel. Wiggle it. It should move easily if done.

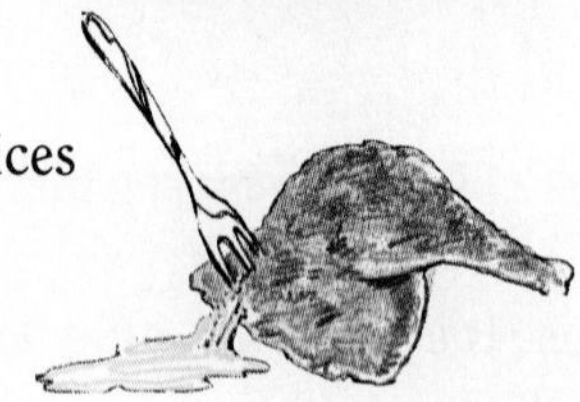

You can also pierce the poultry with a fork. The juices should be a clear yellow, not pink.

## Methods of Cooking Poultry

A number of basic cooking methods can be used for poultry. These include broiling, roasting, braising, frying, and microwaving.

### Broiling Poultry

Chicken halves, quarters, or pieces can be broiled. Leave the skin on to protect the meat from drying out. To reduce fat, remove the skin just before eating.

Place the chicken skin side up on a cold broiler pan. Put it in the broiler unit so the tops of the pieces are about 4 to 6 inches (10 to 15 cm) from the heat. Broil until nicely browned (usually about 20 to 30 minutes). Turn the pieces over with tongs and continue broiling until done. For extra flavor, you can brush the chicken with a sauce, such as barbecue sauce, as it cooks.

**Broiled poultry is a delicious, low-fat alternative to fried poultry.**

Roasted turkey can be served for holiday meals or anytime.

## Roasting Poultry

Roasting, or baking, is a popular cooking method for both chicken and turkey. Leave the skin on during roasting to protect the bird from drying out. You can remove the skin just before eating.

A whole bird can be filled with stuffing before it is roasted. Never stuff a bird the day before and refrigerate it overnight. The stuffing will not chill properly and harmful bacteria will grow. Instead, stuff the bird just before roasting. You can also cook stuffing separately.

A large whole bird takes a long time to cook. Roasting chicken or turkey pieces is often more convenient.

**To roast chicken or turkey pieces . . .**

1. Rinse the pieces carefully and pat dry.

2. Arrange pieces in a single layer in a large roasting or baking pan, skin side up. Use a rack if desired.

3. If you're roasting turkey, brush with melted butter or margarine.
   ▲Turkey pieces are larger and take longer to cook. The butter or margarine helps keep the pieces moist during cooking.

4. Sprinkle lightly with seasoning, such as ground black pepper and dried, crushed marjoram or oregano.

5. Roast uncovered at 350°F (180°C) until parts test done. Cooking time varies with the size of the pieces and amount of bone.
   ▲Turn turkey pieces over after half the cooking time. Baste with pan drippings or melted butter or margarine.

## Braising Poultry

Braising is a common method of cooking poultry. There are endless ways to vary the flavor depending on the ingredients you add.

Braising can be used to tenderize older poultry, such as stewing chickens. Broilers or fryers can also be braised. They cook in less time than older poultry.

You can find many recipes for braised poultry dishes in cookbooks. In general, here are the steps in braising.

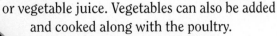

- Brown the chicken in a small amount of oil in a skillet. To reduce fat, you can remove the skin before browning.
- Next, add seasonings and liquid. The liquid might be water, chicken broth, or vegetable juice. Vegetables can also be added and cooked along with the poultry.
- Simmer the mixture until done. Chicken pieces from a broiler or fryer will take about 1 hour to cook.
- If desired, serve over a grain such as rice.

**Braising chicken makes it tender and blends flavors. Try adding tomatoes, onions, and seasonings for Chicken Cacciatore.**

**Start cooking larger poultry pieces first. They have a longer cooking time.**

## Frying Poultry

Poultry can be coated with crumbs or batter and panfried. Remember that frying adds fat and calories because the chicken absorbs fat as it fries.

If you fry chicken, follow these guidelines:

- Wash and dry chicken pieces carefully. If you put moist chicken in hot fat, it will spatter.
- Use only enough oil to cover the bottom of the skillet.
- Start with large, meaty pieces such as the breast and thigh. Place in the skillet skin side down. Once these are partially cooked, add the smaller pieces.
- Turn pieces after half the cooking time.

## Microwave Hints

- When microwaving, do not coat chicken with flour—it gets gummy. If you want a coating, use bread crumbs.
- Remove fat and juices with a baster as they accumulate. They attract microwaves and lengthen the cooking time.

## Microwaving Poultry

Poultry cooked in the microwave will be moist and juicy, but not brown or crisp. Sometimes a coating or sauce is added to give more color.

Before microwaving, be sure the poultry is completely thawed. Pierce or remove the skin to keep it from bursting. When microwaving pieces, put the meatier parts near the outside of the dish and the bonier parts toward the center.

Standing time is needed to allow the center or thicker portions to finish cooking. At the end of the standing time, check the poultry in several thick spots with a meat thermometer. Make sure the poultry has reached an internal temperature of 185°F (85°C) throughout.

**Be sure to arrange poultry properly for even cooking.**

# Chapter 29 Review

### Check the Facts

1. Identify four nutrients found in poultry.
2. List three quality characteristics to look for when buying fresh or frozen poultry.
3. How can you figure the cost per serving of poultry? Why is this important?
4. Describe how to refrigerate fresh poultry.
5. What are five food safety guidelines for properly handling poultry?
6. Describe three ways to test poultry for doneness.
7. When broiling, how far should poultry pieces be placed from the heat?
8. What are two reasons you might braise poultry?
9. Why is standing time needed when microwaving poultry?

### Ideas in Action

1. Chicken breasts with bones are on sale at the supermarket for $2.59 per pound. Boneless chicken breasts cost $3.99 per pound. Whole, cut-up chickens cost $1.29 per pound. What is the cost per serving of each? Which is most economical?
2. Discuss the relationship between safe food handling practices and poultry.
3. Janice is concerned about the amount of fat in her diet. Her family really likes poultry, but has only prepared it fried. What advice would you give Janice about other cooking methods for poultry?

# Recipe Focus

1. Read the recipe below. Why do the microwave directions call for arranging the skewers in a spoke pattern?
2. If boneless chicken breasts are $2.99 per pound, pineapple chunks are 89¢ per can, water chestnuts are two cans for $1.39, and barbecue sauce is $1.79 per jar (you use half of the jar), what would be the total cost of preparing the recipe? The cost per serving?

## Pineapple Chicken Ribbons

| Customary | Ingredients | Metric |
|---|---|---|
| 1 lb. | Boneless, skinless chicken breast | 500 g |
| 20-oz. can | Unsweetened pineapple chunks, drained | 567-g can |
| Two 8-oz. cans | Whole water chestnuts, drained | Two 227-g cans |
| ¾ cup | Barbecue sauce | 175 mL |

**Yield:** About 6 servings (4 skewers per serving)

### Conventional Directions

**Pan:** Broiler pan
**Temperature:** Broiler setting

1. **Cut** chicken breasts lengthwise into ½-inch (13-mm) strips (long ribbons).
2. **Pierce** one end of a chicken strip with a bamboo skewer.
3. **Add** a pineapple chunk to the skewer.
4. **Loop** the chicken strip around the pineapple and pierce again. Add a water chestnut. Continue to alternate the chicken strip with the pineapple chunks and water chestnuts, sliding the pieces down the skewer as you work. (See photo.)
5. **Repeat** the process for the remaining ingredients, making about 24 skewers in all.
6. **Brush** the skewers with half of barbecue sauce.
7. **Place** skewers on broiler pan and position the pan 6 inches (15 cm) from the heat. Broil 10 minutes.
8. **Turn** the skewers and continue cooking 5 to 8 minutes or until done.
9. **Serve** with remaining barbecue sauce.

### Microwave Directions

**Pan:** 10-inch (25-cm) microwave-safe pie plate
**Power Level:** 100%
**Follow** steps 1-6 of conventional directions. Then continue as follows:

7. **Arrange** skewers on the pie plate like the spokes in a wheel.
8. **Microwave**, uncovered, at 100% power 6 to 10 minutes or until cooked through. Rearrange the skewers after 4 minutes.

**Nutrition Information**

**Per serving (approximate): 190 calories, 18 g protein, 23 g carbohydrate, 3 g fat, 44 mg cholesterol, 301 mg sodium**

**Good source of: B vitamins, vitamin C, phosphorus, other minerals**

CHAPTER 30

# Fish and Shellfish

**OBJECTIVES**

**Discover . . .**
- how fish and shellfish fit into a healthful eating plan.
- how to select and store fish and shellfish.
- how to prepare fish and shellfish.

Fish and shellfish are sometimes called "nature's fast food" because they are quick and easy to prepare. They are also nutritious and flavorful.

Fish have fins, a central spinal column, and a bony structure. Cod, catfish, and haddock are fish with fins. Shellfish have a hard outer shell. They do not have bones. Clams, lobsters, crabs, and oysters are examples of shellfish.

## Nutrition Notes

Fish and shellfish are part of the Meat, Poultry, Fish, Dry Beans and Peas, Eggs, and Nuts Group. They are excellent sources of complete protein. As explained in Chapter 5, your body needs protein for growth and repair.

Other nutrients in fish and shellfish vary, depending on the kind of fish and where it was caught. Fish and shellfish may be good sources of:

- Vitamin A and the B vitamins for growth and health.
- Iron for healthy red blood cells.
- Iodine, an essential nutrient supplied by saltwater fish and shellfish.
- Vitamin D, calcium, and phosphorus for healthy bones and teeth. For example, canned sardines and salmon, when eaten with the bones, are excellent sources of calcium.

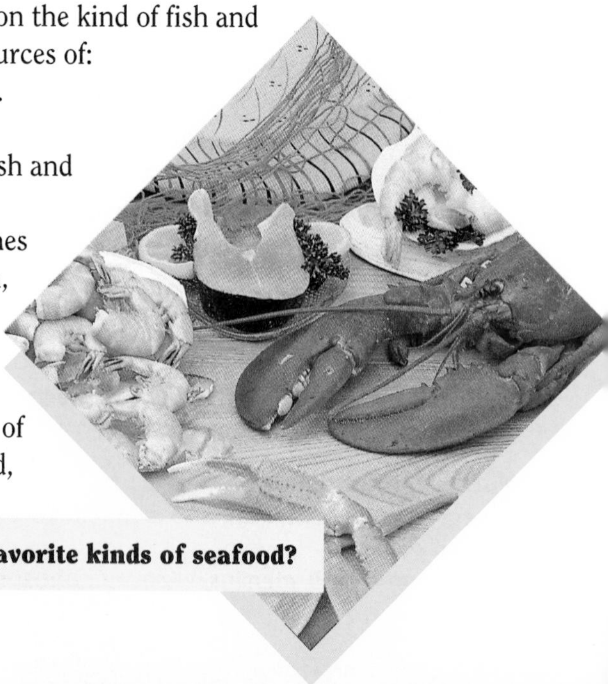

**What are your favorite kinds of seafood?**

Most fish and shellfish are low in fat. Generally, most of the fat is unsaturated. When fish and shellfish are baked, steamed, broiled, or poached, they remain low in fat. Frying fish and shellfish adds both fat and calories.

# Consumer Power

Hundreds of different kinds of fish are available on the market. Some, such as catfish, pollock, bass, halibut, and perch, have light-colored flesh. Others, like trout and salmon, have darker flesh. Generally, you can substitute one kind of fish for another of the same color in a recipe.

## Forms of Fish

Fish is available fresh or frozen. Some of the most common forms of fresh and frozen fish are:

**Whole.** This is the entire fish as it is caught. Whole fish are not frozen.

**Drawn.** The insides have been removed.

**Dressed or pandressed.** Scales and insides have been removed. The head, tail, and fins have been cut off.

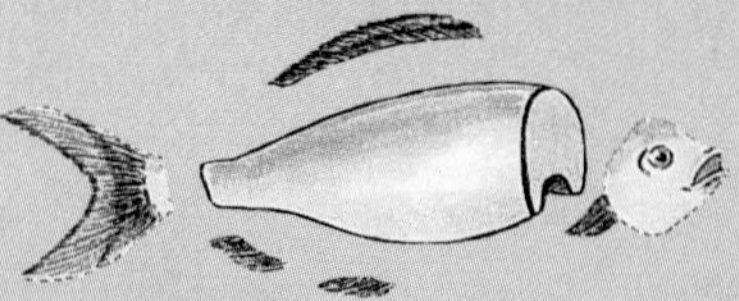

**Steaks.** These are slices cut across a large, dressed fish. They may contain bones.

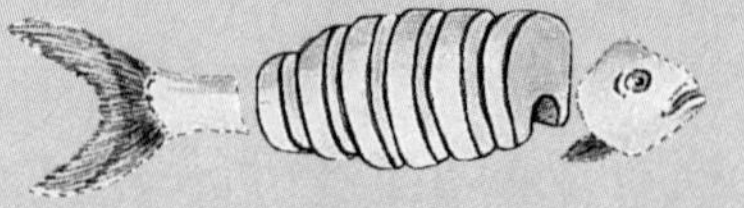

**Fillets.** Sides of fish cut away from the ribs and backbone are called *fillets* (fill-AYS). They are usually boneless, but some may contain tiny bones.

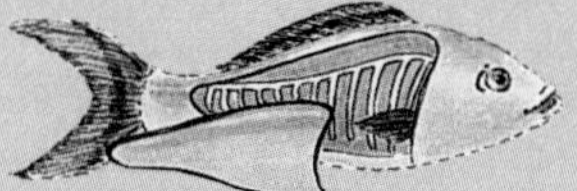

In addition, many convenience forms of fish are available. For example, you can buy canned fish, such as sardines, salmon, and tuna. Frozen fish is available with breading, seasoning, or a sauce. Some products need cooking. Others only need to be heated. There are also frozen or packaged meals made with fish.

**When might you choose canned fish or frozen prepared fish instead of fresh?**

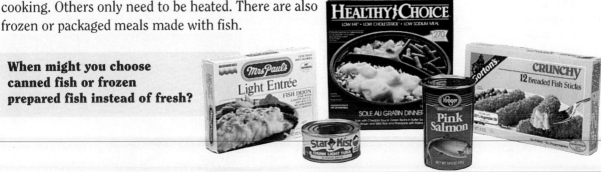

## Buying Fish

Compare prices and the cost per serving of different kinds and forms of fish. Remember the formula:

cost per serving = cost per pound ÷ servings per pound

How many servings can you get from fish?

| 1 lb. (500 g) of . . . | will give you . . . |
|---|---|
| Whole or drawn fish | 1 serving (3 oz. or 84 g fish without bones) |
| Dressed fish | 2 servings |
| Fish steaks or fillets | 3 servings |

When buying fresh fish, check for these signs of quality and freshness:

***Flesh***
Firm and elastic with no dry edges. Press on the flesh with a finger. It should spring back to its original shape.

***Aroma***
Fresh, not fishy or ammonia-like.

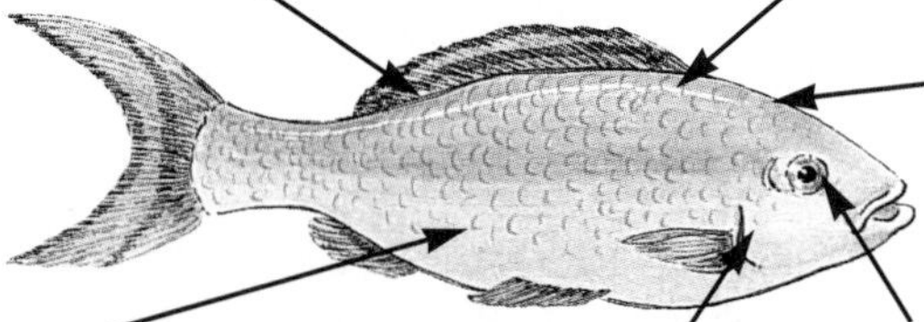

***Skin***
Moist, unbruised, and shiny, with no slime.

***Color***
Good, clear, not faded.

***Gills***
Red, free of slime.

***Eyes***
Full, clear, bulging, with black pupils.

When buying frozen or canned fish, follow the general guidelines explained in Chapter 8. Never buy frozen fish unless it is solidly frozen.

Read labels carefully. Products that have been inspected carry a round seal of inspection. Some fish products are also graded for quality. Grade A fish is the highest grade.

**An inspection seal tells you the fish has been examined to help ensure it is safe to eat.**

## Storing Fish

- ◆ Refrigerate fresh fish up to two days in the coldest part of the refrigerator. Keep the fish covered tightly. Its odor is easily picked up by other foods. For longer storage, freeze the fish.
- ◆ Keep frozen fish solidly frozen.
- ◆ Refrigerate cooked fish in a covered container for up to three or four days. Freeze for longer storage.

## Kinds and Forms of Shellfish

There are many different kinds of shellfish. Some of the most popular include lobster, crab, shrimp, clams, mussels, oysters, and scallops.

Depending on the type, shellfish are sold in different forms. For example, you may find clams and oysters whole in the shell or *shucked*—with the shell removed. Lobster tails and crab legs may be available. Shellfish may be fresh or frozen, uncooked or already cooked. Many shellfish are sold live. You can also buy canned shellfish as well as frozen main dishes and meals.

Imitation shellfish products, such as crabsticks, are made from *surimi.* Surimi contains chopped fish plus other ingredients for flavor and seasoning. It is shaped to resemble shellfish. Surimi products are fully cooked and usually frozen.

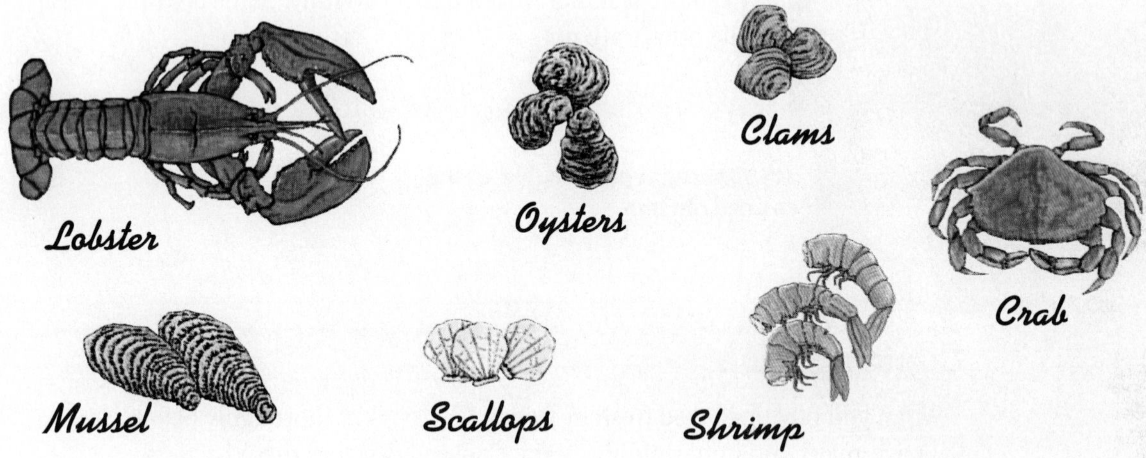


## Buying and Storing Shellfish

**Imitation shellfish products are an economical way to add the flavor of seafood to dishes.**

You don't have to live near a fishing port to enjoy different kinds of shellfish. Most supermarkets carry a wide selection. However, local varieties are likely to be more plentiful and less expensive.

When buying fresh shellfish, look for a good, clear color and fresh aroma. Use fresh shellfish within one day. For longer storage, wrap it tightly and freeze.

Live lobsters and crabs should be active when purchased. Mollusks and clams should have their shells closed tight. Refrigerate live shellfish in a shallow dish covered with a damp towel. Use the shellfish as soon as possible.

Refrigerate cooked shellfish in a covered container for up to three or four days. Freeze for longer storage.

# Food Skills

Preparation of fish and shellfish can be simple or fancy. Clam chowder can warm you up on a cold day. Broiled salmon steaks can be an elegant main dish. With fish and shellfish you can make everything from appetizers to casseroles.

## Using Convenience Forms

Many convenience forms of fish and shellfish are already cooked. For example, canned fish and shellfish are ready to use in salads, sandwiches, casseroles, and other recipes.

Read the labels of frozen items carefully. Some are precooked, while others are not.

**Try making a pasta salad using canned shrimp.**

## Cooking Fish

When you buy uncooked fresh or frozen fish, cook it thoroughly before eating. Raw fish may contain harmful bacteria. Cooking destroys these bacteria.

Frozen fish is often thawed before cooking. This must be done safely. Never thaw fish in warm water or at room temperature. Harmful bacteria will grow. Instead, thaw the fish in the refrigerator or in cold water. You can also use a microwave oven to defrost fish. Follow the directions in the instruction book for the oven. Watch carefully so parts of the fish don't begin cooking while the rest is still thawing. You can also cook fish while still frozen—just add more cooking time.

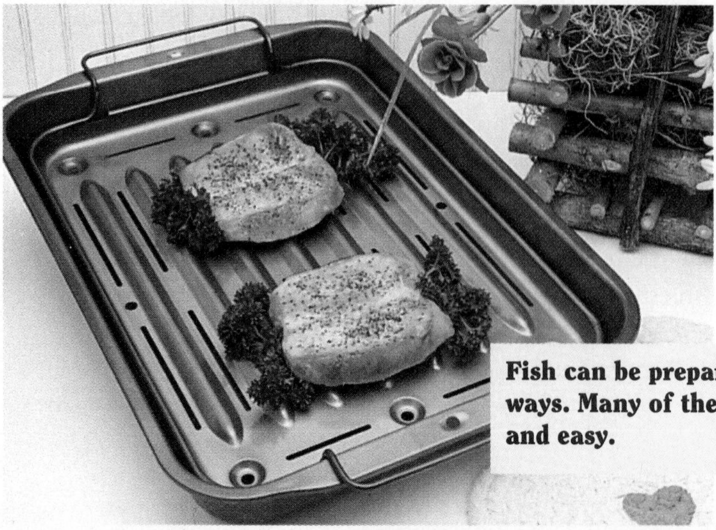

Most frozen convenience foods should be cooked without thawing. Follow package directions.

Before cooking, rinse fish in cold water. Pat it dry with a clean paper towel.

**Fish can be prepared in lots of interesting ways. Many of them are surprisingly quick and easy.**

## Principles of Cooking Fish

Like other protein foods, fish is sensitive to heat. In addition, it has very little connective tissue. This means it is naturally tender. It needs to be cooked only a short time at moderate temperatures.

Raw fish is *translucent*, or semi-clear. As it cooks, it becomes *opaque* (oh-PAKE)—that is, a solid color that you can't see through.

**Notice the appearance of raw fish. As it cooks, the appearance and texture change.**

Properly cooked fish should be opaque throughout. The flesh should flake easily when tested with a fork.

If overcooked, fish becomes dry and mealy. It will also fall apart.

How can you judge how long to cook fish? For conventional cooking, use the 10-minute rule.

**10-Minute Rule for Cooking Fish**

- Measure the thickest part of the fish. Include the stuffing if it is stuffed.
- Cook the fish 10 minutes for every 1 inch (2.5 cm) of thickness.
- If the fish is more than ½ inch (1.3 cm) thick, turn it over after half of the cooking time.

There are many ways to cook fish. Some of the easiest include broiling, baking, and microwaving.

## Broiling Fish

Fish for broiling should be about 1 inch (2.5 cm) thick. Thinner fish will dry out before it is cooked.

1. Brush the grid of a cold broiler pan with oil or use a cooking spray.

2. Rinse the fish and pat dry. Place it on the broiler pan in one layer.

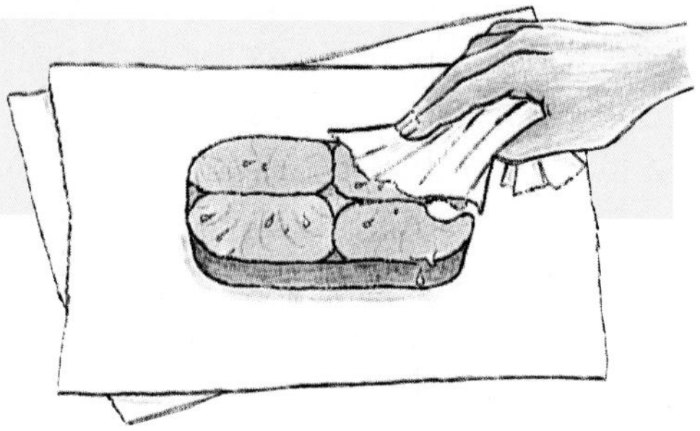

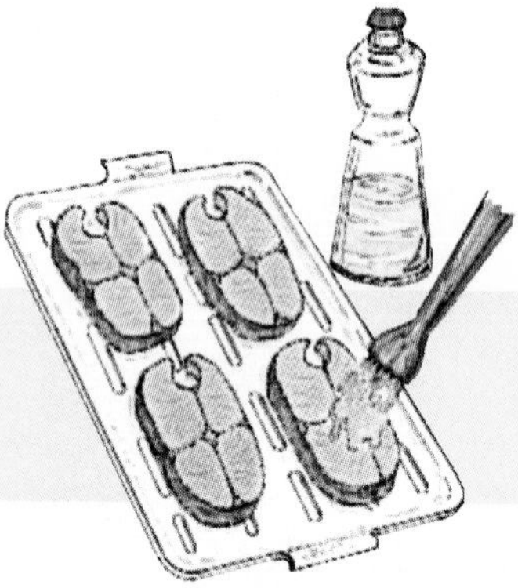

3. If desired, brush the top of the fish lightly with oil, butter, or margarine to help keep the fish from drying out.

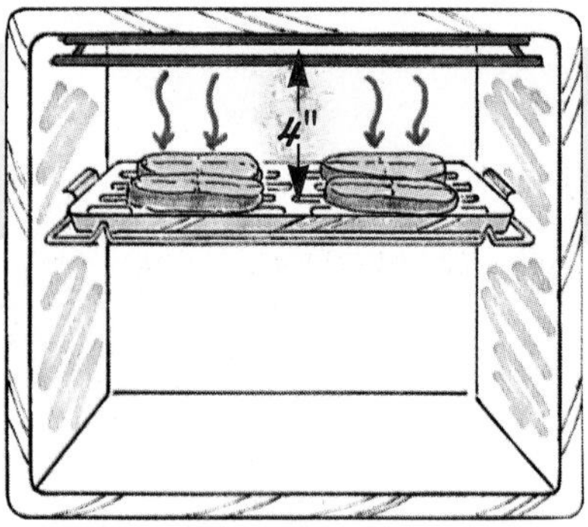


4. Place the broiler pan in the broiler about 4 inches (10 cm) from the heat source.

5. Broil until the fish flakes easily (about 6-10 minutes, depending on the thickness of the fish). Fish steaks or thick fillets should be turned over after half of the cooking time.
   ▲ If desired, brush the fish lightly with oil, butter, or margarine after turning. Thin fillets do not need to be turned.

## Baking Fish

Baking is one of the easiest ways to cook fish. You can add seasonings or a sauce. Whole fish may be stuffed for baking. You can also spread fillets with stuffing and then roll them up.

**Try topping baked fish with vegetables for a flavorful touch.**

## Microwaving Fish

The microwave oven does an excellent job of cooking fish. However, be careful to avoid overcooking. For best results, check the oven's instruction book or a microwave cookbook.

With most microwave recipes, you cover the dish to keep moisture inside. However, fish with a crumb coating usually does not need to be covered. The crumbs keep the fish moist.

To cook fish, microwave at 100% power for 3 to 5 minutes per pound (500 g). If you add liquid or a sauce to the fish, it may need more cooking time. Thick pieces, such as steaks, may need to be turned over after half of the cooking time.

After microwaving, the fish should be slightly underdone in the center. Let stand 5 to 10 minutes to complete the cooking.

Test the fish for doneness after the standing time is completed. Make sure the fish flakes in the center as well as along the edges.

**If you use plastic wrap to cover fish when microwaving, remember to turn back one corner. This lets steam escape.**

### Microwave Hints

- Frozen uncooked fish microwaves best if thawed first.
- You can reheat cooked fish if it has a sauce. Otherwise, it will probably become tough.
- Look for convenience products, such as frozen breaded fish sticks, developed just for microwave cooking. Follow package directions.

**After the standing time, make sure the fish is completely cooked in the center.**

## Cooking Shellfish

Like fish, shellfish are tender and easily overcooked. Cooking times and tests for doneness vary. They depend on the kind of shellfish and the cooking method.

**Shellfish recipes range from simple but tasty dishes to elegant creations like these.**

Lobsters and crabs may be baked, broiled, or simmered. When they are simmered, they are usually put into the water whole and alive.

Clams and oysters may be baked, sautéed, or steamed. Scallops may be broiled, sautéed, or steamed. Shellfish are frequently used in stews and chowders.

To microwave shellfish, follow directions in the owner's manual or recipe book. Different kinds of shellfish require different methods.

## Chapter 30 Review

### Check the Facts

1. Name at least four nutrients contributed by fish and shellfish.
2. What is the difference between a drawn fish and a dressed fish? Between steaks and fillets?
3. Describe at least three ways to tell whether fish is fresh.
4. Give three guidelines for storing fish.
5. What is surimi?
6. How should cooked shellfish be stored?
7. Name two ways to thaw frozen fish.
8. What are two ways to tell whether fish is done cooking?
9. Describe the "10-minute rule" for cooking fish.

### Ideas in Action

1. Discuss surimi. Why do you think this form of imitation shellfish was developed? What are its advantages and disadvantages compared to fresh shellfish?
2. Using cookbooks or other resources, find three recipes that each use a different form of fish or shellfish. Write a meal menu for each recipe.
3. Work in groups to develop a slogan promoting the use of fish and shellfish. Create a plan for a national advertising campaign using your slogan.

# Recipe Focus

1. Read the recipe below. How would you decide what type of fish and which dried herb to use?
2. If you cooked the fish without thawing, what else would you have to change in the recipe?

## Lemon-Herb Fish

| Customary | Ingredients | Metric |
|---|---|---|
| 1 lb. | Fish fillets (sole, cod, perch, or white fish), thawed if frozen | 500 g |
| 1 Tbsp. | Melted butter or margarine | 15 mL |
| ¼ cup | Lemon juice | 50 mL |
| 1 tsp. | Dried herb (such as basil, dill, oregano, tarragon, thyme, or parsley) | 5 mL |

**Yield:** 4 servings

### Conventional Directions

**Pan:** Medium baking dish with cover
**Temperature:** 400°F (200°C)

1. **Preheat** oven to 400°F (200°C).
2. **Wash** fish in cold water and pat dry with paper towel.
3. **Cut** fish fillets into four equal portions.
4. **Place** fish fillets in a single layer in bottom of baking dish.
5. **Combine** melted butter or margarine, lemon juice, and your choice of dried herb. Stir to mix.
6. **Pour** herb mixture over fish fillets.
7. **Cover** the baking dish. Bake 10 to 13 minutes or until fish flakes easily with a fork.

**Note:** Cooking time varies with thickness of the fish fillets.

### Microwave Directions

**Pan:** Medium microwave-safe baking dish with cover
**Power Level:** 100%
**Follow** steps 2-6 of conventional directions. Then proceed as follows:

7. **Cover** baking dish. Microwave at 100% power for 4 to 6 minutes, rotating baking dish after 2 minutes.
8. **Let stand**, covered, for 2 to 3 minutes.
9. **Test** fish for doneness. It should flake easily when tested with a fork in the thickest part. Microwave for an additional minute or two if needed.

**Nutrition Information**
**Per serving (approximate):** 133 calories, 22 g protein, 2 g carbohydrate, 4 g fat, 62 mg cholesterol, 122 mg sodium
**Good source of:** B vitamins, vitamin C, phosphorus

CHAPTER 31

# Meat

OBJECTIVES

Discover. . .
- how meat fits into a healthful eating plan.
- how to select and store meat.
- how to prepare meat.

Meat is a favorite food, and a nutritious one. It is also one of the most expensive foods you can buy. By learning how to select and cook meat well, you can get the most for your money.

The term "meat" has several different meanings. For example, it is common to refer to the "white meat" of chicken. In this chapter, however, "meat" refers to beef, veal, pork, and lamb.

## Nutrition Notes

Meat is part of the Meat, Poultry, Fish, Dry Beans and Peas, Eggs, and Nuts Group. It is an excellent source of:

- Protein for growth and repair of the body.
- Iron for healthy red blood cells.
- B vitamins for a healthy nervous system.

Some meats are also high in total fat, saturated fat, and cholesterol. However, meat can be part of a low-fat eating plan. Just remember these four basic rules:

**Eat meat in moderation.** Remember that a serving is just 2 to 3 oz. (55 to 85 g) of cooked meat. Eat a variety of protein foods, including dry beans and peas.

**Choose lean meat.** Meat varies in its fat content.

**Trim fat before cooking.** You may be able to remove almost half the fat this way.

**Use low-fat cooking methods.** Avoid adding extra fat to meat. Whenever possible, drain off fat during cooking.

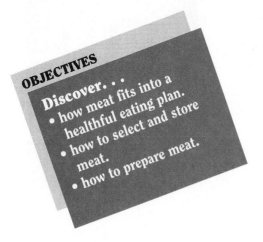

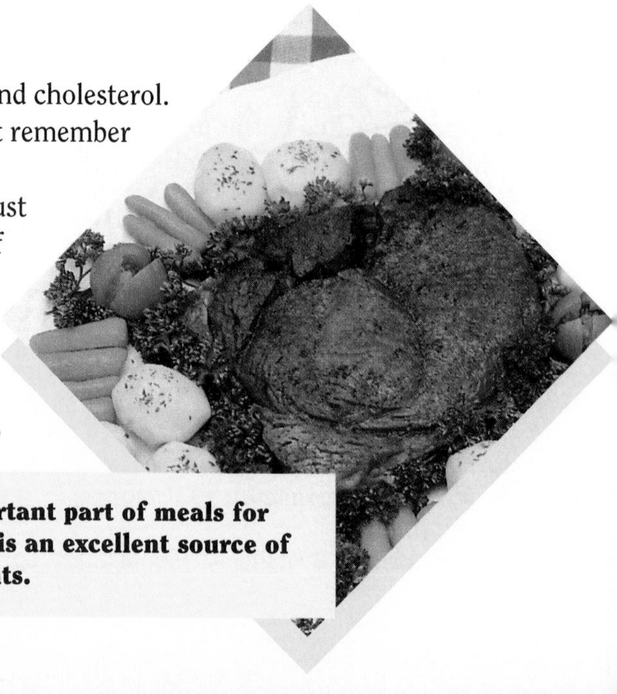

**Meat is an important part of meals for many people. It is an excellent source of valuable nutrients.**

# Consumer Power

Most supermarkets carry these four kinds of meat. Each comes from a different animal.

**Beef** comes from mature cattle over one year old. It has a rich, hearty flavor.

**Veal** comes from young cattle about three months old. The meat has a mild flavor.

**Lamb** comes from young sheep. It has a delicate but distinctive flavor.

**Pork** is meat from pigs or hogs. It has a mild flavor.

At the store, you can buy fresh or frozen meat. In addition, many convenience forms of meat are available. They are described on page 220.

When deciding which to buy, consider cost, nutrition, and how the meat will be used. Your choice will depend on the situation.

## Composition of Meat

Meat is made up of four basic parts:

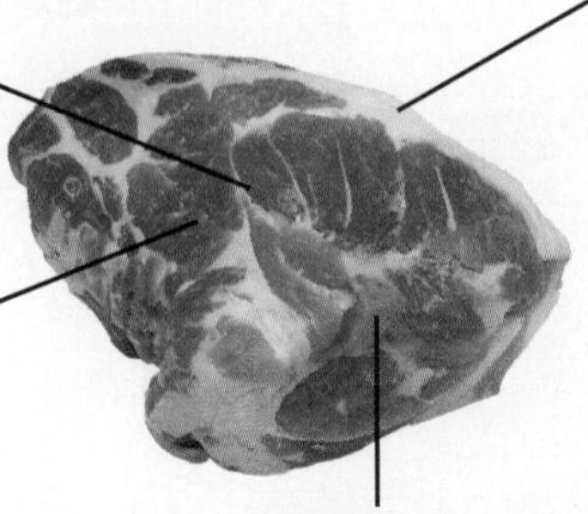

***Connective tissue***
This is tough tissue that surrounds the sections of muscle.

***Fat***
Layers of fat are found between the muscles. In addition, flecks of fat, known as marbling, are found throughout the muscle. Marbling helps make meat flavorful and juicy.

***Muscle***
This is the lean, red or pinkish part of meat.

***Bone***
Many pieces of meat include one or more bones.

## Cuts of Meat

Meat comes in different cuts. A *cut* of meat is a slice or portion from a specific part of the animal.

Meat animals are first divided into large sections called *wholesale cuts*. The drawing below shows the basic wholesale cuts of beef. Pork and lamb have somewhat different wholesale cuts.

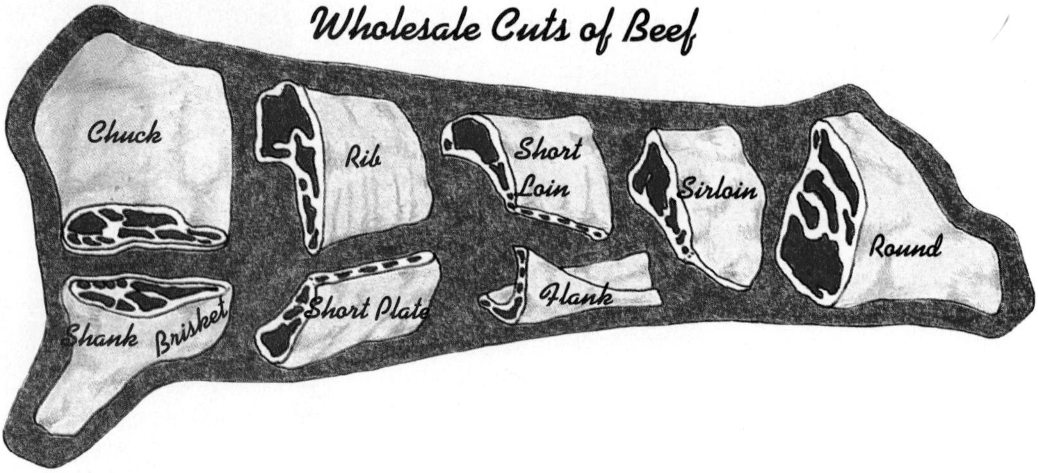


At the supermarket or butcher shop, the wholesale cuts are divided into smaller pieces called *retail cuts*. These are what you buy. For example, round steak and bottom round roast are retail cuts of beef. What wholesale cut do you think they come from?

Cuts of meat differ in tenderness, which affects your choice of cooking method. Cuts also vary in leanness and price. That's why it's important to be able to identify cuts.

You can usually identify cuts of meat by checking the label. It may look like the one shown below. Look for:

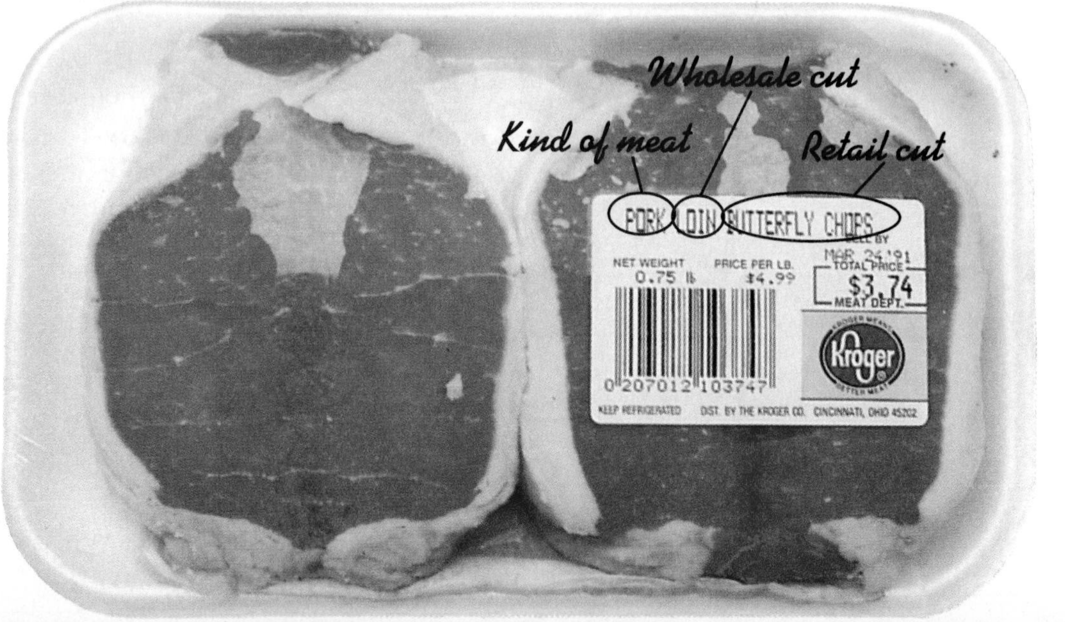

## Buying Fresh Meat

**Meat labeled "Select" has less fat and marbling.**

When buying beef, veal, or lamb, look for a grade stamp or label. Grading is based partly on the amount of fat in the meat. The three top grades are:

**Prime.** Top grade. Has the most marbling and is the most expensive.

**Choice.** High quality. Lower in price and has less marbling than Prime.

**Select.** Just as nutritious as the two top grades, but has less fat and is less expensive.

Check for a "sell by" date on the label. Fresh meat should have good color and aroma. If a package has an odor, don't buy it.

### Getting the Most for Your Money

Smart shopping can help you save money when you buy meat. Compare the cost per serving of different cuts of meat you might buy. Remember the formula:

cost per serving = cost per pound ÷ servings per pound

Look for the cost per pound on the meat label. The number of servings you can get from a pound of meat depends on the amount of bone and fat in the cut.

| 1 lb. (500 g) of . . . | will give you . . . |
|---|---|
| Lean, boneless meat  | 3 to 4 servings |
| Cuts with a moderate amount of bone and/or fat 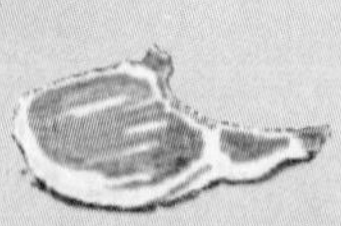 | 2 to 3 servings |
| Cuts with a large amount of bone and/or fat  | 1 to 2 servings |

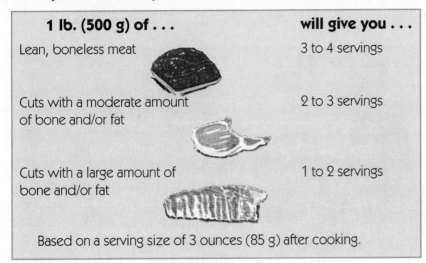

Based on a serving size of 3 ounces (85 g) after cooking.

Here are other tips for saving money:

- Choose meat graded Select.
- Combine a small amount of meat with other ingredients for low-cost main dishes, such as stew.
- Less-tender cuts of meat usually cost less. They can be a good buy if you know how to prepare them. (See page 222.)

## Selecting Lean Meat

By choosing lean meat you can reduce the fat in your diet. Remember that meat graded "Select" or labeled "Lean" is lower in fat than other grades.

Compare the amount of visible fat in different cuts. As a general rule, the following parts of each animal have the least amount of fat:

| | |
|---|---|
| Beef—Round or sirloin | Lamb—Leg |
| Pork—Tenderloin | Veal—All cuts except breast |

**You can sometimes judge whether meat is lean just by looking.**

# Storing Fresh Meat

Store fresh meat in the coldest part of the refrigerator, such as under the freezer compartment or in a meat-keeper drawer. Keep meat in its original package. Put it on a plate or in a plastic bag to catch drippings.

Refrigerated fresh meat should be used within a few days (one to two days for ground meat). For longer storage, wrap the meat properly and freeze it.

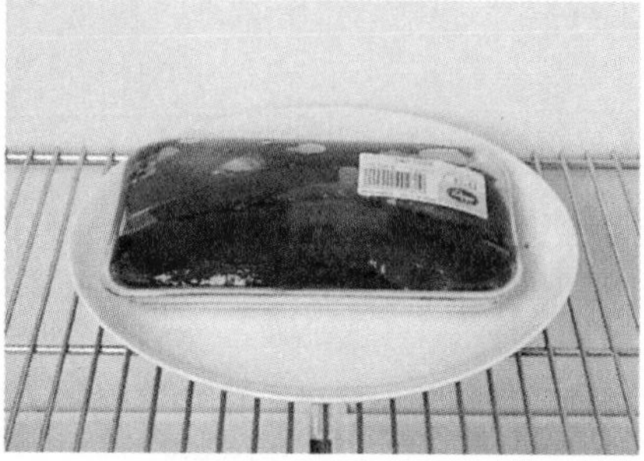

**Why is it important to keep raw meat juices from dripping on other foods?**

# Convenience Meats

**Bacon, sausage, ham, and cold cuts are examples of cured meats. Why is it important to read labels before buying?**

Many convenience meat products can be found on store shelves and in the refrigerated and frozen food sections. They range from canned meats to main dishes, dinners, and microwavable foods.

Cured meats include ham, cold cuts, bacon, corned beef, and sausages. Most cured meat is in the refrigerated section. Some is canned.

When buying convenience meats, read labels carefully. Follow package directions for storage and use. Some types are ready to eat. Others require reheating or cooking. Some frozen meats must be thawed first.

# Food Skills

Meat can be part of the menu at any meal. Sometimes it is a main dish in itself. You can also combine meat with other foods to make soups, stews, stir-fried dishes, casseroles, or sandwiches. A small amount of meat can add flavor and nutrients to a salad or vegetable dish.

## Principles of Cooking Meat

What does cooking do to meat? It makes it tender and brings out the natural flavor. It browns the meat, giving it a pleasant color and aroma. Most important, cooking kills harmful bacteria that might cause food poisoning.

How can you tell whether meat has cooked long enough? When roasting large pieces of meat, use a meat thermometer to check the internal temperature as shown on page 223. Meat that has reached an internal temperature of at least 160°F (75°C) is safe to eat.

For other cooking methods, the appearance of the meat is your clue. Close to the end of the cooking time, cut a small slit in the thickest part of the meat.

- If the meat and its juices are pink or red, cook the meat longer. Some food poisoning bacteria may still be alive.
- If the juices are clear or brown, the meat is done.

How long does it take for meat to cook until done? That depends on the size and shape of the piece and the cooking temperature. Most recipe books have timetables for cooking meat.

Like other protein foods, meat is sensitive to heat. If overcooked, it becomes dry and tough. For flavorful, tender meat, cook at low or moderate temperatures just until done.

**The meat on the left is still pink inside. It needs to be cooked longer until it looks like the meat on the right. Then you can be sure it is safe to eat.**

## Methods of Cooking Meat

There are many cooking methods for meat. Which you choose depends in part on the meat's tenderness.

**Tender cuts** include beef rib, loin, and sirloin; all cuts of pork; and ground meat. Tender cuts can be cooked by dry heat methods, such as roasting and broiling.

**Less-tender cuts**, such as beef chuck, stew meat, and brisket, are tougher because they have more connective tissue. There are several methods you can use to tenderize them:

- Cook them slowly using moist heat methods, such as stewing or braising.
- Pound or make cuts partway through the meat. You may be able to buy meat that has already been tenderized this way, such as cube steak.
- Soak the meat in a marinade before cooking. A *marinade* is a mixture of an acid food, such as citrus juice or vinegar, and seasonings. It adds both flavor and tenderness.
- Buy powdered meat tenderizer. Follow the directions on the package.

No matter what cooking method you choose, you can lower the fat content in meat by trimming it before you start cooking. Using a sharp knife and cutting board, cut away all the visible layers of fat around the outside of the meat. Check for fat separating large sections of muscle. If you find any, cut the meat sections apart and trim away the fat.

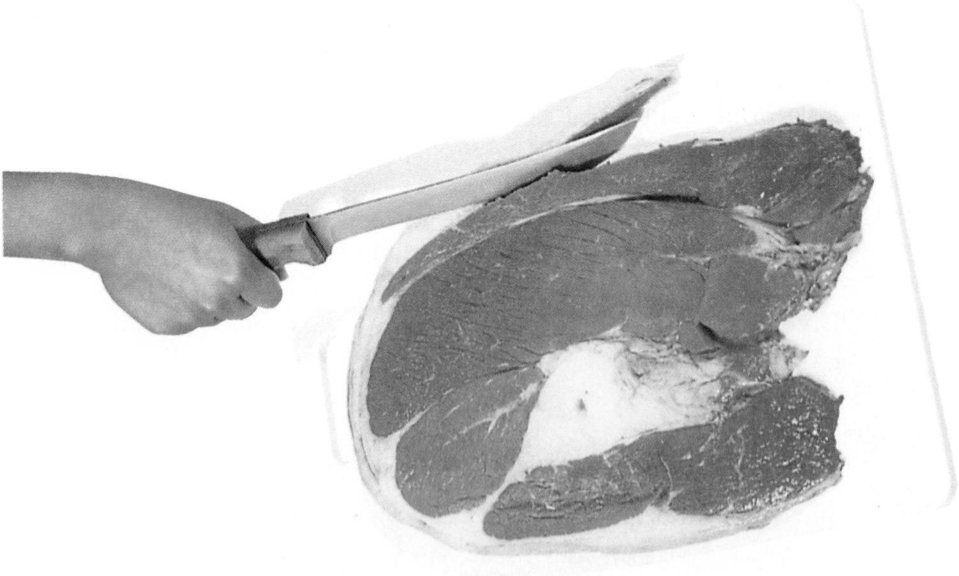

**Trimming away visible fat helps lower the fat content in the meat you eat.**

## Roasting Meat

Only large, tender cuts of meat are roasted, such as rib, loin, and some leg roasts. Leave a thin layer of fat on the meat to keep it from drying out.

1. Place the roast, fat side up, on a rack in a large roasting pan.
   ▲ The rack allows the fat to drain away as it melts.

2. Insert a meat thermometer in the thickest part of the meat away from bone and fat.
   ▲ Bone and fat get hot more quickly and may give you an inaccurate temperature reading.

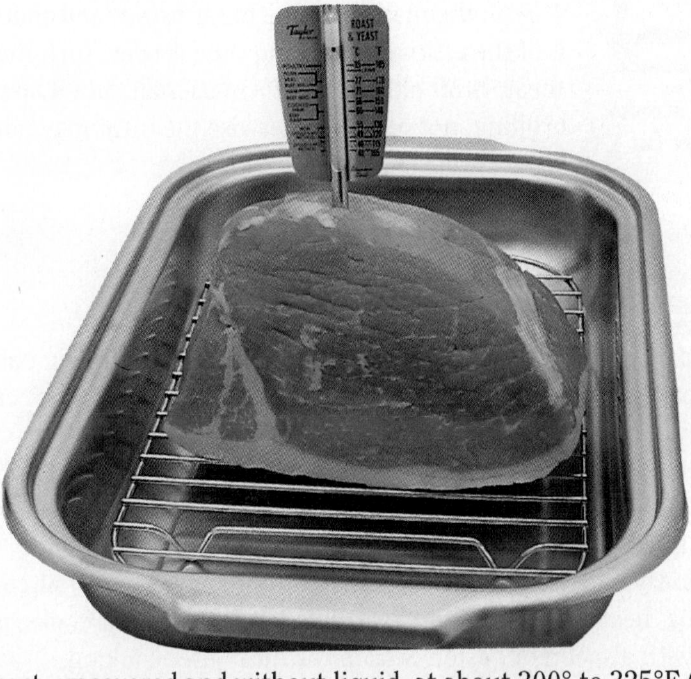


3. Roast, uncovered and without liquid, at about 300° to 325°F (150° to 160°C).
   ▲ For medium doneness, roast until the internal temperature of the meat reaches 160°F (75°C). If you prefer meat that is "well done," cook to an internal temperature of 170°F (80°C).

4. When the roast is done, remove it from the pan. Allow it to stand for 15 to 20 minutes.
   ▲ The roast will carve more easily after standing. Serve immediately after carving.

The juices that drip from meat as it roasts are flavorful and contain nutrients. If you would like to use the drippings, first remove the fat. An easy way is to refrigerate the drippings. The fat floats on the surface and becomes solid. Lift it off and discard it.

## Broiling Meat

Broiling is used for tender cuts of meat such as ground beef, beef steaks, lamb chops, and ham slices. The meat should be at least ¾ inch (2 cm) thick. Thinner pieces may dry out before they are done.

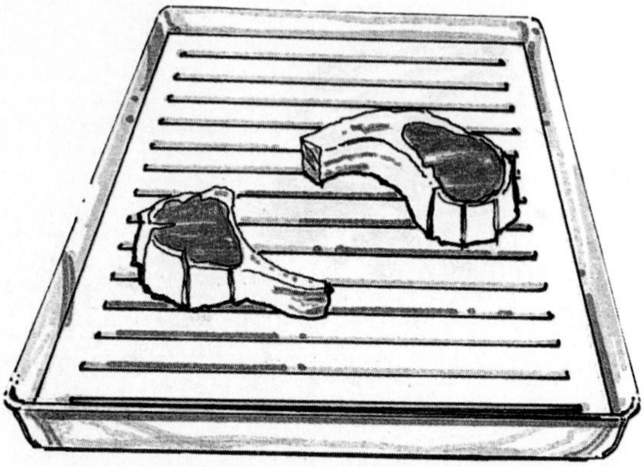

**Broiling is a popular way to cook steaks or lamb chops. Make slashes in the fat to prevent curling.**

Cooking time depends on the distance of the meat from the heat, the meat's thickness, and the doneness you want. Check a cookbook for the approximate cooking time.

Before broiling, make slashes through any remaining fat around the edges of the meat. This helps keep the meat from curling up as the fat melts and shrinks.

Broil the meat until the top is brown and about half the estimated cooking time is over. Turn the meat. Broil until done. If you use salt, add it after broiling, not before. Otherwise the meat may not brown properly.

## Panbroiling Meat

Thin pieces of tender meat can be panbroiled. These include hamburgers, cubed steaks, pork chops, bacon, and liver. The meat should be less than 1 inch (2.5 cm) thick.

Usually, you do not need to add fat. Most meat has enough fat of its own to prevent sticking. If the meat is very lean, you may need to use a nonstick pan, a light coating of cooking spray, or a very small amount of oil.

Brown the meat slowly in a heavy skillet over medium or low heat. Do not cover or add water. Turn the meat occasionally for even cooking. As the meat cooks, pour off fat or skim it off with a spoon or baster. Season the meat after cooking.

**Use a baster or large spoon to remove fat as it accumulates.**

## Braising Meat

Braising is a good choice for less-tender cuts of meat. First the meat is browned to seal in juices and give a flavorful crust. After browning, liquid is added. The rest of the cooking can be done on the rangetop or in the oven. You can also use a slow cooker for braising. Follow the directions in the owner's manual.

If you like, cook vegetables along with the meat. For example, carrots and potatoes can be cut in half and added about an hour before the meat will be done.

1. Brown the meat well in a large, heavy pan or pot using a small amount of oil.

2. Remove the meat to a clean plate. Drain the fat from the pan.
   ▲ Leave the browned, crusty bits of meat in the pan. They will add flavor and color to the cooking liquid.

3. Return the meat to the pan. Add a small amount of liquid, such as water, broth, or vegetable juice.

4. Cover the pan. Cook over low heat on the rangetop or in the oven at about 325°F (165°C).

5. During cooking, turn the meat several times. Skim the fat off the top of the cooking liquid. Add more liquid, if needed.

6. Cook until a fork inserted into the thickest part of the meat comes out easily. If desired, thicken the cooking liquid with flour to make gravy.

### Microwave Hints

- Cover meat loosely with waxed paper to keep it from spattering.
- You can buy a special microwave meat thermometer for use in the microwave. If you don't have one, test the internal temperature with a standard meat thermometer *after* you remove the meat from the microwave.

## Microwaving Meat

Meat will microwave more evenly if it is tender, boneless, and uniform in shape and size. Follow recipe directions for turning and rotating the meat during cooking.

If pork is not cooked thoroughly, it can cause an illness called trichinosis (TRIK-uh-NO-sus). To help pork cook more evenly in the microwave oven, use a plastic oven cooking bag. Follow the directions in the owner's manual or a microwave cookbook.

**A plastic oven cooking bag holds moist heat in so pork cooks all the way through.**

## Chapter 31 Review

### Check the Facts

1. Identify three nutrients found in meat.
2. List four ways meat can be a part of a low-fat eating plan.
3. What is the difference between wholesale and retail cuts of meat?
4. List three characteristics to look for when buying fresh meat.
5. How should fresh meat be stored?
6. Name two ways to tell when meat is done.
7. Give an example of a tender cut and a less-tender cut of meat. Suggest a cooking method for each.
8. Name four methods you can use to tenderize meat.
9. Give at least three guidelines for panbroiling meat.

### Ideas in Action

1. Rico has been asked to pick up some meat on his way home from school. His father is on a low-fat diet. What advice would you give Rico about selecting lean meat?
2. If ground beef is on sale for $1.29 per pound, what is the cost per serving? (Figure on four servings per pound.) How much ground beef would you need to buy in order to make one hamburger each for yourself and five friends?
3. Lynette would like to prepare a special meal for her family. One of their favorites is braised beef chuck roast. She asks you how to prepare it. What would you tell her?

# Recipe Focus

1. Read the recipe below. What are some ways you could save time when preparing the pizza burgers?
2. Describe another way the pizza burgers could be cooked if a broiler or microwave oven were not available.

## Pizza Burgers

| Customary | Ingredients | Metric |
|---|---|---|
| 1 lb. | Ground beef | 500 g |
| ¼ cup | Tomato sauce | 50 mL |
| ¼ cup | Dry bread crumbs | 50 mL |
| 1 | Medium onion, finely chopped | 1 |
| ¼ tsp. | Dried, crushed oregano | 1 mL |
| ¼ tsp. | Pepper | 1 mL |
| ¼ tsp. | Garlic salt | 1 mL |
| 4 slices | Low-fat mozzarella cheese | 4 slices |
| ¼ cup | Grated Parmesan cheese | 50 mL |

**Yield**: 4 servings

### Conventional Directions

**Pan:** Broiler pan
**Temperature**: Broiler setting

1. **Mix** together the ground beef, tomato sauce, dry bread crumbs, chopped onion, oregano, pepper, and garlic salt.
2. **Form** meat into four patties.
3. **Place** meat patties on cold broiler pan. Position the pan so the top of the meat is 3 inches (8 cm) from the heat.
4. **Broil** until desired degree of doneness, turning the patties once. (Burgers broiled to medium doneness will take 10 to 15 minutes depending on thickness.)
5. **Top** each pizza burger with a slice of mozzarella cheese and 1 Tbsp. (about 15 mL) Parmesan cheese.
6. **Return** to broiler only long enough to melt the cheese.

### Microwave Directions

**Pan**: Microwave-safe baking dish with rack
**Power Level**: 100%
**Follow** steps 1-2 of conventional directions. Then proceed as follows:

3. **Place** patties on rack in baking dish.
4. **Make** a thumbprint in center of each burger to aid in even cooking.
5. **Cover** with waxed paper.
6. **Microwave** at 100% power for 2 minutes.
7. **Turn** burgers over.
8. **Continue** microwaving 2 to 3 minutes, depending on degree of doneness preferred.
9. **Top** each burger with a slice of mozzarella cheese and 1 Tbsp. (about 15 mL) Parmesan cheese.
10. **Microwave** at 100% power for 45 to 60 seconds or until cheese melts.

#### Nutrition Information

**Per serving (approximate): 367 calories, 32 g protein, 9 g carbohydrate, 22 g fat, 91 mg cholesterol, 584 mg sodium**
**Good source of: B vitamins, calcium, iron, phosphorus, zinc**

CHAPTER 32

# Eggs

**OBJECTIVES**

**Discover. . .**
- how eggs fit into a healthful eating plan.
- how to select and store eggs.
- how to prepare eggs.

What do meat loaf, egg drop soup, custard, and muffins have in common? All include eggs as an ingredient. Eggs are a bargain—they pack a lot of nutrients into a small package at low cost. With so many ways they can be used, eggs are one of the most versatile foods you can buy.

## Nutrition Notes

Eggs are part of the Meat, Poultry, Fish, Dry Beans and Peas, Eggs, and Nuts Group. They are an excellent source of protein, B vitamins, vitamins A and D, phosphorus, and iron. Review the discussion of these nutrients in Chapter 5.

The egg yolk contains high amounts of fat and cholesterol. For this reason, health experts recommend that people eat no more than four eggs per week. To reduce cholesterol, some people use egg substitutes.

## Consumer Power

Eggs are most commonly sold in cartons of a dozen. They are available in different sizes, such as medium, large, and extra large. The size of the egg has no effect on quality. Most recipes are tested using large eggs.

Eggs are inspected for safety and graded for quality. Grade AA and Grade A are both high quality.

**Did you know that brown eggs have the same nutrients as white ones?**

## Buying and Storing Eggs

When buying eggs, compare unit prices for the different grades and sizes. Buy only refrigerated eggs. Open the egg carton and make sure the eggs are clean. Don't buy broken or cracked eggs.

Eggs lose quality quickly at room temperature. After buying, refrigerate them in their original carton. Don't wash eggs before storing them. Use within 5 weeks.

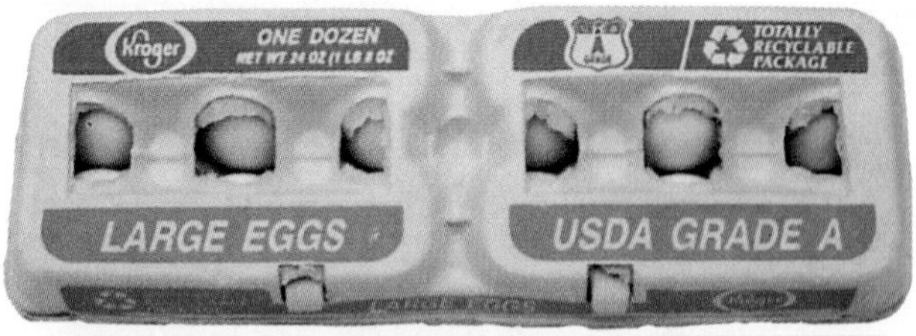


**Look for the grade shield on the egg carton. What else should you look for?**

Egg substitutes come in liquid, frozen, and dried forms. Read the labels for ingredients and storage directions.

**Some egg substitutes are a combination of egg whites and vegetable oil.**

## Food Skills

Eggs are versatile. They can be cooked alone in a variety of ways and served at any meal. For example, hard-cooked eggs often show up in salads or sandwiches and can be eaten as a snack. Egg dishes such as omelets or quiches are popular. Eggs are also an ingredient in many recipes.

Raw eggs may contain salmonella bacteria, which can cause food poisoning. Proper cooking destroys any harmful bacteria. Don't prepare or eat any food that contains raw eggs, such as some ice creams and salad dressings.

**A quiche is a main-dish pie made with eggs.**

## Using Eggs in Recipes

In recipes, eggs are used to:

- Bind ingredients together, as in meat loaf.
- Thicken, as in custard or pumpkin pie.
- Add lightness. Egg whites are beaten to trap air bubbles.

**A soufflé (soo-FLAY) is light and fluffy because of beaten egg whites.**

## Breaking Eggs

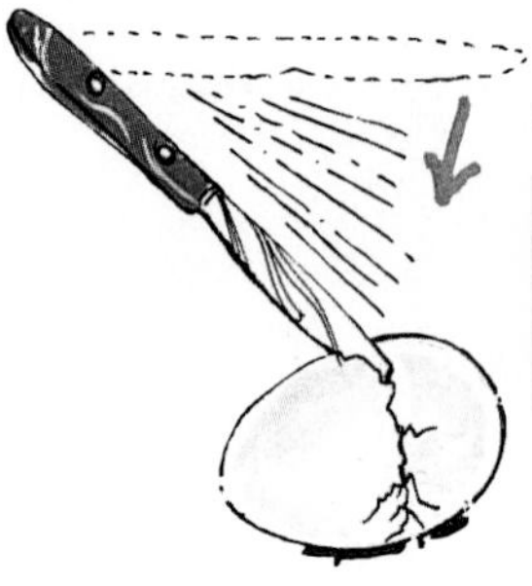

Breaking eggs is a basic cooking skill. With a little practice you will find it easy to do.

1. Tap the egg firmly but gently in the center with the edge of a knife so it cracks.

2. Hold the egg in both hands over a cup, small bowl, or dish.

3. Place your thumbs on the cracked area. Gently pull each end apart. Let the egg fall into the dish.

Never break an egg directly into other ingredients. Break it into a cup or bowl instead. If the egg looks or smells unusual, throw it away. If a piece of egg shell falls into the egg, use a clean spoon to scoop it out.

## Separating Eggs

Some recipes call for only the yolk or the white of the egg. You will have to separate the white from the yolk. Eggs separate more easily when they are cold. You will need two small bowls and one large bowl.

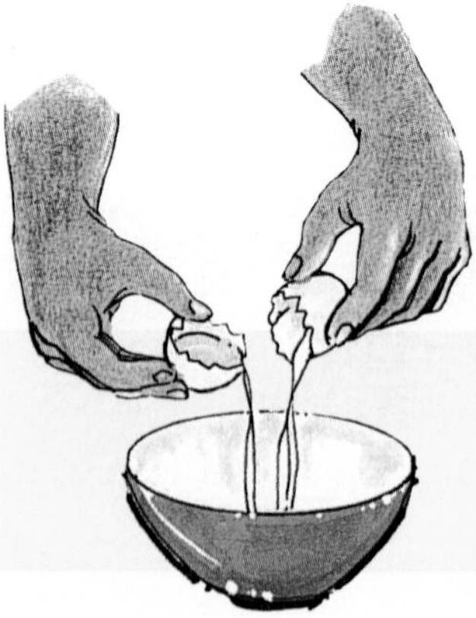

1. Crack the egg in the center.

2. Hold the cracked egg over a small bowl with one end pointed up. Remove the upper half of the shell. The yolk will remain in the bottom half. The white will pour out.

3. Gently move the yolk to the other shell half to allow the white in the bottom half to pour out. Do this several times. Be careful not to break the yolk.

4. Drop the yolk into the other small bowl. If you need to separate more eggs, first pour the white you just separated into the large bowl. That way you will be sure not to get any yolk in it.

## Beating Egg Whites

Many recipes depend on beaten egg whites for their light texture. You can beat egg whites to any consistency called for in a recipe, such as foamy, soft peaks, or stiff peaks.

First separate the egg whites from the yolks. If any yolk falls into the white, save that egg white for another use. The yolk contains fat, which would keep the whites from beating properly.

To beat the egg whites, use a mixer or rotary beater at high speed. This traps air bubbles in the egg whites. Egg whites at room temperature give the best volume.

**Foamy whites.** Air begins to mix into the whites. Bubbles and foam form. The whites are still transparent.

**Soft peaks.** The mixture is white, shiny, and thick. The whites stand up in peaks that bend over.

**Stiff peaks.** The peaks now stand straight up.

Don't beat egg whites past the stiff peak stage. Overbeaten whites are dry and break into pieces. They cannot be used.

Handle beaten egg whites gently so the air bubbles don't break. The whites are usually folded into other ingredients. Review the technique for folding in as shown in Chapter 11.

Some dessert recipes call for *meringue* (mur-ANG). This is made by beating egg whites and sugar until stiff peaks form.

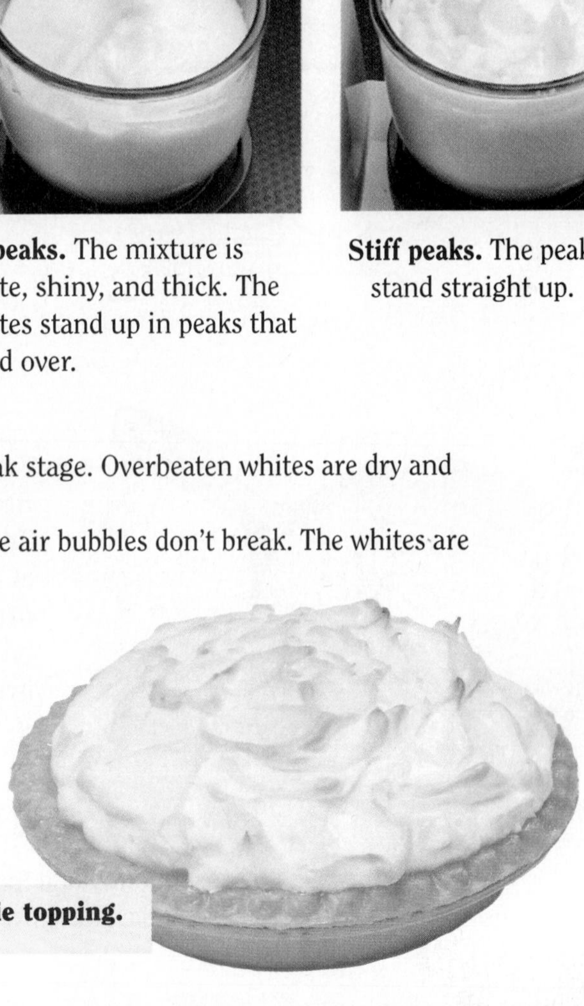

**Meringue is often used as a pie topping.**

## Cooking Eggs

Like other protein foods, eggs are sensitive to heat. Cook them at low or medium temperatures only until done. The yolk should be firm to hard, depending on your taste. If undercooked, the yolk is runny. Harmful bacteria may still be present. If overcooked, eggs turn tough and rubbery.

There are many ways to cook eggs. For example:

- Poached eggs are cooked in simmering water or in a special poaching pan. The shell is removed before the eggs are cooked. Poached eggs are usually served on toast.

- Eggs can be cooked in the shell in hot water. Place the eggs in a saucepan and cover with cold water. Bring the water to a boil, turn off the heat, and cover the pan. The hot water provides enough heat to cook eggs. Experiment with different standing times to find out how long it takes the yolk to become firm.

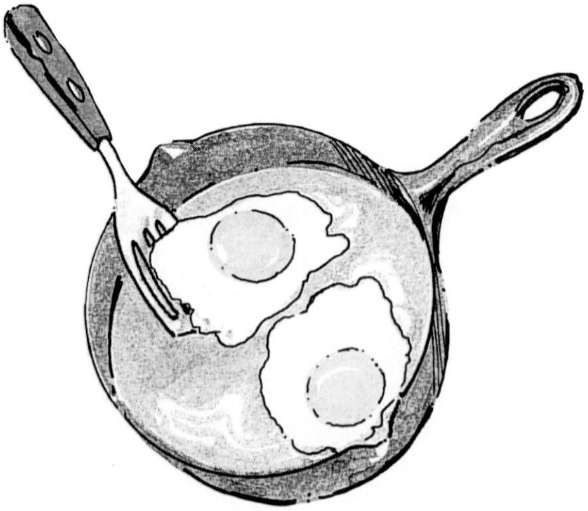

- Frying is a quick way to prepare eggs. Break the eggs into a hot, greased skillet. Try to keep the yolks whole. Cook the eggs at a low temperature until the yolks are firm. To finish cooking the yolks, put a lid on the skillet or carefully turn the eggs over with a turner.

Other methods include scrambling and making omelets. In addition, some egg dishes can be prepared in the microwave oven.

## Scrambling Eggs and Preparing Omelets

Scrambled eggs and simple *omelets* (AHM-lets) are very similar. They are made from the same basic ingredients—eggs plus milk or water. Both make a filling main dish for any meal.

The main difference is in the way they are cooked. Scrambled eggs are gently stirred as they cook to make them light and fluffy. Omelets are cooked without stirring, like a large egg pancake. After cooking, an omelet is usually folded in half with a filling in the middle. Compare the directions for scrambling eggs (which follow) with those on page 235 for preparing an omelet.

There are dozens of ways to vary scrambled eggs and omelets by adding extra ingredients. Try adding herbs to scrambled eggs before cooking. Chopped, cooked vegetables can be added to omelets or scrambled eggs.

**To scramble eggs. . .**

1. Heat 1 Tbsp. (15 mL) butter or margarine in a skillet.
   ▲ The fat should be just hot enough so a drop of water sizzles.

2. For one serving, mix two eggs in a bowl with 2 Tbsp. (30 mL) skim milk or water and a dash of pepper.

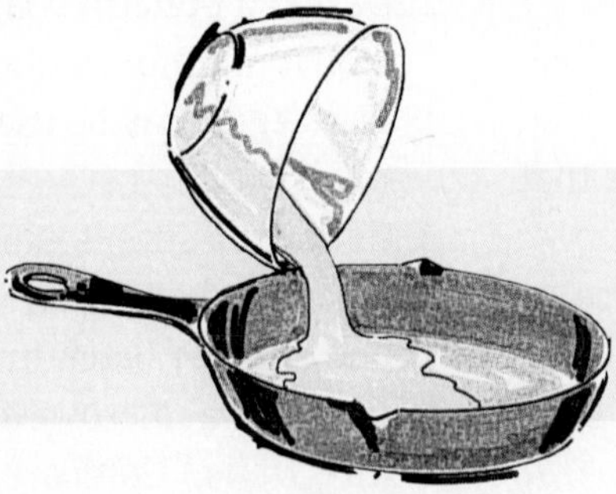

3. Pour the egg mixture into a hot skillet. Do not stir.

4. As the eggs begin to set, gently draw a turner or spoon completely across the bottom of the skillet.
   ▲ Large, soft curds will begin to form. The uncooked portion will flow to the bottom.

5. Repeat as needed until eggs are firm. Avoid constant stirring—the mixture will get mushy.

### Microwave Hints

- In the microwave, egg yolks cook faster than whites. Microwave just until the yolk is cooked. During the standing time, the white will finish cooking.
- Avoid overcooking—it causes rubbery eggs.

## Microwaving Eggs

Before cooking eggs in the microwave oven, check a microwave cookbook. The microwave works well for some methods of cooking eggs, such as scrambling. Other methods do not work as well. Some can even be dangerous.

Heat and steam pressure can build up inside whole eggs and yolks. They may explode while they are cooking or after you take them out of the microwave. Never use the microwave to cook eggs in the shell or reheat whole cooked eggs. When microwaving whole egg yolks, pierce the yolks with a toothpick to let steam escape.

## Chapter 32 Review

### Check the Facts

1. Name four nutrients found in eggs.
2. Why do health experts recommend limiting the number of eggs eaten per week?
3. Identify three quality characteristics to look for when buying eggs.
4. Why shouldn't you prepare or eat foods that contain raw eggs?
5. How are eggs used in recipes? Give three examples.
6. At what temperature should eggs be cooked? Why?
7. Name two tips to remember when microwaving eggs.

### Ideas in Action

1. Discuss the advantages and disadvantages of using eggs for family meals.
2. Design a bulletin board about eggs. Include nutrition information as well as different ways eggs may be used in meals and in other foods.
3. Conduct a simple experiment. Prepare scrambled eggs in a skillet on the range and another batch in the microwave. (Consult a microwave cookbook for directions.) Compare the eggs for cooking time, appearance, texture, and flavor. What conclusions can you draw?

# Recipe Focus

1. Read the recipe for "Vegetable Blend Omelet." What changes could you make to reduce the calories from fat in this recipe?
2. Estimate the cooking time for the conventional method and the microwave method. Which method would you choose and why?

# Vegetable Blend Omelet

| Customary | Ingredients | Metric |
|---|---|---|
| 1 Tbsp. | Butter or margarine | 15 mL |
| 1 cup | Frozen mixed vegetables | 250 mL |
| 1 clove | Garlic, minced | 1 clove |
| 4 | Eggs | 4 |
| 2 Tbsp. | Water | 30 mL |
| 2 Tbsp. | Butter or margarine | 30 mL |
| 1 Tbsp. | Grated Parmesan cheese | 15 mL |

**Yield:** 4 servings

### Conventional Directions

**Pan:** 10-inch (25-cm) skillet with cover

1. **Melt** 1 Tbsp. (15 mL) butter or margarine.
2. **Add** vegetables and garlic. Cook over high heat 1 to 2 minutes, stirring constantly.
3. **Reduce** heat and cover skillet. Continue cooking 2 to 3 minutes.
4. **Remove** vegetables to a bowl. Set aside.
5. **Beat** eggs and water until blended.
6. **Heat** 2 Tbsp. (30 mL) butter or margarine in skillet over medium heat until a drop of water sizzles when added to the pan.
7. **Pour** egg mixture into skillet. Cook over medium-low heat until eggs begin to set.
8. **Lift** cooked mixture with spatula, allowing uncooked portion to flow underneath.
9. **Continue** cooking until omelet is set, but still moist on the surface.
10. **Place** vegetables and cheese on omelet.
11. **Fold** omelet in half. Continue cooking 2 to 3 minutes or to desired doneness.
12. **Slide** omelet onto a warm plate. Cut into quarters and serve immediately.

### Microwave Directions

**Pan:** 10-inch (25-cm) microwave-safe pie plate

1. **Combine** 1 Tbsp. (15 mL) butter or margarine, vegetables, and garlic in pie plate.
2. **Microwave** at 100% power 4 to 6 minutes or until vegetables are tender-crisp. Stir every 2 or 3 minutes.
3. **Remove** vegetables to a bowl. Set aside.
4. **Beat** eggs and water until blended.
5. **Melt** 2 Tbsp. (30 mL) butter or margarine in pie plate at 100% power for 35 seconds.
6. **Pour** egg mixture into pie plate. Cover with waxed paper and cook at 100% power for 2 minutes.
7. **Stir** cooked outer edges of omelet to center. Rotate dish ¼ turn.
8. **Cover** again with waxed paper. Continue cooking at 100% power for 3 to 4 minutes, rotating dish after 2 minutes. Cook until center is set, but still moist.
9. **Place** vegetables and half of cheese on omelet. Loosen the edges of the omelet with spatula and fold in half to cover vegetables and cheese.
10. **Sprinkle** remaining cheese on top of omelet. Microwave 35 to 45 seconds at 100% power or until cheese is melted.
11. **Slide** omelet onto a warm plate. Cut into quarters and serve immediately.

### Nutrition Information

**Per serving (approximate): 169 calories, 8 g protein, 3 g carbohydrate, 14 g fat, 215 mg cholesterol, 205 mg sodium**
**Good source of: vitamin A, vitamin C, B vitamins, phosphorus**

CHAPTER 33

# Salads

**OBJECTIVES**

**Discover . . .**
- how salads fit into a healthful eating plan.
- how to select and store salad ingredients.
- how to prepare salads.

Salads can add flavor, variety, and nutrients to your daily food choices. Almost any type of food can be used to make an attractive, interesting, and delicious salad.

Salads can be used in many ways. A large, filling salad can serve as a main dish. A fruit salad can be a dessert. A salad can also be a snack, an appetizer, or an accompaniment to the main dish.

## Nutrition Notes

Salads can give a nutritional boost to a meal. Many salad ingredients are high in nutrients but low in fat and calories.

- Vitamins and minerals can be supplied by including greens, vegetables, sprouts, fruits, cooked grains, cheese, and eggs.
- Fiber and complex carbohydrates can be added with fruits, whole grains, cooked dry beans, and vegetables.
- Good sources of protein include cooked beans, lean meat, poultry, fish, cheese, and eggs.

Some foods, such as eggs and many cheeses, are high in fat or cholesterol. Use them sparingly. Choose salad dressings that are low in fat and sodium.

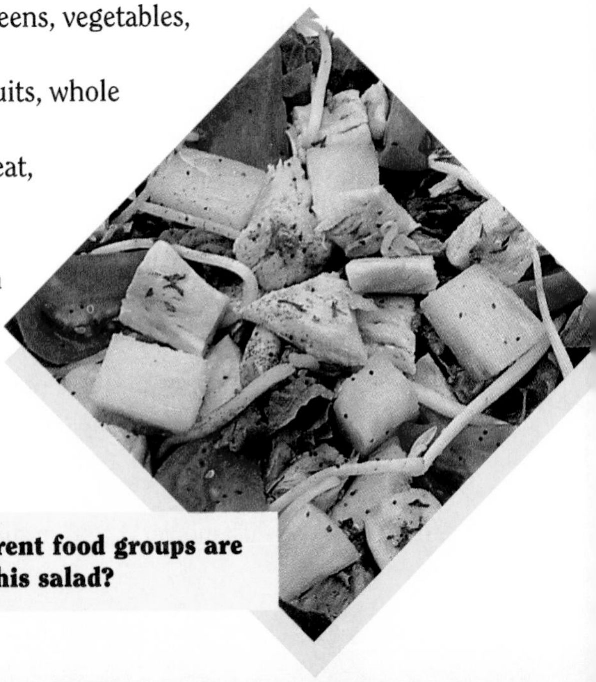

**How many different food groups are represented in this salad?**

# Consumer Power

Good salads start with good ingredients. Chapters 24–32 tell how to select and store many fresh salad ingredients such as fruits, cheese, pasta, and meat. Two foods that play a part in many salads are salad greens and dressings.

## Buying and Storing Salad Greens

You can choose from a wide variety of salad greens. Each has a different color, shape, and texture. A combination of greens can give a salad a pleasing, distinctive flavor.

When buying greens, follow the guidelines on pages 181-182 for buying fresh vegetables. After you take them home, wash the greens carefully in plain cool water. Shake out the excess. Store the greens in the refrigerator in a plastic bag or container.

Before washing and storing iceberg lettuce, remove the core.

**To core and wash lettuce . . .**

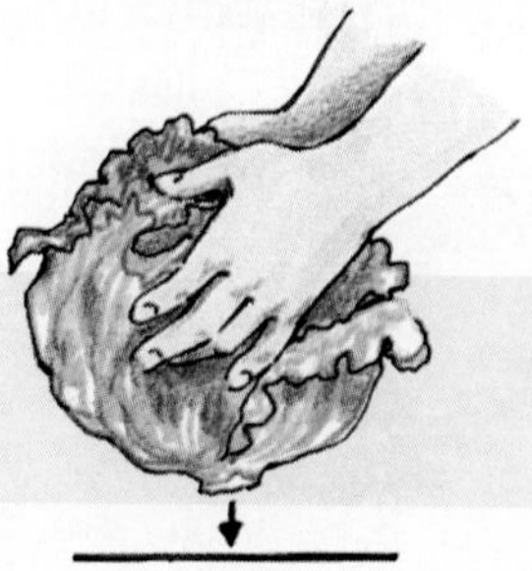

1. Hold the head with both hands, bottom side down. Hit the bottom hard against a flat surface. This will loosen the core.

2. Remove the core with your fingers.

3. Run cold water into the hole.

4. Let the lettuce drain, hole side down.

Bean sprouts

Alfalfa sprouts

You might also enjoy sprouts in a salad. Sprouts are tiny plants which have just started to grow from seeds. Not all can be eaten. The most popular edible ones are alfalfa sprouts and bean sprouts.

Look for sprouts in the produce section of the store. Refrigerate them in their original containers. Use within a few days.

## Buying and Storing Salad Dressings

A dressing adds flavor to a salad and can help hold the mixture together. Many varieties of prepared dressings are available at the store. For good nutrition, look for dressings that are low in fat, sodium, and calories.

You can also make your own dressing. Keep in mind that there are many no-fat ways to add flavor to a salad. Try mixing plain nonfat yogurt with seasonings such as mustard. On a tossed green salad, you might use lemon juice or an herb-flavored vinegar, such as tarragon vinegar.

## Food Skills

To store salad dressings, follow label instructions. Many dressings, including homemade ones, need refrigeration.

With a little imagination you can make meals more interesting with creative salads. There are many ways to put together a salad. For example, the ingredients can be:

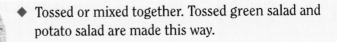

- Tossed or mixed together. Tossed green salad and potato salad are made this way.

- Arranged in an attractive pattern. You might arrange fresh fruit wedges in a fan shape on lettuce with a mound of cottage cheese.

- Molded in a decorative container. A molded salad is firm enough to hold its shape after it is removed from the mold. Molded salads are often made with gelatin.

## Making a Tossed Green Salad

A tossed green salad can be made in one large bowl or individual servings. In spite of its name, a tossed salad isn't just "thrown together." You begin by properly preparing the ingredients.

1. Wash fresh vegetables and fruits carefully. Drain thoroughly.
   ▲If water is left on the foods, it will thin the dressing.

2. Tear greens into bite-size pieces.
   ▲When greens are cut with a knife, the edges brown quickly.

3. Cut other ingredients. For example, you might grate carrots, slice cucumbers, dice green peppers, and separate sliced onions into rings. Remember to use a cutting board.

4. Toss the ingredients together gently. If the salad won't be served right away, cover and refrigerate it so it stays fresh and crisp.

5. Add the dressing just before serving, or serve it separately so people can add their own.
   ▲ Dressing can make greens wilt if added too far ahead of time.

You can vary a tossed green salad every time you make one. Think of all the different vegetables and dressings you could use. If you like, add toppings, such as sunflower seeds, raisins, or croutons (seasoned, toasted bread cubes) for extra flavor and texture.

## More Salad Ideas

- Create a mini salad bar in your refrigerator by keeping several containers of fresh, ready-to-use salad foods on hand.
- By combining gelatin with other ingredients, you can make dozens of interesting salads. You can buy gelatin in different flavors or unflavored.
- Arranging a salad gives you a chance to use your creativity. Most arranged salads have three parts: base, body, and dressing. The *base* is the foundation of the salad. Leaf lettuce makes a good base. The *body*, or main part of the salad, is arranged attractively on the base. The dressing goes on top of the salad or can be served alongside. The recipe on the opposite page is an example of an arranged salad.

**Keeping salad ingredients ready in your refrigerator allows you to make a salad easily at any time.**

## Chapter 33 Review

### Check the Facts

1. Name at least three nutrients that salads can contribute to your diet.
2. Give two examples of ingredients that would add protein to a tossed salad.
3. Identify three steps to follow when storing fresh greens.
4. List two ways of adding dressing to a salad without using a bottled dressing.
5. Describe the five-step process in making a tossed green salad.
6. Describe the three parts of an arranged salad.

### Ideas in Action

1. Make a salad poster. Look through magazines for pictures of salads and recipes. You may want to group the salads according to type (such as main dish, fruit, appetizer, accompaniment). Emphasize healthful salad choices. Use the posters to make a display.
2. Write a simple salad recipe to serve four people. Keep in mind the serving sizes recommended in the Daily Food Guide. Choose ingredients that appeal to you. What dressing would you serve with your salad?
3. With a partner, plan a short demonstration on how to prepare a simple tossed salad. Consider the ingredients and equipment you would need. What can you talk about as you demonstrate? How much time do you think the demonstration would take?

# Recipe Focus

1. Read the recipe for "Sunshine Salad." How much of each ingredient would you need to prepare six servings?
2. What could you substitute for honey in this recipe? What other fruits might be appealing?

## Sunshine Salad

| Customary | Ingredients | Metric |
|---|---|---|
| 1 cup | Plain, low-fat yogurt | 250 mL |
| 1 Tbsp. | Honey | 15 mL |
| ¼ tsp. | Dried, crushed mint | 1 mL |
| | Crisp lettuce leaves | |
| 4 | Canned pineapple slices, drained | 4 |
| 1 | Banana, sliced | 1 |
| 1 | Medium orange, peeled and sectioned | 1 |
| | Fresh mint leaves or watercress (for garnish) | |

**Yield:** 4 servings

### Directions

1. **Prepare** dressing the day before so flavors blend. Combine yogurt, honey, and mint. Refrigerate overnight.
2. **Arrange** lettuce leaves as a base on four salad plates.
3. **Arrange** pineapple slices, banana slices, and orange sections in an attractive design on the lettuce.
4. **Top** with dressing.
5. **Garnish** with fresh mint leaves or watercress.

**Nutrition Information**

**Per serving (approximate): 134 calories, 4 g protein, 29 g carbohydrate, 1 g fat, 4 mg cholesterol, 45 mg sodium**

**Good source of: vitamin C, B vitamins, calcium, phosphorus**

# CHAPTER 34

# Soups

**OBJECTIVES**

**Discover . . .**
- how soups fit into a healthful eating plan.
- how to select and store convenience forms of soup.
- how to prepare simple soups.

Soups come in many varieties. There are clear, light soups and creamy ones made with milk. Heartier soups are full of cooked vegetables, meat, poultry, or fish. Some thick soups made with vegetables, fish, or seafood are called *chowder*.

Soup might be served as an appetizer or a snack. A cup or bowl of soup plus a sandwich or salad makes a light meal. Hearty soups can be a main dish or even a meal in themselves.

## Nutrition Notes

When soups are made with nutritious ingredients, they are an excellent source of the nutrients you need for good health. The liquid in soup—called *broth*—contains water-soluble vitamins and minerals. (These are often lost with other foods because the cooking water is thrown away.) Vegetables or fruits in soup boost the vitamins and minerals. Meat, poultry, or fish adds protein. Dry beans can supply both protein and fiber.

Soups made with meat or poultry may contain fat. Chilling soup in the refrigerator allows the fat to come to the surface and harden. Simply remove the hardened fat and you will have a nutritious, low-fat soup. Another way to make soups more healthful is to use herbs for flavoring instead of salt.

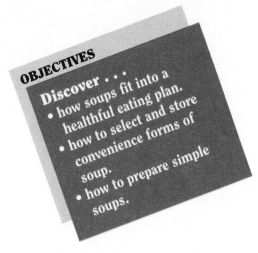

**A cup of soup makes a delicious, nutritious snack.**

# Consumer Tips

In Chapters 23-32, you learned how to buy and store many foods that can be used to make soup. When you don't have time to make soup from scratch, you can choose from a wide variety of convenience forms:

**Canned and frozen soup.** These only need to be heated and served. Check the labels. Water or milk must be added to some.

**Bouillon cubes or granules.** *Bouillon* (boo-YOWN) is clear, flavorful broth. The convenience version is made by adding the cubes or granules to hot water.

**Dried soup mixes.** These come in packages and are usually just mixed with hot water.

Follow the general guidelines in Chapter 8 for buying these products. Read labels carefully. Many convenience soups, like other convenience foods, are high in sodium. Look for low-sodium varieties.

Store canned soups and packaged mixes in a cool, dry place. Keep frozen soups in the freezer until you are ready to prepare them. Cooked soups can be kept in a covered container in the refrigerator for two or three days. Freeze for longer storage.

# Food Skills

Have you ever made soup from scratch? Bony pieces of meat or poultry are cooked in water with a few seasonings. Long, slow cooking will give a flavorful broth that is often called *stock*. Add a few vegetables, the meat from the bones, and perhaps some pasta. The result—a tasty, filling meal.

**Low-cost ingredients, such as less-tender meat or poultry, can be used to make soup. What other advantages does homemade soup offer?**

## Managing with Soup

You can practice good management when you make soup. Manage time by making a large batch of soup and freezing portions to use as needed. Soups are also a good way to use up foods that might go to waste. Many leftovers are perfect additions to soup. Even vegetables that have lost some of their freshness are fine for soup.

Long, slow cooking isn't the only way to make soup. There are many quick and easy possibilities.

## Using Convenience Soups

Convenience soups are easy to prepare—just follow package directions. But you don't have to stop there. You can use your creativity to liven up canned soups or mixes.

One way is to combine several different kinds of canned soups. Choose flavors that go together—perhaps a vegetable soup with chicken soup, or two different vegetable soups. Add the amount of liquid specified on each can.

You can also give convenience soups more flavor and nutrients by adding your own ingredients. You might mix in leftover cooked meat, poultry, fish, vegetables, or pasta. Herbs and other seasonings can lend a special flavor. Try topping soup with chopped chives, snipped parsley, or croutons.

## Simple Cream Soup

Cream soups can be easy to make. They often have a white sauce base.

Refer to the directions for making white sauce on pages 154-155. Vary the amount of flour and margarine or butter to get the thickness you want. Add cooked vegetables such as corn, chopped broccoli, or diced carrots. Season to taste.

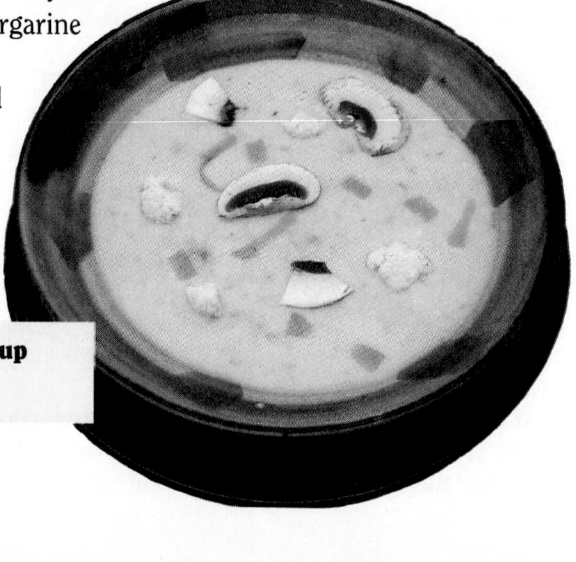

**If you like, you can garnish cream soup with chopped fresh vegetables.**

## Quick and Hearty Soup

You can make an easy homemade soup using canned broth or vegetable juice as a base. Add an assortment of vegetables and other ingredients. To save time, you can use frozen vegetable combinations.

1. Chop or dice fresh vegetables that need longer cooking time, such as onion, potato, and celery. Precook them by sautéing in a small amount of oil or simmering in broth or water.

2. Add vegetable juice and thawed frozen vegetables. If desired, add cooked meat, poultry, or fish. Season with herbs and spices such as marjoram, thyme, basil, pepper, and allspice.

3. Bring the mixture to a boil. Lower the heat and cover the saucepan.

4. Simmer 10 to 15 minutes or until vegetables are cooked, stirring occasionally.

Would you like a thicker soup? Use one of the following techniques to thicken it.

- Puree cooked potatoes or cooked dry beans in a blender or food processor. Add them to the soup.
- Add a grain, such as pasta, rice, or barley, to the soup. As the grain cooks, it will absorb liquid. The directions on the grain package can help you decide how much to add.

**Microwave Hints**

- If you have a temperature probe, use it to bring soup to 170°F (80°C).
- Soups bubble around the edges before they are done in the microwave.
- For even heating, stir soups once or twice during cooking.

## Microwaving Soups

You can use the microwave oven to make homemade soups in less time than by conventional cooking. Check a microwave cookbook for directions.

If you make homemade soup and freeze it, you can defrost and reheat it in the microwave for a quick meal. Most convenience soups can also be heated in the microwave oven. Check the package for directions.

Use a large container for cooking soups in the microwave to allow room for boiling and stirring. For example, use a 1½ quart (1.5 L) container for 1 quart (1 L) of soup.

**Soup can easily be heated in the microwave for a quick meal.**

## Chapter 34 Review

### Check the Facts

1. Describe two ways you can make soup that fits into a healthful eating plan.
2. Give four tips for selecting and storing convenience soups.
3. What is stock?
4. What are three ways to be a good manager when preparing soup?
5. Give an example of how to improve convenience soups.
6. What are two ways to thicken soups?
7. Why should you stir soup while it is being cooked in the microwave?

### Ideas in Action

1. Write a news bulletin suggesting ways to quickly prepare soups as part of a healthful eating plan.
2. You belong to a group concerned about people in your area who often go hungry. You would like to offer a meal twice a week to those in need. Someone has suggested serving different kinds of soups at the community center. Why might soup be a good choice? (Identify as many reasons as possible.) Where might you get the ingredients? What might you serve with the soup for a nutritious meal?
3. Develop a booklet containing simple soup ideas and recipes. You may want to include recipes for several varieties of soups, such as creamy soups, hearty soups, clear soups, and chowders.

# Recipe Focus

1. Plan a menu using "Mexican Corn Chowder" as part of the meal. Use the meal planning information in Chapter 20.
2. What could you use to garnish this soup instead of green onions?

## Mexican Corn Chowder

| Customary | Ingredients | Metric |
|---|---|---|
| ½ cup | Pared, finely diced potato | 125 mL |
| ½ cup | Chopped onion | 125 mL |
| ½ cup | Chopped tomato | 125 mL |
| ¼ cup | Water | 50 mL |
| 1 tsp. | Butter or margarine | 5 mL |
| 2 Tbsp. | All-purpose flour | 30 mL |
| 3 cups | Skim milk | 750 mL |
| 1 cup | Frozen whole-kernel corn, thawed | 250 mL |
| ¼ tsp. | Ground cumin | 1 mL |
| | Chopped green onions (for garnish) | |

**Yield:** 4 servings

### Conventional Directions

**Pan:** 2-qt. (2-L) saucepan with cover

1. **Combine** potato, onion, tomato, water, and butter or margarine in saucepan.
2. **Cook,** covered, over medium heat until potatoes are tender (about 10 minutes).
3. **Stir in** flour.
4. **Add** milk, corn, and cumin. Stir to mix.
5. **Cook,** uncovered, over medium heat, stirring occasionally, until mixture boils and thickens.
6. **Serve** garnished with chopped green onions, if desired.

### Microwave Directions

**Pans:** 1-qt. (1-L) and 2-qt. (2-L) microwave-safe containers

**Power Level:** 100%

1. **Microwave** milk at 100% power, uncovered, in 1-qt. (1-L) container for 2 to 3 minutes or until hot.
2. **Combine** potato, onion, tomato, water, and margarine in 2-qt. (2-L) container.
3. **Microwave** at 100% power, uncovered, for 7 to 8 minutes or until potatoes are tender. Stir after 4 minutes.
4. **Stir in** flour.
5. **Add** hot milk gradually. Stir in corn and cumin.
6. **Microwave** at 100% power, uncovered, for 11 to 12 minutes or until boiling and thickened. Stir three times during cooking.
7. **Serve** garnished with chopped green onions, if desired.

### Nutrition Information

**Per serving (approximate): 150 calories, 9 g protein, 27 g carbohydrate, 2 g fat, 3 mg cholesterol, 110 mg sodium**

**Good source of: vitamin A, B vitamins, vitamin C, calcium, phosphorus**

CHAPTER 35

# One-Dish Meals

**OBJECTIVES**

**Discover . . .**
- how one-dish meals fit into healthful eating.
- the role of convenience products.
- how to prepare one-dish meals.

One-dish meals combine meat or other protein foods, vegetables, grains, and flavorings into one dish that serves as the main food for a meal. They include recipes such as stir-fried dishes, casseroles, and pizza.

One-dish meals have several advantages. Because different foods are combined, only a small amount of meat, poultry, or fish is needed. As a result, the meals are usually economical. In addition, many are quick and easy to prepare.

## Nutrition Notes

One-dish meals include foods from several food groups. For example, a chicken casserole may be made with chicken and mixed vegetables in a seasoned white sauce and topped with biscuits. Can you identify the basic food group each of these ingredients represents?

As you can see, one-dish meals can supply a wide range of nutrients. They are generally high in vitamins, minerals, protein, and complex carbohydrates. If whole grains are used, they also provide fiber.

These dishes can also be high in fat, sodium, and calories if the foods are not chosen wisely. To lower the fat, choose ingredients such as lean meat, cooked dry beans, low-fat cheeses, and skim milk.

To complete the meal, add foods from other groups. For example, you might eat a fruit salad and beverage with the chicken casserole described earlier. With other dishes, you might add a tossed salad, a whole-grain bread, and a beverage of juice or milk.

**What one-dish meals do you enjoy?**

# Consumer Power

Your shopping skills can help you choose ingredients for one-dish meals. Refer to Chapters 23-32 for information on how to buy and store specific foods.

People often use a combination of fresh ingredients and convenience foods to create one-dish meals quickly. Many convenience foods discussed in other chapters, such as canned fish or dried soup mix, can be used in one-dish meals. In addition, look for products such as packaged main-dish mixes and ready-to-use stir-fry vegetables. These can be combined with fish, poultry, or meat for a quick one-dish meal.

**How could these foods help you prepare one-dish meals quickly?**

You can also buy already prepared one-dish meals. Look for them on store shelves and in the frozen, refrigerated, and deli sections. Most simply need reheating.

Use your consumer and decision-making skills when considering whether to buy convenience foods. Remember that convenience foods often cost more than foods you prepare yourself. Many are high in fat and sodium.

You can make your own "convenience foods" to use in one-dish meals. How? Refrigerate or freeze leftovers such as cooked vegetables, dry beans, grains, meat, poultry, or fish. You can also prepare extra batches of these foods when you have time and freeze them to use later.

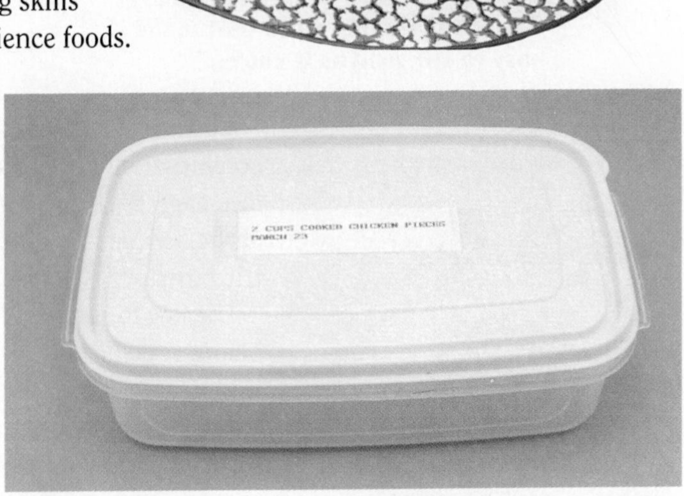

**Keeping ready-to-use ingredients in the freezer lets you put one-dish meals together easily.**

# Food Skills

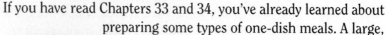

If you have read Chapters 33 and 34, you've already learned about preparing some types of one-dish meals. A large, filling salad can be a one-dish meal, as can a hearty soup. Another type—stew—is similar to soup, but less liquid is used.

**Stew makes a nutritious, satisfying meal. Check a cookbook for recipes. What would you serve with this stew?**

Many one-dish meals are cooked on top of the range. The recipe on page 255 is an example of this type of dish, which is sometimes called a skillet meal.

The following pages will help you get started in creating other one-dish meals. You will will learn about making stir-fried meals, casseroles, and pizza.

## Stir-Fried Meals

As you learned in Chapter 14, stir-frying is a method of cooking food quickly in a small amount of oil. The food is stirred as it cooks. You can stir-fry in a large skillet, an electric skillet, or a wok. A *wok* is a large pan with a rounded bottom. It has a separate metal ring to hold the pan on the heating unit.

**A wok has sloping sides that make it easy to stir food as it cooks.**

A stir-fried meal usually includes lots of vegetables in any combination. For protein, include fish, poultry, meat, or tofu (see page 191). You can also add flavorings such as ginger, garlic, thyme, soy sauce, or prepared mustard. Often the stir-fried mixture is served with hot cooked rice.

The key to successful stir-frying is preparing the ingredients before you start cooking. The actual cooking takes just a few minutes.

To prepare the ingredients, cut foods into small uniform pieces so they cook quickly and evenly. Keep each ingredient separate. Line up the ingredients in the order they will be cooked. Foods that take longer to cook, such as meat, will go in the pan first. Liquids are added near the end.

**To prepare a stir-fried meal . . .**

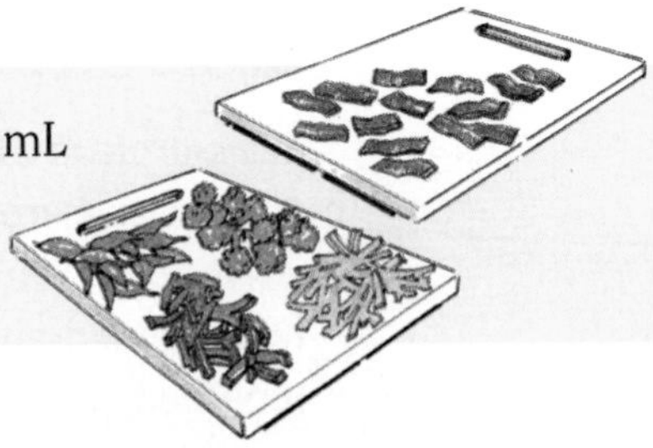

1. Cut vegetables into small, uniform pieces (about 3 cups or 750 mL total). On a separate cutting board, cut meat, poultry, or fish into thin strips (about 1 cup or 250 mL).

2. Measure 1 Tbsp. (15 mL) cornstarch into a small bowl. Gradually add a small amount of cold water, stirring constantly. Set this mixture aside.

3. Heat 1 Tbsp. (15 mL) oil in a skillet or wok, using high heat. Cook the pieces of meat, poultry, or fish using high heat and stirring constantly. When done, remove the pieces to a clean plate.
   ▲If you are using already-cooked meat, poultry, or fish, skip this step.

4. Begin cooking the vegetable pieces. Start with the tougher ones, like carrots. They'll take longer to cook than tender ones, like tomatoes. Cook and stir over high heat until the vegetables begin to wilt.

5. Add 1 cup (250 mL) liquid, such as broth or vegetable juice, along with any seasonings. Cover the pan and allow the vegetables to steam until tender-crisp.

6. Add the cooked meat, poultry, or fish.

7. Pour the cornstarch mixture slowly into the pan, stirring constantly. Cook and stir over medium heat only until the mixture thickens and becomes clear.
   ▲If overcooked, cornstarch loses its thickening power.

8. Serve over hot cooked rice, if desired. Makes 4 to 6 servings.

# Casseroles

A *casserole* is a mixture of foods baked together in a casserole or baking dish. A main-dish casserole generally includes the following types of foods:

**Protein food.** You can use cooked meat, poultry, fish, cheese, dry beans, or tofu. Brown and drain ground beef before use. Cut other foods into small pieces, if needed.

**Casserole ingredients are often precooked and mixed together in a saucepan. Final cooking is done in the oven.**

**Vegetables.** Vegetables add variety, flavor, texture, and nutrients to the casserole.

**Binder.** The binder helps thicken the casserole and holds the ingredients together. It also adds flavor, texture, and nutrients. You can use foods such as cooked pasta, rice, grits, potatoes, or dry beans.

**Liquid.** The liquid helps the binder work and adds flavor and nutrients. Try liquids such as skim milk, vegetable juice, broth, canned soup, or white sauce.

**Other ingredients.** For flavor and texture, add small amounts of foods such as chopped celery, green pepper, parsley, onions, grated cheese, chopped nuts, or seeds. Try different combinations of seasonings.

Sometimes a topping is added, such as buttered bread crumbs, grated cheese, or biscuits. The topping keeps the casserole from drying out and adds flavor and texture.

In a conventional oven, casseroles are usually baked at about 350°F (180°C). The cooking time varies, depending on the foods used. If a topping is not used, cover the casserole during baking. Check about 10 minutes before the casserole is done. If the mixture is too thin, remove the cover so some of the liquid evaporates.

# Pizza

Pizza is a variation of a pie. It consists of a crust or base, sauce, your choice of toppings, and cheese. Instead of a pie pan, a flat, round, or rectangular baking pan is used.

The crust is usually made of yeast dough, rolled or patted thin. To save time, you can buy a ready-to-use pizza crust. It is generally found in the refrigerated section in a supermarket. Follow the package directions for preparing the crust. Some types are already rolled out into a circle. Others are folded and need to be pressed into a pan.

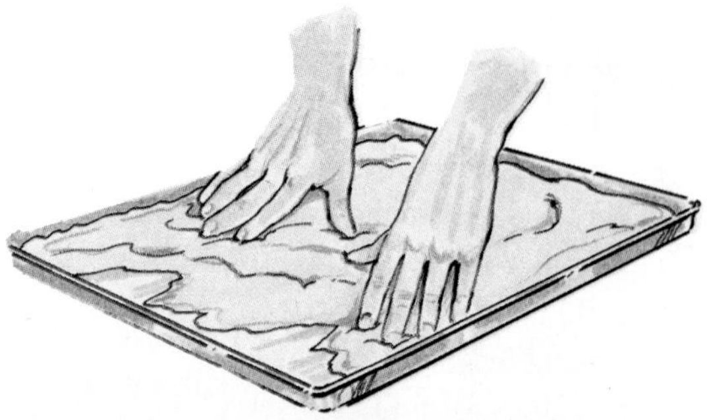

**When making pizza, press the crust evenly into the baking sheet.**

You could also use other foods as a base for the pizza. Try French bread sliced lengthwise or English muffin halves. (See the recipe for mini-pizzas on page 163.)

Next, spread a seasoned sauce evenly over the crust. You can make your own or use a prepared sauce. Then add your choice of toppings. You might try fresh vegetables such as green or red peppers, mushrooms, onions, zucchini, or steamed broccoli or cauliflower. You can also add cooked meat, poultry, or fish, thinly sliced or diced.

Sprinkle grated cheese over the toppings. You can use mozzarella, Swiss, or Parmesan, or combine two or more cheeses for variety. When possible, choose low-fat cheese.

Finish the pizza by baking in a conventional oven until lightly brown. This generally takes about 20 minutes at 425°F (220°C).

**Pizza is a delicious one-dish meal that can be quickly and easily prepared.**

### Microwave Hints

- Defrost frozen casseroles in the microwave to save time.
- You can sauté chopped vegetables in the microwave. For 1 cup (250 mL) vegetables, use 1 Tbsp. (15 mL) oil. Microwave in a covered container at 100% power for 3 to 4 minutes.

## Microwaving One-Dish Meals

The microwave can save time and energy in preparing one-dish meals. You can use it to thaw or precook ingredients such as meat or vegetables.

The microwave can also handle final cooking of many casseroles. Spread the mixture evenly in the pan. Stir or turn the dish halfway through the cooking time and again at the end. Cover the casserole to hold in moisture.

For pizzas and stir-fried dishes, look for recipes in microwave cookbooks or the owner's manual.

**Microwaving casseroles saves time when preparing family meals.**

## Chapter 35 Review

### Check the Facts

1. Give an example of a one-dish meal that includes foods from at least four food groups. Explain how each food group is represented.
2. Give two examples of how convenience foods may be used in one-dish meals.
3. Name two ways stir-fried meals are different in preparation from other types of one-dish meals.
4. Identify the basic types of foods used in casseroles. Give an example of each type.
5. Name four ingredients you would choose when preparing a low-fat pizza.
6. List three ways to use the microwave in preparing one-dish meals.

### Ideas in Action

1. In small groups, brainstorm a list of foods that could be put into a casserole. From this list, select up to 10 ingredients that your group thinks would be good together. As a group, write the recipe for your casserole. Check cookbooks to estimate the amount of each ingredient.
2. Discuss the advantages and disadvantages of using convenience foods in one-dish meals.
3. Choose a one-dish meal recipe from a cookbook or one you have used at home. How well do you think this recipe fits in with nutrition guidelines? How could this recipe be adapted to make it more nutritious?

# Recipe Focus

1. Read the recipe for "Skillet Chicken and Rice." What could you substitute for boneless chicken breast in this recipe?
2. Refer to the nutrition information for this recipe. Identify the ingredient(s) that are the main source of each vitamin and mineral listed.

## Skillet Chicken & Rice

| Customary | Ingredients | Metric |
|---|---|---|
| 1 lb. | Boneless, skinless chicken breast | 500 g |
| 1 Tbsp. | Oil | 15 mL |
| ½ cup | Chopped onion | 125 mL |
| 2 cups | Broccoli florets | 500 mL |
| 1¼ cups | Low-salt chicken broth | 300 mL |
| 1½ cups | Instant rice | 375 mL |
| Dash | Pepper | Dash |
| 1 cup | Shredded reduced-fat mild cheddar cheese | 250 mL |

**Yield:** 4 servings

### Conventional Directions

**Pan:** 10-inch (25-cm) skillet with lid

1. **Cut** chicken into strips about ¼ inch (6 mm) wide.
2. **Heat** oil over medium-high heat until a drop of water dropped into the skillet sizzles.
3. **Add** chicken and onion to hot oil. Cook, stirring constantly, about 2 minutes or until chicken is lightly browned.
4. **Add** broccoli and broth. Bring to a boil.
5. **Stir** in rice and pepper. Cover pan and remove from heat.
6. **Let stand** 3 minutes, then stir.
7. **Top** with shredded cheese. Cover again and let stand 2 minutes or until cheese is melted.

### Microwave Directions

**Pan:** 1½-qt.(1.5-L) casserole dish with cover
**Power Level:** 100%

**Ingredients:** Reduce onion to ¼ cup (50 mL). Omit oil.

1. **Cut** chicken into strips about ¼ inch (6 mm) wide.
2. **Stir** together chicken and onion in casserole dish. Cover.
3. **Microwave** at 100% power 5 to 6 minutes or until chicken is no longer pink. Stir after 3 minutes.
4. **Stir in** broccoli, broth, rice, and pepper. Cover.
5. **Microwave** at 100% power 6 to 8 minutes or until most of liquid is absorbed. Stir after 4 minutes.
6. **Top** with shredded cheese. Cover. Microwave at 100% power 1 to 2 minutes or until cheese is melted.

### Nutrition Information

**Per serving (approximate):** 405 calories, 38 g protein, 35 g carbohydrate, 12 g fat, 67 mg cholesterol, 520 mg sodium
**Good source of:** vitamin A, B vitamins, vitamin C, calcium, iron, phosphorus, other minerals

CHAPTER 36

# Snacks

**OBJECTIVES**

**Discover . . .**
- how snacks fit into a healthful eating plan.
- how to choose snacks wisely.
- how to prepare nutritious snacks.

If you are like most people, you enjoy snacks. Did you know that snacks can be good for you? They can help boost your energy between meals. When chosen wisely, they can add nutrients and fill in missing servings from the food groups. The trick is to choose and prepare nutritious snacks.

When it comes to snack foods, you have a wide variety of choices. Too often, people forget that snacks need to be chosen with the same care as meals. They are part of your daily food intake.

## Nutrition Notes

How can you choose snacks that are good for you? Just remember that snacks, like meals, should be based on foods from the five main food groups in the Daily Food Guide (pages 42-43). Foods such as fruits, vegetables, and yogurt make excellent snacks. They are full of flavor and important nutrients, yet can be low in fat, sugar, and sodium.

What about chips, candy bars, and soft drinks? They are high in calories, fat, sugar, or sodium. At the same time, they have little or no protein, vitamins, minerals, or fiber. Enjoy them as an occasional treat, not an everyday choice.

Here are some tips for smart snacking:

- If you snack all day long, it's easy to lose track of what you're eating. You might eat too much or miss out on important nutrients.
- Frequent snacking can lead to tooth decay. Brush your teeth after snacks whenever possible.
- Consider your individual needs when planning snacks. If you are active in sports, you may need extra calories to fuel your body. If you are overweight, choose snacks that are nutritious but low in calories.

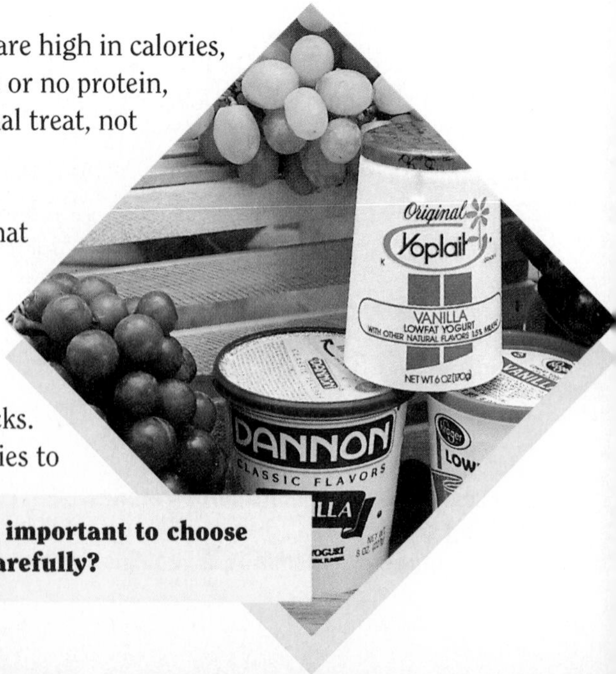


**Why is it important to choose snacks carefully?**

# Consumer Power

You can buy snack foods almost anywhere—not just at the supermarket, but at sports events, movie theaters, shopping malls, and from vending machines. Remember to use your nutrition knowledge and consumer skills wherever you go. Many choices look tempting, but how will they fit into your total eating plan? Would plain popcorn or unsalted nuts be a better choice than potato chips or pork rinds?

**Look for healthful snack choices, such as fruit juice, when you are away from home.**

One way to beat the pitfalls of "impulse snacking" is to plan ahead. You can find many nutritious, low-fat snack foods at the grocery store. Here's a sample shopping list:

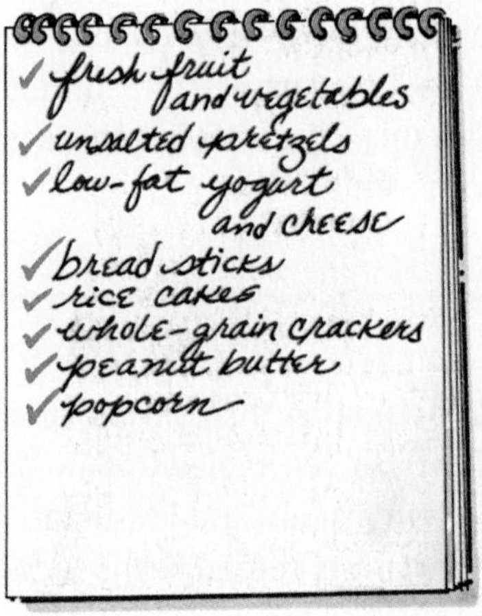


Keep snack foods like these at home. When you have the urge for something sweet or crunchy, you'll have nutritious foods to choose from. You can also bring your own snacks from home to eat at school or when you go out with friends. You'll probably save money, too.

When you shop for snack foods, read labels carefully. For example, many crackers look healthful but are high in fat and sodium. Look for varieties with better nutrition. Refer to Chapters 23–32 for more information on buying and storing nutritious foods.

**Read snack labels carefully. Avoid snacks high in fat, sodium, and sugar. What does this label tell you?**

# Food Skills

Many snacks come ready to eat. You may just open a package of crackers or grab an apple. Other tasty snacks require only a few simple steps. Here are some to try.

## Popcorn

Popcorn is an ideal snack. It's a good source of fiber. It combines the sweet flavor of corn with a crunchy texture.

**Sprinkle flavorful seasonings over popcorn instead of salt.**

You can buy already-popped corn or packaged, ready-to-pop corn for microwaving. However, read labels carefully. Some products are high in calories, fat, and sodium. For the least fat, make your own popcorn using a hot-air popper or a special microwave popper.

If you don't enjoy plain popcorn, try seasoning it with herbs or spices. You might also mix dry roasted peanuts with plain popcorn. This gives a delicious peanut flavor.

## Spreads

*Spreads* are seasoned mixtures of meat, poultry, fish, beans, or cheese. They can be spread on breads, rolls, crackers, fruits, or vegetables.

Bean spread is a good choice. It's high in protein and low in fat. Try it on crackers topped with salsa, in pita pockets, or in place of refried beans in tacos and tostadas.

**To make a bean spread . . .**

1. Drain a 15½-oz. (439-g) can of red kidney beans or other beans. Save the liquid for making soup or sauce.
2. Mash the beans in a medium bowl or use a blender.

3. Add a small chopped onion, a minced garlic clove, ¼ tsp. (1 mL) each dried crushed rosemary and thyme, and a dash of hot pepper sauce.
4. Mix well. Refrigerate in a covered container overnight to blend the flavors.

## Fruit and Vegetable Snacks

Fresh fruits and vegetables make great snacks. Keep both on hand.

For a flavorful dip to eat with vegetables, mix low-fat cottage cheese or plain yogurt with seasonings. You might use minced onion, garlic powder, chopped parsley, dill weed, chopped chives, or chili powder.

**For quick snacks, keep an assortment of cleaned and cut raw vegetables in the refrigerator.**

Try this fruit dip: Blend ½ cup (125 mL) mashed fresh fruit (such as strawberries) with 1 cup (250 mL) vanilla low-fat yogurt. Add 1 Tbsp. (15 mL) honey and mix well. Serve with fruit chunks or small whole fruits.

To make fruit kabobs, place chunks of fruit and low-fat cheese on skewers. Dip the fruit in lemon juice first to prevent browning.

## Hot Snacks

In just a few minutes you can make delicious hot snacks. Try the recipe for Cheesy Mini-Pizzas on page 163 or the Tostada Melt recipe on page 195. You might also enjoy these:

**Tortilla treats.** Spread a corn tortilla with a very thin coating of margarine. Sprinkle with 1 Tbsp. (15 mL) Parmesan cheese and 1 tsp. (5 mL) sesame seeds. Cut the tortilla into triangles. Bake in the oven at 350°F (180°C) until cheese melts and tortillas are crisp.

**Roasted pumpkin or sunflower seeds.** Rinse all the pumpkin fibers from the seeds. For sunflower seeds, remove the hulls. Sprinkle ½ tsp. (2 mL) salt in the bottom of a microwave-safe baking dish. Place the damp seeds on top of the salt in the baking dish and microwave at 100% power about 6 minutes. Stir twice during cooking time. Seeds should be crispy when ready to eat.

## More Snack Ideas

- Make a small salad. Refer to Chapter 33 for ideas.
- Have a cup of soup along with some crackers or breadsticks.
- Make a mini-sandwich. See the sandwich ideas in Chapter 22.
- Have a small serving of leftovers, such as a slice of pizza.
- Make a nutritious blender shake. You'll learn how in the next chapter.
- Mix cereal with pretzels, nuts, seeds, and dried fruit. Use the recipe on the next page or make your own combination.
- Add fresh or canned fruit to plain yogurt or cottage cheese.
- Make your own frozen yogurt pops. Mix 8 oz. (250 mL) plain low-fat yogurt with a thawed 6-oz. (177-mL) can of your favorite frozen juice concentrate. Add chopped fruit if you wish. Pour into paper cups and place a popsicle stick in the middle. Freeze. To eat, simply peel away the cup.

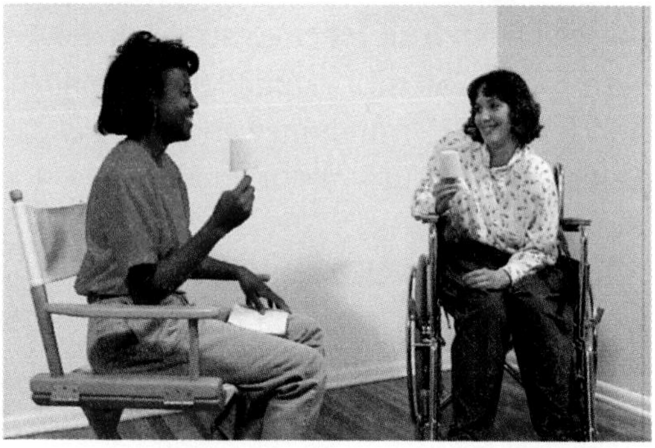

## Chapter 36 Review

### Check the Facts

1. Name at least two factors to consider when choosing foods for snacks.
2. Identify at least four nutritious snacks from each of the five main food groups.
3. How can you avoid "impulse snacking"?
4. Why should you read snack food labels?
5. Identify two flavorings, other than butter and salt, that you can use on popcorn.
6. Give three suggestions for using fruits and vegetables as snacks.

### Ideas in Action

1. Write an article for the school newspaper convincing students to make healthful snack choices.
2. In small groups, brainstorm different snack possibilities to meet the needs of the following types of individuals. List at least four possibilities for each.
   - A long-distance runner on the track team.
   - A person struggling to lose five pounds.
   - An underweight person.
   - A member of the marching band.
   - A person who watches TV every day after school.
3. Look through cookbooks for snack recipes. Evaluate each recipe for nutrition, ease of preparation, and cost.

# Recipe Focus

1. Read the recipe for "Snack Mix." Name two nutritious alternatives for each ingredient in the recipe.
2. Why might "Snack Mix" be a good snack choice to keep on hand?

## Snack Mix

| Customary | Ingredients | Metric |
|---|---|---|
| 1 cup | Pretzels, broken into pieces | 250 mL |
| 1 cup | Unsalted, roasted peanuts | 250 mL |
| 1 cup | Raisins | 250 mL |
| 1 cup | Ready-to-eat, whole-grain cereal | 250 mL |
| ½ cup | Unsalted sunflower seeds | 125 mL |

**Yield:** About 9 servings (½ cup or 125 mL each)

### Directions

1. **Mix** pretzels, peanuts, raisins, cereal, and sunflower seeds.
2. **Store** in an airtight container.

**Nutrition Information**

**Per serving (approximate): 229 calories, 7 g protein, 27 g carbohydrate, 12 g fat, 0 mg cholesterol, 165 mg sodium**

**Good source of: B vitamins, phosphorus, other minerals**

CHAPTER 37

# Beverages

**OBJECTIVES**

**Discover . . .**

- how beverages fit into a healthful eating plan.
- how to select and store nutritious beverages.
- how to prepare blender shakes and fruit punches.

Beverages are part of any meal, but they can also be enjoyed as a snack or refreshment. When you reach in the refrigerator at home, eat at a fast-food restaurant, or snack with friends, do you automatically choose a soft drink? Consider your alternatives. This chapter will help you choose and prepare flavorful, healthful beverages.

## Nutrition Notes

Beverages help fill your body's need for water. In fact, plain water is the best beverage when it comes to quenching your thirst. For good health, drink at least six to eight glasses of water each day.

If you choose beverages wisely, they can also help meet your body's need for other nutrients.

- Milk supplies protein, calcium, phosphorus, and vitamins D and A. (For information on buying, storing, and using milk, see Chapter 23.) Beverages such as cocoa and milk shakes can also provide these nutrients because they are made from milk. However, they have more sugar, fat, and calories as well.
- Fruit and vegetable juices provide the same vitamins and minerals as those found in the fruit or vegetable. For example, orange juice is high in vitamin C and potassium.

**Many hot and cold beverages are nutritious as well as delicious.**

Coffee, tea, and soft drinks such as cola are beverages to be enjoyed only occasionally. Although they are refreshing, they supply few or no vitamins and minerals. Instead, they may supply too much of what you don't need, such as sugar and sodium. Many of these beverages also contain *caffeine* (kaff-EEN), a chemical that can cause nervousness and other problems.

Too often, soft drinks are chosen instead of nutritious beverages such as milk. That can be a problem—especially for children and teens, who need plenty of calcium while their bones are still growing. What beverages do you choose most often? What improvements can you make in your beverage choices?

**A typical soft drink has about 10 tsp. (50 mL) sugar in a 12-ounce (375-mL) can.**

**Why is fruit juice a better choice than a soft drink such as cola?**

## Consumer Power

The shopping skills and nutrition information you have already learned will help you choose beverages. Here are more tips to help you be a wise consumer.

### Juices and Fruit Drinks

Many different kinds of fruit are used to make juice. You can also buy vegetable juices, such as tomato.

Only products that are pure juice can be called "juice" on the label. What if the label uses another term, such as fruit drink or punch? These products typically contain from 5% to 50% juice. The rest is water and sugar or another sweetener. Some are fortified with vitamin C.

You'll find juices and fruit drinks on the store shelves as well as in the refrigerated section. They may be packaged in bottles, cartons, or cans. Also look for frozen juice concentrate and powdered mixes. Before using these products, you must reconstitute them by adding water as directed on the label.

**A variety of juices and juice drinks are available at the supermarket. Read the labels carefully to be sure you are getting the type of product you want.**

## Buying and Storing Beverages

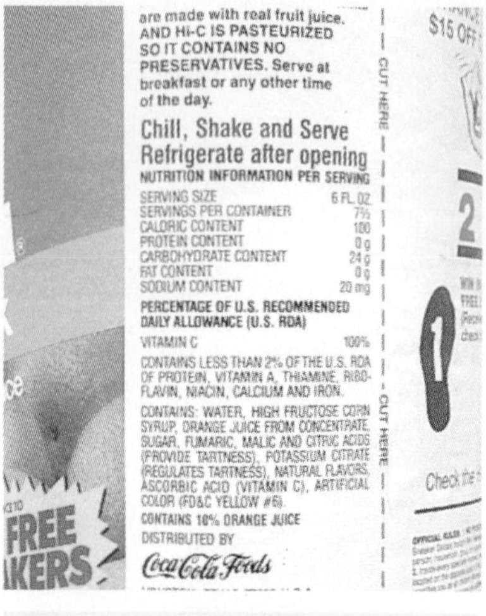

are made with real fruit juice.
AND HI-C IS PASTEURIZED
SO IT CONTAINS NO
PRESERVATIVES. Serve at
breakfast or any other time
of the day.
Chill, Shake and Serve
Refrigerate after opening
NUTRITION INFORMATION PER SERVING
SERVING SIZE 6 FL. OZ.
SERVINGS PER CONTAINER 7½
CALORIC CONTENT 100
PROTEIN CONTENT 0 g
CARBOHYDRATE CONTENT 24 g
FAT CONTENT 0 g
SODIUM CONTENT 20 mg
PERCENTAGE OF U.S. RECOMMENDED DAILY ALLOWANCE (U.S. RDA)
VITAMIN C 100%
CONTAINS LESS THAN 2% OF THE U.S. RDA OF PROTEIN, VITAMIN A, THIAMINE, RIBOFLAVIN, NIACIN, CALCIUM AND IRON.
CONTAINS: WATER, HIGH FRUCTOSE CORN SYRUP, ORANGE JUICE FROM CONCENTRATE, SUGAR, FUMARIC, MALIC AND CITRIC ACIDS (PROVIDE TARTNESS), POTASSIUM CITRATE (REGULATES TARTNESS), NATURAL FLAVORS, ASCORBIC ACID (VITAMIN C), ARTIFICIAL COLOR (FD&C YELLOW #6).
CONTAINS 10% ORANGE JUICE
DISTRIBUTED BY
Coca-Cola Foods
CUT HERE
CUT HERE
$15 OFF
FREE


**Is this product a fruit juice or a fruit beverage? How can you tell?**

When shopping for beverages, read labels carefully. What nutrients does the product provide? How much sugar, sodium, and caffeine does it contain?

Unless you read carefully, it may not be easy to tell the difference between pure fruit juice and other fruit beverages. A product that says "100% natural" may not be 100% juice. Remember, the label must list any added ingredients.

Like other foods, beverages need to be stored properly to maintain their nutrients and fresh flavor.

- Juice from the refrigerated case should be kept cold. Most other unopened products can be stored in a cool, dry area.
- Refrigerate opened containers of juice. Use within a few days.
- Keep fruit juice concentrates frozen until you are ready to use them. After they are reconstituted, refrigerate them.

# Food Skills

With a few simple steps, you can make a variety of tasty beverages for snacks or special occasions.

## Blender Shakes

You can use a blender or food processor to make nutritious low-fat shakes. Try creating your own combinations of fresh fruit, fruit juice, skim milk, and yogurt. Here are some ideas to get you started.

- Banana Shake—Cut an overripe banana into chunks and freeze solid. Combine the frozen banana chunks with ⅔ cup (150 mL) skim milk in a blender or food processor. Blend on high speed until smooth.
- Lemon-Strawberry Smoothie—Blend ½ cup (125 mL) lemon yogurt, ½ cup (125 mL) skim milk, ¼ cup (50 mL) sliced strawberries, and 1 tsp. (5 mL) sugar.
- Sunshine Shake—Blend ¾ cup (180 mL) chilled pineapple or orange juice, ¼ cup (50 mL) plain nonfat or low-fat yogurt, 2 tsp. (10 mL) honey, and 3 crushed ice cubes.

## Fruit Punch

It's fun to create your own fruit juice combinations. Choose juices that will blend well in color and flavor. A mixture of fruit juices is sometimes called *fruit punch*. Here's an idea for a bubbly fruit punch you can serve at a party.

1. Ahead of time, thaw a 6-ounce (177-mL) can frozen lemonade concentrate. Mix with 2 qt. (2 L) cranberry juice cocktail in a large pitcher or punch bowl. Chill to allow flavors to blend. Also chill a 1-qt. (1-L) bottle of plain seltzer water.

2. Just before serving, slowly add the chilled seltzer water to the punch.

3. For a garnish, float lemon or orange slices in the punch.

## Hot Beverages

Fruit juice or punch can also be served hot. If spices such as cinnamon or cloves are added, the hot mixture is called a *mulled* beverage. "Mulled Citrus Punch," the recipe on page 267, is an example.

When making a mulled beverage, simmer the mixture at least 10 minutes to blend the flavors. Serve the beverage piping hot in mugs. For a garnish, you can use a stick of cinnamon or a slice of orange or lemon.

Cocoa is a popular hot beverage. Making hot beverages with milk requires special care. Follow the guidelines for cooking with milk in Chapter 23. You will find a cocoa recipe on page 157.

**When might you serve a hot mulled fruit punch?**

## Microwave Hints

- Microwave beverages at 100% power unless the recipe specifies a different level.
- You can reheat hot beverages that have cooled to room temperature. One serving takes about 1½ minutes at 100% power. Two servings take about 3 minutes.

## Microwaving Beverages

Some beverages, especially those made with milk, need careful attention when microwaved. They can develop a film on the surface of the liquid. This acts as a cover and lets steam build up under the surface. The hot liquid may spurt out of the container and cause burns. Stir before and during microwaving to prevent this problem. Also stir after microwaving to mix hotter and cooler parts of the liquid.

**When should microwaved beverages be stirred? Why?**

# Chapter 37 Review

### Check the Facts

1. Give three examples of healthful beverage choices. Briefly explain why they are healthful.
2. Name two drawbacks of soft drinks such as cola.
3. What is the difference between fruit juices and fruit drinks?
4. What juice products must be refrigerated?
5. Give three examples of ingredients that can be used to make nutritious blender shakes.
6. What is a mulled beverage?

### Ideas in Action

1. Soft drinks recently surpassed milk as the most popular beverage consumed in the United States. What are some reasons this may have happened? Do you think people should make changes in the beverages they choose to drink? Why or why not?
2. Make a poster for your school cafeteria showing nutritious beverage choices. Your poster should convince other students to make healthful choices.
3. Assume you are a nutrition consultant. Write a one-minute persuasive speech on the need for choosing healthful beverages. Imagine you are writing this speech to present to a group of students on the track team.

# Recipe Focus

1. Read the recipe for Mulled Citrus Punch. Suppose you want to serve this recipe cold. What would you do to be sure the flavors had developed before serving?
2. If you did not have cinnamon sticks and whole cloves on hand, what could you use to flavor the punch?

## Mulled Citrus Punch

| Customary | Ingredients | Metric |
|---|---|---|
| 2 cups | Orange juice | 500 mL |
| 1 cup | Cranberry-apple drink | 250 mL |
| 3 Tbsp. | Packed brown sugar | 45 mL |
| ½ tsp. | Whole cloves | 2 mL |
| 1 | Cinnamon stick | 1 |
| Dash | Ground nutmeg | Dash |
| 6 | Orange slices (for garnish) | 6 |

**Yield:** 6 servings (about ½ cup or 125 mL each)

### Conventional Directions

**Pan:** 1-qt. (1-L) saucepan

1. **Combine** orange juice, cranberry-apple drink, brown sugar, cloves, cinnamon stick, and ground nutmeg in saucepan.
2. **Bring** to a boil.
3. **Reduce** heat. Simmer for 10 minutes.
4. **Strain** into mugs or coffee cups.
5. **Garnish** each serving with an orange slice.

### Microwave Directions

**Pan:** Microwave-safe 1-qt. (1-L) liquid measuring cup or bowl

**Power Level:** 100%

1. **Combine** orange juice, cranberry-apple drink, brown sugar, cloves, cinnamon stick, and ground nutmeg in measuring cup or bowl.
2. **Microwave** at 100% power for 4 to 6 minutes. If you are using a temperature probe, heat the mixture to 150°F (70°C).
3. **Strain** into mugs or coffee cups.
4. **Garnish** each serving with an orange slice.

### Nutrition Information

**Per serving (approximate): 92 calories, 1 g protein, 23 g carbohydrate, 0 g fat, 0 mg cholesterol, 5 mg sodium**

**Good source of: vitamin C**

CHAPTER 38

# Principles of Baking

**OBJECTIVES**

**Discover . . .**
- the purpose of ingredients in baking.
- what happens during mixing and baking.
- guidelines for successful baking.

Baked goods such as cakes and breads use basically the same ingredients. Their differences are caused by the amounts of the ingredients used and how they are put together and then baked.

In this chapter, you will learn information and skills that will be helpful for any baked product. You will put these general skills to work to make specific baked products in Chapters 39 and 40.

## The Chemistry of Baking

A recipe for a baked product is like a chemical formula. In fact, chemical reactions that take place during mixing and baking give the product its final appearance, texture, and flavor.

### What Ingredients Do

Each ingredient in baking has a specific purpose. They all work together to make a product with the desired texture and flavor. You will learn more about some of these ingredients as you study the rest of this unit.

**Flour** provides proteins and starch that make up the structure of baked products.

**Leavening agents**, such as baking powder, make products rise. They do this by causing air or gas to be trapped in the mixture. Without leavening agents, products would be flat with a dense texture.

**Understanding basic principles can help your baked goods turn out right.**

**Liquids** help flour form the structure of baked products. They also make possible many of the chemical changes which take place in the mixture. Water, milk, fruit or vegetable juice, yogurt, and sour cream are some of the liquids used in baked products.

**Fats and oils** make products rich and tender. They also add flavor and help to brown the crust.

**Sweeteners**, such as sugar, give flavor. They also help the crust to brown.

**Eggs** make baked products tender, add flavor and richness, and can help bind mixtures together so they don't separate. Beaten eggs may be used as a leavening agent.

**Flavorings** include chocolate, spices, herbs, and extracts such as vanilla and almond.

**Each type of ingredient in baking has a specific job to do.**

If you look at a recipe for muffins or other baked goods, you'll see most or all of these types of ingredients. If you use a convenience mix, some of the ingredients are already included in the mix. You add what's missing, such as liquid.

You have already learned how to buy and store some ingredients, such as milk and eggs. In Chapters 39 and 40 you will find consumer information for other ingredients.

## How Ingredients Are Combined

The ingredients are combined and mixed in a specific way, depending on the type of baked product. Proper mixing helps give the desired texture.

The mixture of ingredients is called dough or batter, depending on how thick it is.

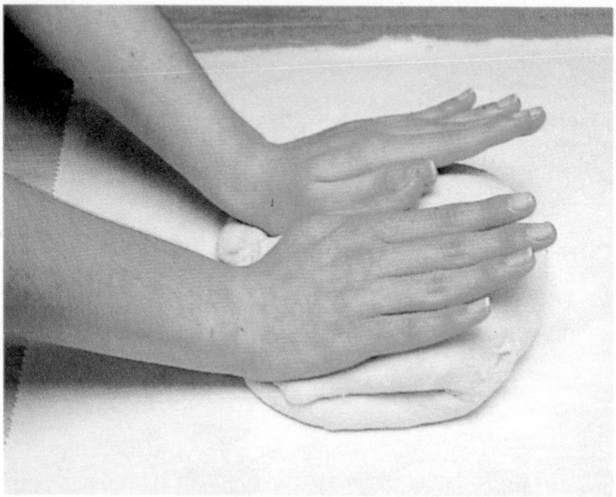

**Dough** is thick enough to be shaped by hand or cut into shapes. Biscuits, cookies, pie crust, and some breads are made from dough.

**Batter** is thin enough to be poured or dropped from a spoon. Pancakes, muffins, and cakes are made from batter.

One of the reasons for mixing ingredients is to distribute them evenly. Another is to develop gluten. *Gluten* is an elastic substance formed by the protein in flour. It forms the structure of the product. The more the dough is mixed, the stronger the gluten becomes. Some baked products, such as yeast bread, must have strong gluten. Others, such as cakes, do not need strong gluten.

## How Leavening Agents Work

As mentioned earlier, most baked products need a *leavening agent* to help them rise. Recipes use one or more of these four basic leavening agents:

**Trapped air.** Air is trapped in a mixture when you sift flour, cream fat and sugar together, beat egg whites, or beat batter.

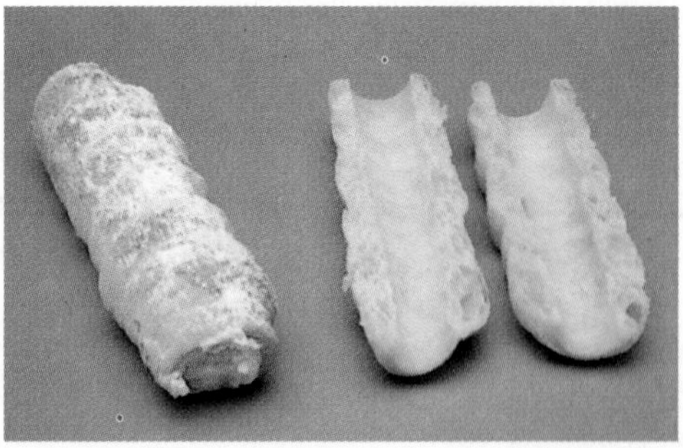

**Steam**. When steam is used as a leavening agent, the product must be baked at a high temperature. The high heat causes water in the mixture to turn to steam and the product rises. Cream puffs are an example.

**Chemical leavening**. There are two common chemical leavening agents—baking soda and baking powder. Baking soda forms carbon dioxide gas when it is combined with an acid. It is used in recipes that contain naturally acid foods, such as buttermilk, yogurt, or citrus juice. Baking powder is a combination of baking soda and a dry acid. It forms carbon dioxide when mixed with a liquid.

**Yeast**. Yeast is a microscopic plant that gives off gas as it grows. It reproduces quickly if it has warmth, food (such as sugar), and moisture. Yeast gives the baked product a distinctive flavor. It's the reason baked yeast bread smells and tastes so good.

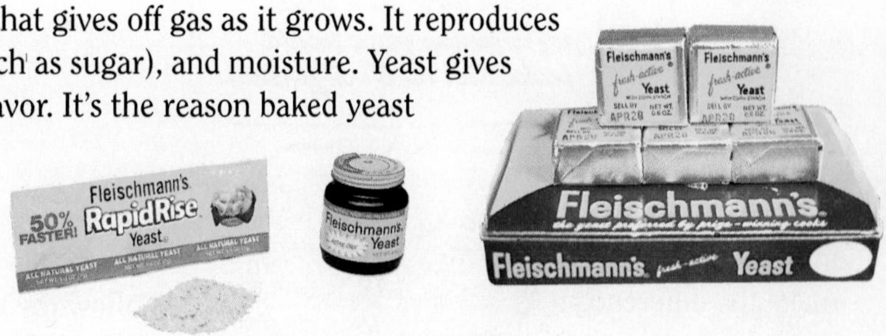


Leavening agents work together with gluten. As the batter or dough is mixed, the gluten strengthens to form an elastic mesh. The air or gas from the leavening agent forms tiny cells or pockets within the mesh. When the batter or dough is baked, heat causes the air or gas to expand. The gluten stretches and the product rises. As baking continues, the heat causes the proteins and starch in the flour to set (become firm). As they set, they give the product its final shape.

**The action of leavening agents, gluten, and heat combine to give baked goods their final structure. The tiny holes in bread are spaces left by bubbles of gas produced by yeast.**

# Successful Baking

The chemical reactions that take place during baking are sensitive. They depend on the ingredients and amounts used, the way they are mixed together, and the baking temperature and time. Baking success depends on accurately following the recipe.

## Follow the Recipe

**Use the exact ingredients called for.** Different types of flour, fats and oils, sweeteners, and other ingredients are available. Each type gives a different flavor and texture to the finished product. If you substitute one type for another, the results may not be what you expect.

What happened? All I did was use oil instead of shortening.

I never thought a little extra lemon juice would make that much difference!


**Measure accurately.** Even a few extra drops of an ingredient can make the difference between success and failure.

I just threw everything in the bowl and mixed it up real good.


**Follow the mixing directions in the recipe.** Don't take shortcuts.

**Use the correct type and size of pan.** If you use a pan that is too small, the mixture will flow over the side as it rises. If you use a pan that is too large, the product will be thin and may not brown on top.

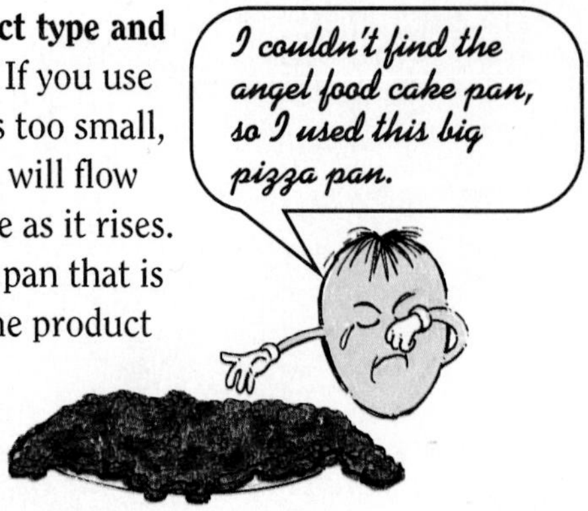

I couldn't find the angel food cake pan, so I used this big pizza pan.


**Use the correct oven temperature.** Too high a temperature causes overbrowning, poor volume, and a tough texture. Too low a temperature causes a pale color, soggy texture, uneven grain, and a sunken center.

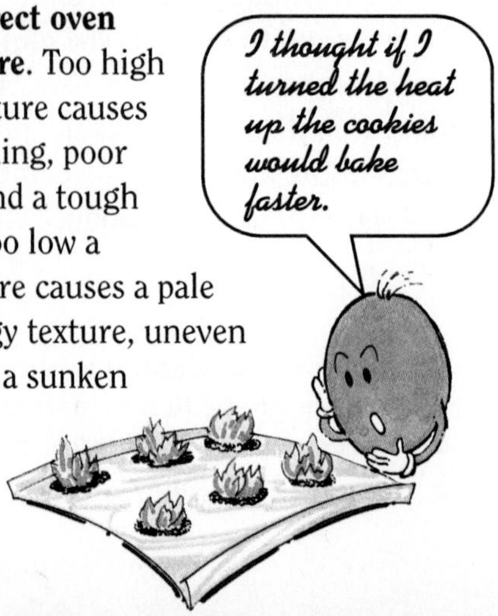

I thought if I turned the heat up the cookies would bake faster.

## Setting the Oven Temperature

The correct oven temperature may depend on the type of pan you use. Some pan materials retain more heat than others. Unless they state otherwise, recipes are usually based on using shiny metal pans. If you use dull metal pans, lower the oven temperature about 10°F (6°C). If you use glass pans, lower the oven temperature about 25°F (14°C).

For best results, preheat the oven. About 10 minutes before you are ready to put the pan in, turn the oven control to the desired temperature. Preheating ensures that the oven will be at the correct temperature. The mixture will start to bake right away and will rise properly.

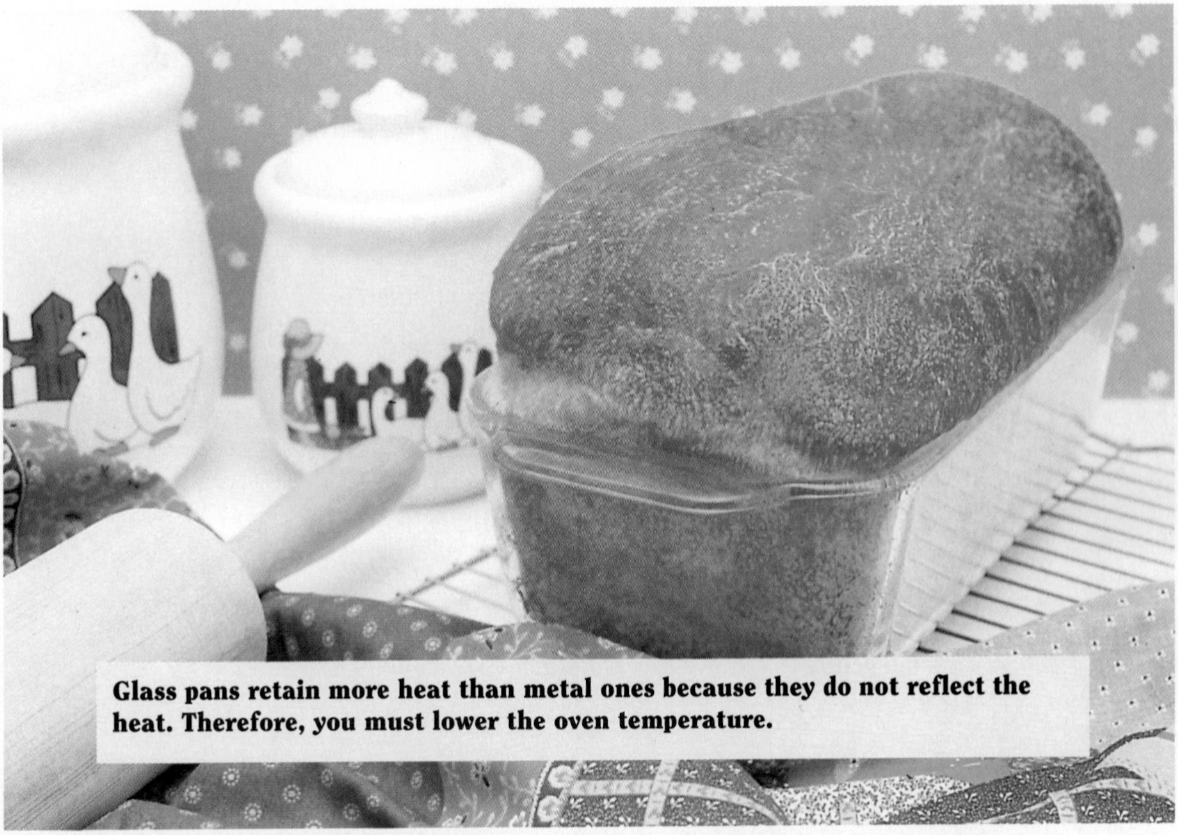

**Glass pans retain more heat than metal ones because they do not reflect the heat. Therefore, you must lower the oven temperature.**

## Preparing Pans for Baking

Pans must be properly prepared for baking. Otherwise the baked product may be difficult to remove. Follow the directions in the recipe. Some recipes call for greased pans, others for ungreased pans.

When greasing pans, use unsalted shortening or a cooking spray. The salt in butter or margarine could cause the crust to overbrown and stick to the pan.

Some recipes call for greased and floured pans. The flour makes the product easier to remove. It also absorbs the fat and keeps it from soaking into the crust.

**To grease and flour a pan . . .**

1. Using waxed paper or a paper towel, spread shortening in a thin, even layer over the bottom and sides of the pan. Be sure corners and the areas where the bottom and sides meet are well greased.

2. Sprinkle about 1 tablespoon (15 mL) all-purpose flour into the pan.

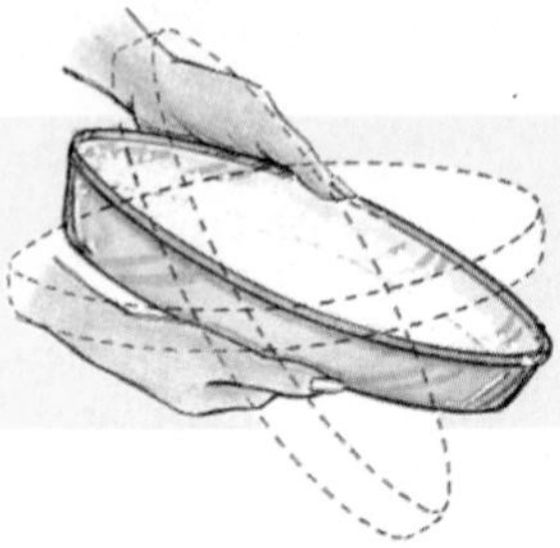

3. Hold the pan in both hands. Gently turn it at different angles to spread the flour evenly over the bottom and sides. Tap the pan gently to help spread the flour.

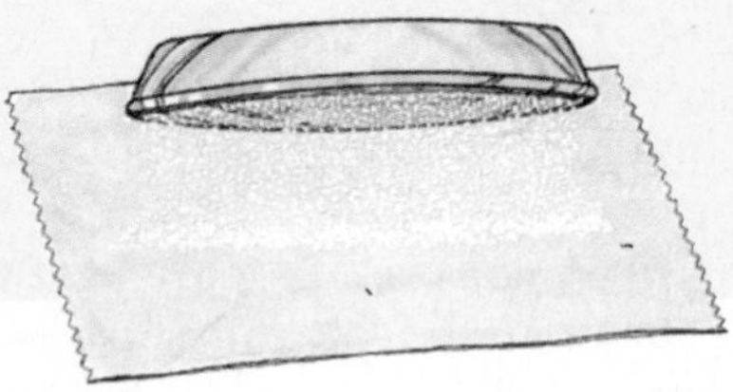

4. When the flour is spread evenly over the pan, hold the pan over a large piece of waxed paper. Turn the pan upside down and tap gently to remove excess flour.

## Placing Pans in the Oven

Before placing pans in the oven, wipe off the pan sides and bottom. Food particles on the pan will burn.

In the oven, air must be able to circulate freely. If you are baking only one pan, place it in the center of the oven.

If you are baking several pans at a time, use two racks. Stagger the pans, as shown on the next page, so that one is not directly above another. Leave at least 1 inch (2.5 cm) space between pans and between the pans and oven walls.

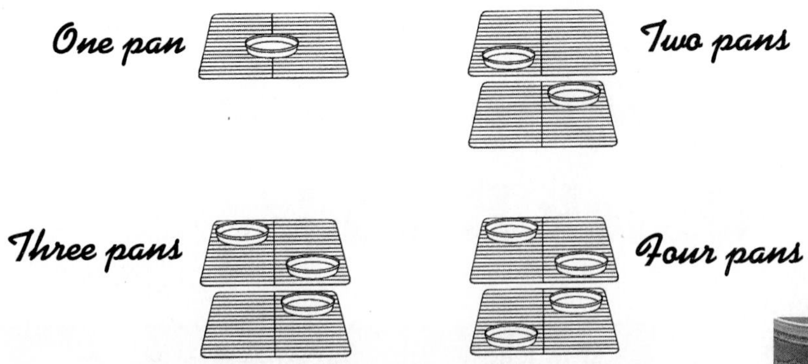


## Removing Baked Products from Pans

The recipe should tell you when to remove the baked product from the pan. Some baked products should be taken out of the pans as soon as they are removed from the oven. Others must first cool for a few minutes. After products are taken out of the pan, they are usually placed on a wire rack or other surface to cool completely.

## Chapter 38 Review

### Check the Facts

1. Identify one function of each of the following ingredients: flour, leavening agents, liquids, fats and oils, sweeteners, eggs, and flavorings.
2. What is the difference between batters and doughs? Give an example of each.
3. What is gluten? How is it affected by mixing?
4. What are the four main types of leavening agents? Briefly describe how each works.
5. What are five general guidelines to follow when preparing any recipe for baked products?
6. Why should you preheat the oven?
7. If you were baking three pans at one time, how would you place them in the oven? Why?

### Ideas in Action

1. Find a recipe for a baked product such as bread, muffins, cake, or cookies. Does it include all seven types of ingredients discussed in this chapter? Explain.
2. Choose one of the principles of baking explained in this chapter. Make a poster using words and pictures to illustrate that principle.
3. Discuss the following: "I've watched my grandmother bake for years. She never measures anything—she just scoops out the ingredients. Her things turn out okay. Why should I bother to measure accurately?"
4. Prepare a demonstration on the proper placement of pans in the oven.

CHAPTER 39

# Quick Breads

**OBJECTIVES**

**Discover . . .**

- how quick breads fit into a healthful eating plan.
- how to select and store baking ingredients and convenience forms.
- how to prepare quick breads.

Quick breads are "quick" because they do not take as long to prepare as breads made with yeast. (For more about yeast breads, see page 281.) Quick breads include pancakes, waffles, muffins, biscuits, and some loaf breads and coffee cakes. They usually use baking powder as a leavening. As soon as they are mixed, they are put in the oven to bake.

## Nutrition Notes

Quick breads provide complex carbohydrates along with some B vitamins and iron. If made with whole grain flour, they give you some fiber, too. Using milk in quick breads adds calcium. Nuts, fruits, and vegetables in the recipe add flavor and nutrients.

The amount of sugar, fat, cholesterol, and calories in quick breads depends on the recipe. For example, a muffin made with skim milk and vegetable oil will be lower in saturated fat and cholesterol than one made with whole milk and butter. A nutritious, low-fat quick bread makes a tasty snack or dessert. It can be a more healthful choice than cake, cookies, or pie.

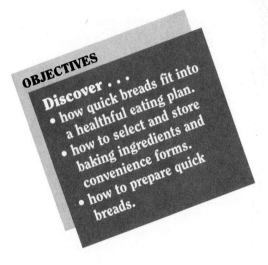

**Eating quick breads is a delicious way to add breads and grains to your daily food plan. What are some of your favorites?**

# Consumer Power

Quick breads can be made from scratch or with convenience products. In either case, use your consumer skills to select the products you want and store them properly.

## Buying and Storing Baking Ingredients

As you learned in Chapter 38, each ingredient in baked products has a specific job to do. Here is more information about buying and storing some of those ingredients.

### Flour

Many types of flour are available, such as:

- All-purpose flour—enriched white flour made from wheat.
- Whole wheat flour—made from the entire wheat kernel.
- Self-rising flour—has leavening and salt added.

**Check labels carefully to be sure you use the right type of flour.**

Use the type of flour called for in the recipe. If the recipe does not specify a type, use all-purpose flour.

Store flour in a cool, dry place. After opening the bag, put the flour in a tightly covered container.

### Sweeteners

Here are some of the most common sweeteners used in baking. All should be stored in tightly closed containers in a cool, dry place.

- Granulated sugar is white table sugar.
- Brown sugar is granulated sugar with molasses added. Dark brown sugar has a stronger flavor than light brown.
- Powdered, or confectioner's, sugar has a fine texture.
- Honey is a liquid sweetener with a distinct flavor. Use it only when the recipe calls for it.

You can also buy artificial sweeteners. Use these only in recipes that have been specifically developed for them.

**Sweeteners provide flavor and make baked products brown.**

### Leavening Agents

Most quick bread recipes call for either baking powder or baking soda. Check packages of baking powder for a "use by" date. After that date, the products will not give good results.

Store baking soda and baking powder in a cool, dry place. Baking powder must always be kept dry, so cover it tightly.

### Fats and Oils

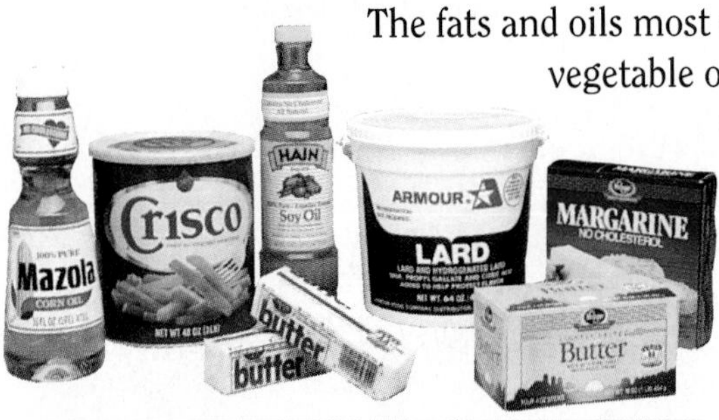

**Why can't all of these products be substituted for one another in baking?**

The fats and oils most commonly used in baking are butter, margarine, vegetable oil, lard, and shortening. Each one gives a slightly different flavor and texture. Lard is highest in saturated fat, while vegetable oil is lowest.

Solid fats and liquid fats cannot be used in place of one another in baking. The results will not be the same.

Butter, margarine, and lard should be stored in the refrigerator. Vegetable oil and shortening should be stored in a cool, dry place. If oil is refrigerated, it thickens and becomes cloudy.

## Convenience Forms

If you don't have time to prepare quick breads from scratch, you can use convenience forms. For example, refrigerated biscuits are ready to bake. With boxed mixes, you mix in the liquid and bake according to package directions.

You can also buy ready-made quick breads, fresh or frozen. However, preparing your own can be creative and satisfying. What are some other reasons for choosing to bake your own quick breads?

**Convenience quick bread products are available for the busy consumer.**

## Storing Quick Breads

Wrap prepared quick breads tightly and store at room temperature. Use within a few days. For longer storage, freeze them.

# Food Skills

Quick breads differ in the way they are mixed. The two most common mixing methods are called the muffin method and the biscuit method.

**Lumpy batter (above) will give you a muffin that is well-shaped and evenly textured (below, left).**

*Properly mixed muffin*

*Over-mixed muffin*

## Muffin Method

The muffin method of mixing is used for muffins, pancakes, waffles, cornbread, and loaves like banana bread. First the dry ingredients are mixed together in a bowl. Then the liquid ingredients are combined and added to the dry. The recipe for Streusel Top Muffins on page 283 gives specific directions.

The batter is mixed only long enough to moisten the dry ingredients. The batter should be lumpy, not smooth. Too much mixing can cause an irregular shape, a tough crust, and tunnels.

To check muffins and quick bread loaves for doneness:

- Check the appearance. The crust should be golden brown, slightly rough, and shiny.
- The sides of the quick bread should have pulled away slightly from the sides of the pan.
- When the top is tapped gently, it should feel firm.

Check the recipe to see whether the product should cool in the pan. Some quick breads are best when served warm. Before removing muffins and loaves from the pan, first loosen them by running a spatula around the product.

## Biscuit Method

Biscuits are mixed in a different way. The biscuit method of mixing gives biscuits their flaky texture.

1. Sift the dry ingredients together in a mixing bowl.

2. Add the shortening to the dry ingredients. Cut it in using a pastry blender, two table knives, or a fork. Stop when the mixture looks like large crumbs.

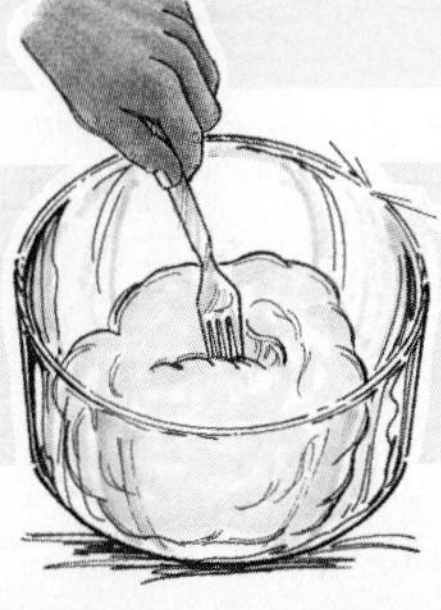

3. Add the milk. Mix with a fork to make a soft dough. The dough should come away from the sides of the bowl.

After biscuit dough is mixed, it is kneaded. To *knead* means to work or press the dough with your hands. Kneading helps gluten, the elastic structure of the dough, to form.

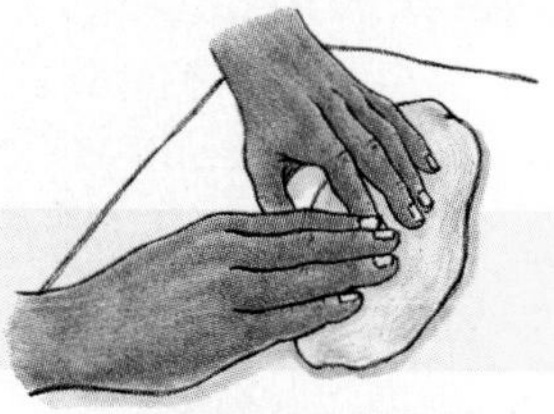

1. Turn the dough out onto a clean, lightly floured surface.

2. Gently fold the dough in half.

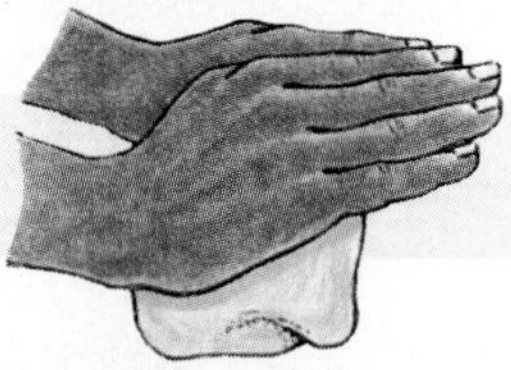

3. Push down on the dough with the heels of both hands.

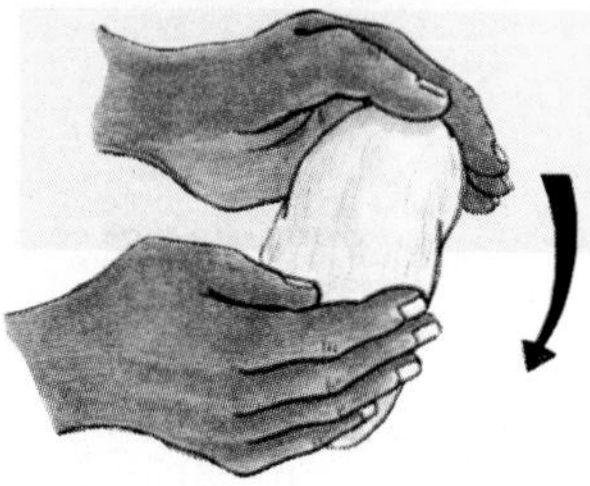

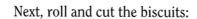

4. Give the dough a quarter turn. Continue to knead by repeating the folding and pushing process.

Biscuit dough should be kneaded for only about 30 seconds. If you knead too long, the biscuits will be tough.

Next, roll and cut the biscuits:

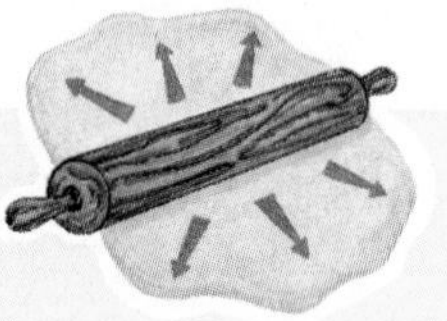

1. Roll the dough out into a circle ½ inch (1.3 cm) thick. Use light, gentle strokes.

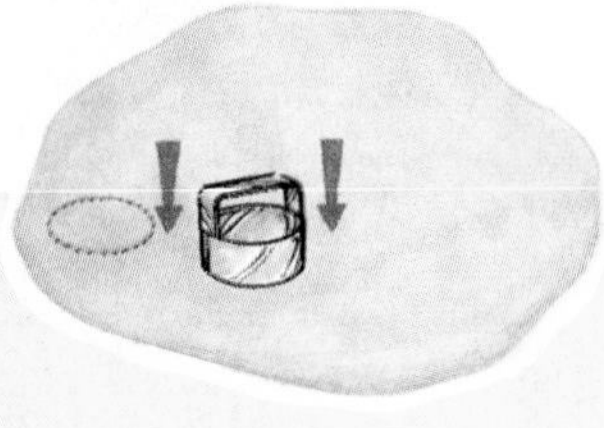

2. Cut the biscuits. Dip the cutter in flour first. Cut straight down so the biscuits will be even.

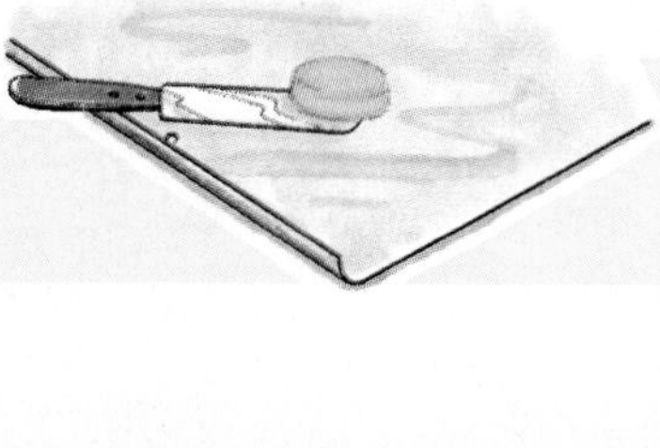

3. Use a spatula or turner to move the biscuits to the baking sheet. Leave about 1 inch (2.5 cm) space between the biscuits.

4. Push the leftover dough together. Do not knead it. Roll and cut more biscuits.

Bake the biscuits in a preheated oven for the time given in the recipe. To test them for doneness:

- ◆ Check the color. The biscuits should be lightly browned on top. The sides will be a lighter, creamy color.
- ◆ Check the shape and height. The sides should be straight. The biscuits should be doubled in size.

Serve the biscuits while still warm or let them cool on a wire rack before storing.

## Yeast Breads

Yeast breads are leavened with yeast. It gives the breads a much-liked flavor and fragrance.

Active dry yeast is the most common type. It is sold in a package and does not need refrigeration. You can buy regular or quick-acting. Use yeast by the date on the package.

Yeast breads take considerably longer to make than quick breads. After the dough is mixed, it is kneaded for several minutes. Then it is allowed to rise for about an hour to give the yeast time to grow. Next, the dough is shaped. After the dough rises again, it is baked until the crust is golden brown.

For homemade taste in less time, you can buy refrigerated or frozen yeast dough. Refrigerated dough is ready to bake. Frozen dough is usually placed in a greased pan to thaw and rise before baking.

**How do quick breads (left) differ in appearance from yeast breads (right)?**

## Microwave Hints

- If you don't have a microwave-safe muffin pan, arrange custard cups in a circle on a plate.
- To reheat quick breads, microwave uncovered at 100% power. One muffin takes about 10 seconds if at room temperature or 15 seconds if frozen. Do not overheat or the bread will be tough.

## Microwaving Quick Breads

You can make muffins and other quick breads in the microwave oven. Usually a round or ring-shaped pan is used. Follow the directions in a microwave cookbook.

Quick breads made in the microwave have a heavier and coarser texture. In addition, they do not brown. To make up for the lack of color, you can add a topping, such as chopped nuts, toasted coconut, or a sugar and cinnamon mixture. After microwaving biscuits, you can brush them with melted butter or margarine and broil in a conventional oven.

**When microwaving, fill muffin cups only half full.**

# Chapter 39 Review

### Check the Facts

1. Name two differences between quick breads and yeast breads.
2. Name at least three nutrients that can be found in quick breads.
3. Are all quick breads more healthful than cake or cookies? Explain.
4. Describe how to store flour, sweeteners, baking soda, baking powder, fats, and oils.
5. Identify three convenience forms of quick breads.
6. Name at least two signs that muffin batter has been overmixed.
7. Describe how to knead biscuit dough. What happens if you knead too long?
8. What are two ways to tell whether biscuits are done baking?
9. How does a microwaved muffin compare to a conventionally baked one?

### Ideas in Action

1. Discuss the advantages and disadvantages of using convenience quick bread products.
2. Ton Nguyen is new to the United States. In Ton's native country, muffins are not common. How would you describe to Ton what a muffin is like? Include appearance, doneness, and flavor in your description.
3. Form teams for a game of charades. Choose one member of your team to act out one of the steps in making biscuits. The rest of the team should try to guess what is being pantomimed. Take turns acting out different steps in biscuit making.
4. Develop a scorecard for evaluating muffins or biscuits. Include specific standards for how the product should look and taste.

# Recipe Focus

1. Read the recipe for "Streusel Top Muffins." Make a list of the equipment you would need.
2. This recipe is an example of the muffin method of mixing. How does the muffin method differ from the biscuit method?

## Streusel Top Muffins

| Customary | Ingredients | Metric |
|---|---|---|
| ⅓ cup | Brown sugar | 75 mL |
| 3 Tbsp. | All-purpose flour | 45 mL |
| 1 tsp. | Ground cinnamon | 5 mL |
| 1 Tbsp. | Melted butter or margarine | 15 mL |
| ¼ cup | Chopped nuts | 50 mL |
| 1¾ cup | Sifted, all-purpose flour | 425 mL |
| ¼ cup | Sugar | 50 mL |
| 2½ tsp. | Baking powder | 13 mL |
| ½ tsp. | Salt | 2 mL |
| 1 | Egg | 1 |
| ¾ cup | Skim milk | 175 mL |
| ⅓ cup | Butter or margarine, melted | 75 mL |

**Yield:** 10 to 12 muffins

### Conventional Directions

**Pan:** Muffin pan
**Temperature:** 400°F (200°C)

1. **Preheat** oven to 400°F (200°C).
2. **Grease** muffin cups.
3. **Combine** first five ingredients in a small bowl. Set aside for streusel topping.
4. **Combine** 1¾ cup (425 mL) sifted flour, sugar, baking powder, and salt in a large mixing bowl. Set aside.
5. **Beat** the egg in a small bowl.
6. **Add** milk and ⅓ cup (75 mL) melted butter or margarine to the beaten egg. Mix well.
7. **Make** a well in the center of the dry ingredients.
8. **Pour** the liquid mixture all at once into the center of the dry ingredients.
9. **Stir** until the dry ingredients are just moistened, about 15 strokes. Do not overmix. Batter will be lumpy.
10. **Spoon** batter into muffin cups until they are ⅔ full.
11. **Sprinkle** streusel topping mixture over each muffin.
12. **Bake** about 20 minutes or until a toothpick inserted in the center of a muffin comes out clean.

### Microwave Directions

**Pan:** Microwave-safe muffin pan
**Power Level:** 100%

1. **Line** muffin pan with paper liners.
2. **Follow steps 3-11** of conventional directions, then continue with step 12 below.
12. **Microwave** at 100% power. For 4 to 6 muffins, microwave 2 minutes or until no longer doughy and top of muffin springs back when touched.

**Nutrition Information**

**Per muffin (approximate): 195 calories, 4 g protein, 27 g carbohydrate, 8 g fat, 34 mg cholesterol, 229 mg sodium**

**Good source of: B vitamins**

CHAPTER 40

# Cookies, Cakes, and Pies

**OBJECTIVES**

**Discover . . .**
- how cookies, cakes, and pies fit into a healthful eating plan.
- convenience forms of cookies, cakes, and pies.
- how to prepare and store different kinds of cookies, cakes, and pies.

How many different kinds of cookies can you think of? What about cakes and pies? In all, there are hundreds of varieties. Many originated centuries ago. Every country and culture has its own special baked sweets, which are often a traditional part of celebrations. What are some of your favorites?

## Nutrition Notes

Cookies, cakes, and pies are delicious treats. Although they are high in calories, fat, and sugar, they can be part of a healthful eating plan when eaten in moderation. Most people enjoy cookies, cakes, and pies on special occasions or just now and then.

When you do eat these treats, choose wisely. Look for sweets with some nutritious ingredients. Try carrot or oatmeal cookies, banana or date cake, and pumpkin or strawberry pie.

Some cookies, including fig bars and gingersnaps, are low in fat. Angel food cake is too. You can also save fat and calories by choosing pies with only one crust instead of two.

## Consumer Power

Cookies, cakes, and pies can be made from the same basic ingredients as other baked goods. Review the buying and storing information on pages 277-278. Remember to use the specific type of product called for in the recipe. For example, some cake recipes require cake flour.

**Baked treats can be artistic creations.**

## Buying and Storing Convenience Forms

There are many products to help you prepare cookies, cakes, and pies more quickly and easily.

- Packaged cookie and cake mixes are usually dry. They require the addition of liquids and often other ingredients, such as oil or eggs.
- Refrigerated cookie dough is ready for baking.
- Convenience pie crusts can be found in several forms: packaged mixes, dough sticks, ready-to-use rolled pastry, and ready-to-fill frozen pastry shells.
- Pie fillings may be canned or made from packaged mixes.

**Products such as these can save time in baking. How else might using these products differ from scratch baking?**

When buying, read the labels on these products carefully. Are low-fat varieties available? How do calories and nutrition compare? If you have time, could you bake from scratch and save money?

## Storing Cookies, Cakes, and Pies

Check the labels of convenience products for storage instructions. Proper storage will also let home-baked treats keep their quality longer.

Store crisp cookies and soft cookies in separate containers. For crisp cookies, use a loose-fitting cover. Soft cookies should have a tight-fitting cover to keep them moist.

Cakes with cream fillings are perishable. Store them in the refrigerator. Other cakes can be stored in tightly closed containers at room temperature. Cakes can be frozen for longer storage.

Refrigerate custard and cream pies immediately after baking. If they stand at room temperature, harmful bacteria can grow rapidly. Store fruit pies in the refrigerator and reheat them to serve warm.

**For crisp cookies, use a container with a loose-fitting cover. Soft cookies should be in a tightly sealed container.**

# Food Skills

Baking cookies, cakes, and pies lets you be creative. Many people gain satisfaction from baking treats for special occasions and to give as gifts.

## Cookies

Most cookies are a variation of one of six basic types. The main difference in these types is the way they are shaped.

**Bar cookies** are baked in a square or rectangular pan, just like a cake. After baking, the cookies are cut into bars or squares. Brownies are a popular bar cookie.

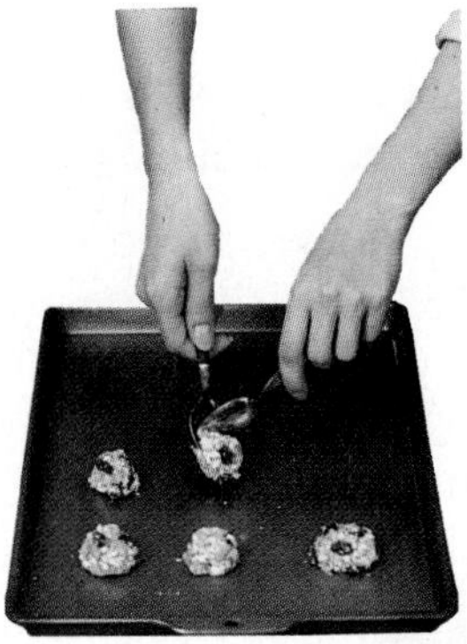

**Drop cookies** are made by dropping teaspoonfuls of batter onto a baking sheet. Chocolate chip cookies are usually made by this method.

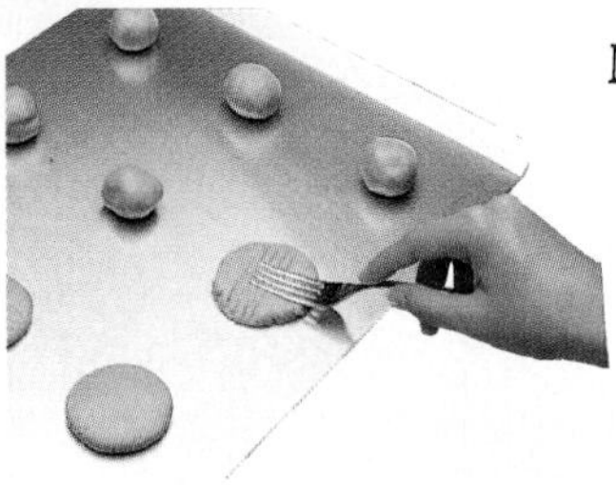

**Molded cookies** are made from a stiff dough and shaped by hand. One common method is to roll the dough into balls about the size of walnuts. The balls are spaced on a baking sheet and flattened with a fork or the bottom of a glass. Some peanut butter cookies are molded this way.

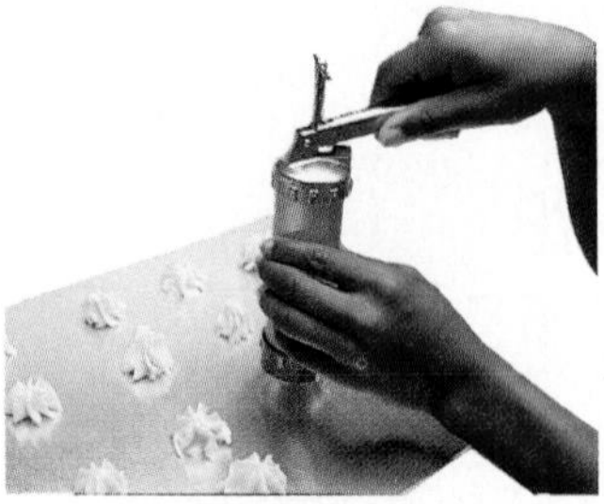

**Pressed cookies** are made by pushing the dough through a cookie press onto a baking sheet. The cookie press comes with several design plates to give the cookies different shapes. The dough must be stiff enough to keep the shape of the design. Spritz cookies are an example.

**Rolled cookies** are made by rolling out a stiff dough to the thickness specified in the recipe. Then cookie cutters are used to cut shapes. Sometimes the cookies are decorated with colored sugar or frosting.

**Refrigerator cookies** are sliced from a long roll of chilled dough and baked on a cookie sheet.

## Tips for Making Cookies

Cookies should be well shaped and delicately browned with a pleasing flavor and texture. Here are some tips for good-looking, good-tasting cookies.

Sometimes dough sticks to the fork, rolling pin, or cookie cutters. Try dipping utensils in flour or sprinkling some on the rolling pin. Use just a little flour. Too much will make the cookies tough and dry.

Make all cookies in a batch the same shape and thickness. If some are thin and some thick, the thin ones will be done before the thick ones.

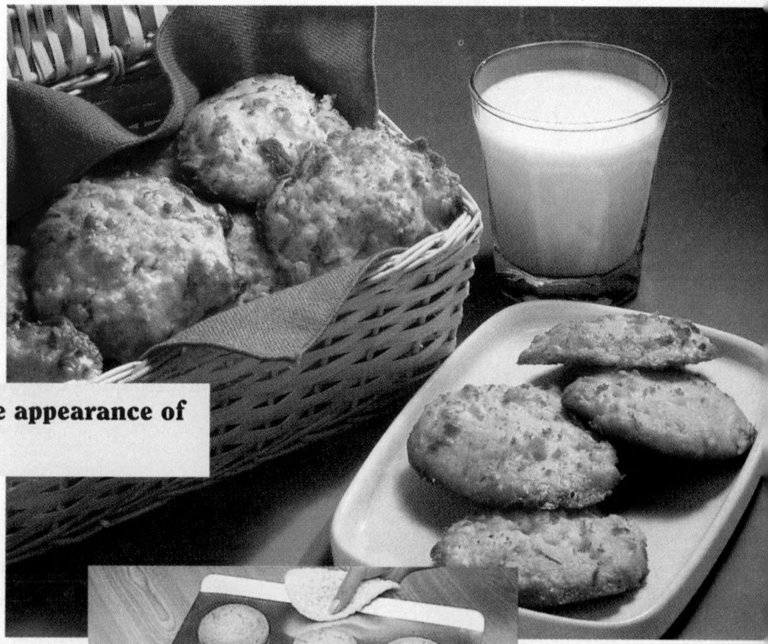

**How would you rate the appearance of these cookies?**

Check the recipe for how to space cookies on the sheet. Some types of cookies spread as they bake.

Prepare the pan according to recipe directions. Allow hot cookie sheets to cool before using them again. If you put cookie dough on a hot baking sheet, the dough will melt and spread. If you have two cookie sheets, one can cool while the other is in the oven.

An extra minute or two of heat can overbrown cookies. Watch them carefully. Test bar and drop cookies for doneness by pressing lightly with your finger. The imprint of your finger should show slightly.

Follow recipe directions for cooling cookies. Some can cool in the pan. Others are removed while hot and cooled on a wire rack. Use a wide spatula or turner.

**Warm cookies are fragile, so handle them gently.**

# Cakes

There are two basic types of cakes:

- *Shortened cakes* contain fat, such as shortening, margarine, or oil. For leavening, they use baking powder or baking soda. Shortened cakes can be baked in round, square, rectangular, or specially shaped pans. Two or more layers may be put together with frosting.

- *Unshortened cakes* do not include fat or oil. Angel food cake and sponge cake are examples. For leavening, they use the air beaten into egg whites. Most unshortened cakes are baked in a tube pan—a deep, round pan with a tube in the center. The tube helps the heat get to the center quickly so the cake bakes evenly. The pan is left ungreased so the cake can cling to the sides. That helps it rise.

## Tips for Baking Cakes

A properly made cake should have a smooth, slightly rounded top. The inside should be finely textured without tunnels or air bubbles. When you taste it, the cake should be moist, tender, and pleasantly flavored.

Proper mixing is one key to a successful cake. The mixing method will vary depending on the type of cake and the recipe. Follow directions carefully. Review the other baking principles discussed in Chapter 38.

**If the top springs back, the cake is done.**

To test a cake for doneness, check the top. It should be evenly browned. When you tap the top gently, it should spring back. Look at the area where the top meets the sides of the pan. A shortened cake should be pulled away from the sides of the pan. An unshortened cake will continue to cling to the sides of the pan.

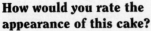

**How would you rate the appearance of this cake?**

## After Baking

Unshortened cakes, such as angel food cakes, are cooled in the pan. The pan is turned upside down so the cake won't fall.

**Most tube pans rest on metal legs when upside down. You can also slip the tube over the neck of an empty bottle.**

Shortened cakes are removed from the pan after baking and cooled on a wire rack.

**To remove a cake from the pan . . .**

1. Run a spatula around the sides of the pan between the cake and the pan.

2. Place a wire rack over the top of the cake. Hold the cake and rack securely with pot holders.

3. Turn the cake and rack upside down. Place the wire rack on a level surface, such as a table or counter.

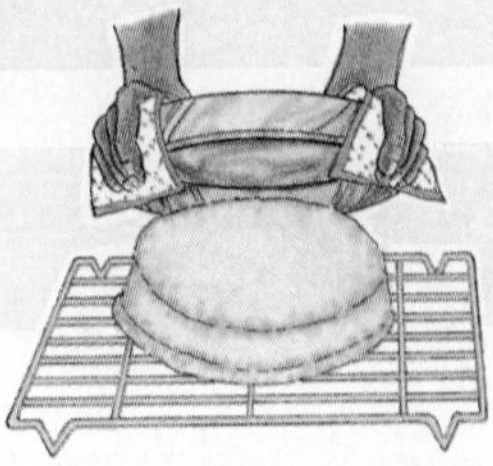

4. Lift off the cake pan. It should come off easily.

5. The cake is now upside down. Quickly place another wire rack on the cake. Grasp both wire racks with both hands and turn them so the cake layer is right side up.

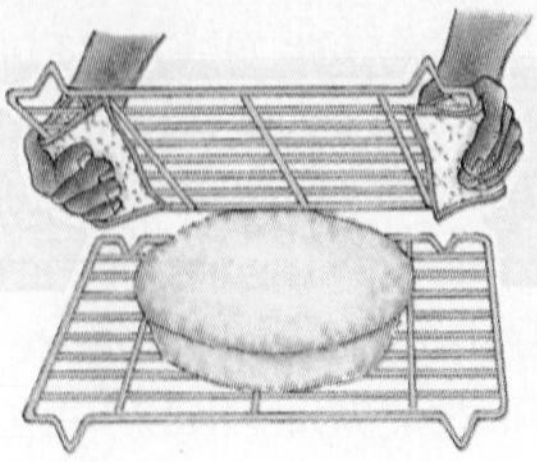

6. Remove the top wire rack. Allow the cake to cool on the bottom wire rack.

Once the cake has completely cooled, it can be decorated with frosting or powdered sugar. You can also top cake with fresh fruit.

**Special, decorated cakes are favorites for birthdays and weddings.**

# Pies

A pie is a combination of a crust and a flavorful filling.

- A two-crust pie has a bottom and top crust with a filling in between. Usually a fruit filling, such as apple, is used.
- A one-crust pie has a bottom crust only. Sometimes the crust is baked first. Then a ready-to-eat filling, such as chocolate pudding, is poured into the baked crust. One-crust pies often have toppings such as whipped cream or meringue (a mixture of sugar and stiffly beaten egg whites).
- A deep-dish pie is a fruit pie with only a top crust. Fruit filling is placed in a baking dish, covered with a crust, and baked. The pie is often served hot.

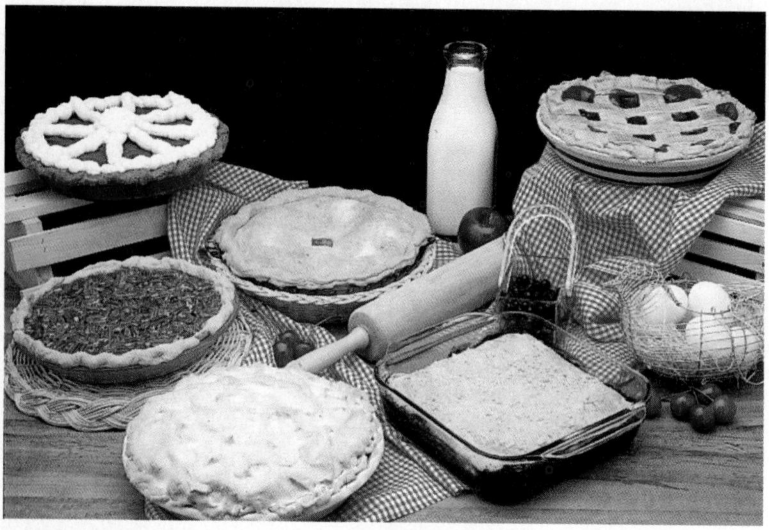

**Pies may have one crust or two and a variety of fillings. Can you identify the basic types shown?**

No matter what type of pie you're making, it should have an even, tender crust that is nicely browned. The crust should have a delicate, crisp texture. Pastry crusts should be flaky. The filling should be thick, not sticky. The whole pie should have a rich, delicate flavor.

## Crusts

The most common pie crust is made from pastry. Pastry is a mixture of flour, fat, cold water, and salt. When mixed properly, the pastry forms flaky layers as it bakes.

If you are making a one-crust pie that doesn't have to be baked, you can use a crumb crust. It can be made from finely crushed graham crackers, gingersnaps, vanilla wafers, or chocolate cookies. The crumbs are mixed with melted butter or margarine and sugar. The mixture is pressed into a pie pan, baked, and cooled. Then the filling is added. You can also buy a ready-to-bake crumb crust.

**To make a pastry crust, roll the dough out into a circular shape. Then gently place it in the pie pan.**

## Fillings

Pie fillings can be made from scratch or prepared from convenience products.

- Fruit is the most popular filling for pie. You can use fresh, frozen, or canned fruit. Follow recipe directions for sweetening and thickening. Canned fruit pie filling is ready to use.
- Cream pies have a pudding-type filling. The mixture is poured into a baked pie shell. Packaged mixes for puddings and pie fillings sometimes have to be cooked first. Others are instant mixes.
- The filling in custard pies contains eggs and milk. They are baked with the crust.
- Chiffon pies are made with gelatin and flavored with fruit. Beaten egg whites make the pie lighter.

**Making homemade pie goes more quickly with the help of a friend or family member. One person can make the crust while the other prepares the filling.**

# Microwave Methods

Some types of cookies, cakes, and pies can be prepared in the microwave oven. Remember that microwaving differs from conventional baking. Recipes developed for microwave use should give good results if you follow directions carefully.

Bar cookies and shortened cakes adapt well to microwaving. Some can be mixed and microwaved in the same dish. For best results, use a microwave-safe round pan or ring mold. If you use a pan with corners, the batter in the corners will cook faster. Those parts may get hard and dry.

To microwave a one-crust pie, precook the crust before adding the filling. Otherwise, the crust will not be done. Two-crust pies should be baked in a conventional oven.

**Microwave Hints**

- Microwave cookies until they are set. When done, they look dry.
- For cakes and pies, use the tests for doneness given in the recipe. Standing time may be needed to complete the cooking.

Microwaved products will not brown. To make up for the lack of browning, you might choose recipes that are a dark color, such as chocolate cookies or spice cake. You can also top foods with chopped nuts, frosting, or a sprinkling of cinnamon and sugar. Try adding yellow food coloring to the water when mixing pie crust. You can also microwave the crust, then broil in a conventional oven until lightly browned.

**Toppings can help make microwaved cakes look more like conventionally baked ones.**

# Chapter 40 Review

## Check the Facts

1. Give three suggestions for fitting cookies, cakes, and pies into a healthful eating plan.
2. Name at least three convenience products that can be used in making baked treats.
3. How should pies and cream-filled cakes be stored? Why?
4. What are the six basic types of cookies?
5. Name three guidelines to follow in placing cookies on the baking sheet.
6. Identify three differences between shortened and unshortened cakes.
7. What are two ways to test a cake for doneness?
8. What ingredients are used in pastry pie crust?
9. Name two ways to add color to microwaved cookies, cakes, or pies.

## Ideas in Action

1. Brainstorm ways to make cookies, cakes, and pies more nutritious.
2. Debate the use of cookies, cakes, and pies as a regular part of your food plan. What are the pros and cons? What are some ways to compromise on this issue?
3. In a cookbook, find two recipes for shortened cakes and two for unshortened cakes. Compare ingredients, mixing methods, and baking instructions. What conclusions can you draw?
4. Demonstrate how to remove a cake layer from the pan. You may want to use a folded towel in the pan in place of the cake.
5. Using cookbooks or other sources, find examples of the different kinds of cookies and pies mentioned in this chapter.

# Recipe Focus

1. Read the recipe for "Carrot Drops." If you wanted to make eight dozen cookies, how much would you need of each ingredient?
2. How would you test these cookies for doneness?

## Carrot Drops

| Customary | Ingredients | Metric |
|---|---|---|
| 2 cups | Sifted, all-purpose flour | 500 mL |
| 2 tsp. | Baking powder | 10 mL |
| ¾ cup | Butter or margarine | 175 mL |
| ¾ cup | Sugar | 175 mL |
| 1 | Egg | 1 |
| 7½ oz. jar | Junior baby food carrots* | 215-g jar |
| ¾ cup | Chopped walnuts | 175 mL |
| 1 Tbsp. | Grated orange rind | 15 mL |
| 1 Tbsp. | Orange juice | 15 mL |
| 1 tsp. | Vanilla | 5 mL |

*You may substitute 1 cup (250 mL) cooked, mashed carrots.

**Yield:** About 4 dozen cookies

### Directions

**Pan:** Cookie sheets

**Temperature:** 350°F (180°C)

1. **Preheat** oven to 350°F (180°C).
2. **Sift** together flour and baking powder. Set aside.
3. **Cream** butter or margarine and sugar together in a large bowl.
4. **Add** the egg to creamed mixture and beat until light and fluffy.
5. **Add** carrots, walnuts, orange rind, orange juice, and vanilla to creamed mixture. Mix well.
6. **Blend** in dry ingredients.
7. **Drop** by teaspoonfuls onto ungreased cookie sheets. Space about 2 in. (5 cm) apart.
8. **Bake** in preheated oven for 13 to 15 minutes.
9. **Remove** cookies from cookie sheet and cool on wire rack.
10. **Frost** with Orange Glaze when cool.

## Orange Glaze

| Customary | Ingredients | Metric |
|---|---|---|
| 1 cup | Confectioner's sugar | 250 mL |
| 2 Tbsp. | Orange juice | 30 mL |

### Directions

1. **Combine** sugar and orange juice.
2. **Use** as glaze on cookies.

**Nutrition Information**

**Per cookie (approximate): 70 calories, 1 g protein, 8 g carbohydrate, 4 g fat, 12 mg cholesterol, 50 mg sodium**

**Good source of: vitamin A**

# Glossary

## A

**aerobic** (uh-ROE-bik). Helping the body use and take in more oxygen than it normally does. Used to describe certain types of exercise, such as running. (Ch. 4)

**al dente** (ahl-DEHN-tay). Italian phrase meaning "to the tooth." Used to describe pasta that is tender but still firm in the center. (Ch. 25)

**amino acids.** Chemical "building blocks" that combine to make different kinds of *protein*. (Ch. 5)

## B

**bacteria** (bak-TEER-ee-uh). Tiny living things that can be seen only with a microscope. Some are helpful, while others are harmful. (Ch. 17)

**base.** The foundation of a salad. (Ch. 33)

**baste.** To brush or pour liquid over food as it cooks. (Ch. 11)

**beat.** To stir with a quick, over-and-over motion. (Ch. 11)

**body.** Main part of a salad. (Ch. 33)

**boil.** To heat a liquid until bubbles rise to the surface and break; or to cook food in boiling liquid. (Ch. 11)

**bouillon** (boo-YOHN). Clear, flavorful *broth*. (Ch. 34)

**braising.** Browning food in a small amount of hot fat, then cooking it slowly in *moist heat*. (Ch. 14)

**bran.** The outer covering of a grain kernel. (Ch. 25)

**broth.** The liquid in soup. (Ch. 34)

## C

**caffeine** (kaff-EEN). A chemical, often found in coffee, tea, and soft drinks, that can cause nervousness and other problems. (Ch. 37)

**carbohydrates.** A type of *nutrient* that is your body's main source of energy. Carbohydrates include starches and sugars and are found mainly in plant foods. (Ch. 5)

**career.** The work you choose to do for a long period or in a specific field. (Ch. 3)

**casserole.** A mixture of foods baked together; also, the type of dish the food mixture is baked in. (Ch. 10, Ch. 35)

**cholesterol.** Fat-like substance that helps the body carry out its many processes. Having too much cholesterol in the blood is believed to raise the risk of heart disease. (Ch. 5)

**chop.** To cut food into small, irregular pieces. (Ch. 11)

**chowder.** Thick soup made with vegetables, fish, or seafood. (Ch. 34)

**colander.** A bowl-shaped utensil with many small holes; used to drain liquid from foods. (Ch. 10)

**complete proteins.** *Proteins* that contain all the essential *amino acids* in the right amounts. (Ch. 5)

**complex carbohydrates.** One of two types of *carbohydrates*. Also known as starches. (Ch. 5)

**convection oven.** Oven in which fans circulate heated air at high speed. Cooks food faster than a *conventional oven*. (Ch. 9)

**conventional oven.** Oven in which heated air flows naturally around the food and cooks it. (Ch. 9)

**cooking power.** The amount of electricity a *microwave oven* uses to create *microwaves*. Measured in watts. (Ch. 15)

**cream.** To combine shortening and sugar until soft, smooth, and creamy. (Ch. 11)

**cross-contamination.** Letting harmful *bacteria* spread from raw foods to other foods. (Ch. 17)

**cube.** To cut food into same-size pieces about ½ inch (13 mm) or more on each side. (Ch. 11)

**curd.** The solid part of milk after it has been thickened. Used to make cheese. (Ch. 24)

**curdle.** To become separated into many small lumps and a watery liquid. Milk may curdle if improperly cooked. (Ch. 23)

**cured.** Treated with *ingredients* that slow spoilage and add a distinctive flavor. (Ch. 29)

**customary system.** Most commonly used system of measurement in the United States. (Ch. 12)

**cut in.** To mix shortening and flour using a pastry blender or two knives and a cutting motion. (Ch. 11)

**cut.** Slice or portion of meat from a specific part of an animal. (Ch. 31)

## D

**dice.** To cut food into same-size pieces about ¼ inch (6 mm) on each side. (Ch. 11)

**disposables.** Products that are used once or a few times and then thrown away. (Ch. 19)

**dovetailing.** Working ahead on some steps in a *recipe* while others are still going on. For example, while waiting for water to boil, you can be measuring foods. (Ch. 18)

**dry heat methods.** Methods used to cook foods without adding any liquid or fat. They include broiling, panbroiling, and baking or roasting. (Ch. 14)

## E

**endosperm.** The middle portion of a grain kernel, beneath the outer *bran* layers and surrounding the *germ*, or inner portion. Made up mostly of *carbohydrates* and *proteins*. (Ch. 25)

**enriched.** A term used to describe foods with added *nutrients*. (Ch. 8)

**entry-level job.** A job which does not require experience or a college degree. (Ch. 3)

**equivalent.** Equal in value; the same. For example, 12 inches is equivalent to one foot. (Ch. 12)

**evaluate.** To judge how well you reached your goal. (Ch. 2)

## F

**fiber.** A substance, found in some foods, that is an important part of a healthy diet. Consists of plant materials that do not break down completely during digestion and are not absorbed by the body. (Ch. 5)

**fillets** (fill-AYS). Sides of fish cut away from the ribs and backbone. (Ch. 30)

**flammable.** Burns easily. (Ch. 16)

**flatware.** Dinner knives, forks, and spoons. (Ch. 21)

**fold in.** To combine two foods, such as beaten egg whites and batter, with a very gentle motion. (Ch. 11)

**food guides.** Simple guidelines to help you make healthy food choices. Two examples are the Dietary Guidelines for Americans and the Daily Food Guide. (Ch. 6)

**fortified.** A term used to describe foods with added *nutrients*. (Ch. 8)

**fruit punch**. A mixture of fruit juices. (Ch. 37)

## G - H

**garnish.** To decorate a food or dish with a small, colorful food, such as parsley or a lemon slice. (Ch. 11)

**generic.** Term used to describe plain label products that are less expensive than brand name products. (Ch. 8)

**germ.** The innermost portion of a grain kernel; the sprouting section from which a new plant can grow. (Ch. 25)

**gluten.** An elastic substance formed by the *protein* in flour. (Ch. 38)

**grate.** To rub food on a grater to make very fine particles. (Ch. 11)

**homogenized** (huh-MAH-jen-ized). Term that describes milk processed so that the cream does not separate. Fat is broken into tiny drops and mixed permanently with the milk. (Ch. 23)

**hydrogenated oil** (hy-DRAH-juh-nay-ted). Oil that has been turned into a more solid fat. In the process, it becomes more *saturated*. (Ch. 5)

## I - J - K

**impulse buying.** Buying an item you don't need just because it seems appealing at the moment. (Ch. 8)

**incomplete proteins.** *Proteins* that lack one or more of the essential *amino acids*. Plant proteins are incomplete. (Ch. 5)

**ingredients.** Foods used in a *recipe*; also, substances that make up a product you buy. (Ch. 8, Ch. 11)

**knead.** To work or press dough with your hands. (Ch. 39)

## L

**leavening agent.** Substance that helps a baked product rise. May be baking powder, baking soda, yeast, trapped air, or steam. (Ch. 38)

**legumes** (leh-GYOUMZ). Seeds that grow in a pod. Dry beans and dry peas are legumes. (Ch. 28)

**long-term goal.** Something you plan to accomplish in the far future. It may be made up of several *short-term goals*. (Ch. 1)

## M

**management.** Using *resources* wisely to meet goals. (Ch. 2)

**marbling.** Flecks of fat in meat. (Ch. 31)

**marinade.** Liquid in which meat may be soaked before cooking to add flavor and tenderness. Usually a mixture of an acid food, such as citrus juice or vinegar, and seasonings. (Ch. 31)

**meal management.** Using basic *management* skills, such as planning, making decisions, and using time wisely, to help you prepare good meals. (Ch. 20)

**meal pattern.** The pattern of how many meals and snacks you eat throughout the day and when you eat them. (Ch. 7)

**menu.** List of foods that you plan to serve at a meal. (Ch. 20)

**meringue** (mur-ANG). Topping for some desserts which is made by beating egg whites and sugar until stiff peaks form. (Ch. 32)

**metric system.** Standard system of measurement in most of the world. (Ch. 12)

**microwave oven.** Oven in which tiny waves of energy cause molecules in the food to vibrate against each other. This results in friction, which produces the heat that cooks the food. (Ch. 9)

**microwaves.** Tiny waves of energy produced by a *microwave oven*. (Ch. 15)

**mince.** To *chop* food until the pieces are as small as possible. (Ch. 11)

**moist heat methods.** Methods for cooking foods using a hot liquid, steam, or a combination of both. (Ch. 14)

**mulled.** Term describing a beverage, such as fruit juice or punch, that is spiced and served hot. (Ch. 37)

## N - O

**natural resources.** Materials that are provided by nature, such as air, fuel, water, and land. (Ch. 2)

**nutrient density.** A way of relating the amount of energy, or calories, supplied by a food with the *nutrients* it provides. Foods with low nutrient density are relatively high in calories, but limited in important nutrients. Foods with high nutrient density are good sources of nutrients. (Ch. 6)

**nutrients.** Chemicals in food that the body needs to work properly. (Ch. 4)

**omelet** (AHM-let). A dish made by cooking beaten eggs without stirring. Usually folded in half with a filling, such as chopped cooked vegetables. (Ch. 32)

**opaque** (oh-PAKE). Not clear; solid color that you can't see through. Fish turns opaque as it cooks. (Ch. 30)

## P - Q

**pare.** To cut a very thin layer of peel from fruits or vegetables. (Ch. 11)

**pasta.** General term for spaghetti, macaroni, noodles, and similar products. Usually made from flour and water. (Ch. 25)

**pasteurized** (PASS-tyoor-ized). Term describing milk that has been heat treated to kill harmful *bacteria*. (Ch. 23)

**perishable.** Spoils easily. Perishable foods, such as milk, are stored in the refrigerator. (Ch. 17)

**pesticide.** A poison which kills insects and other pests. (Ch. 16)

**place setting.** The arrangement of tableware for each individual who will be served a meal. (Ch. 21)

**poison control center.** A place you can call on the telephone that has a staff specially trained to deal with poison emergencies. (Ch. 16)

**poultry.** Birds raised for food, such as chickens and turkeys. (Ch. 29)

**pre-preparation.** Getting food or equipment ready to use in a *recipe.* (Ch. 18)

**processing.** Steps that are taken to prepare and package food for sale. (Ch. 8)

**proteins.** A type of *nutrient* that the body uses to build new cells and repair injured ones. Proteins are made up of *amino acids*. (Ch. 5)

**puree** (pure-RAY or pure-EE). To put food through a blender, food processor, food mill, or strainer so that it becomes a smooth, thick mass. (Ch. 11)

## R

**recipe.** A guide to help you prepare a certain food. (Ch. 11)

**reconstitute.** To replace water that has been removed from a food. (Ch. 23)

**resource.** Something you can use to help meet your goals. (Ch. 2)

**retail cuts.** The *cuts* of meat that you can buy in the store; come from dividing *wholesale cuts* into smaller pieces. (Ch. 31)

**ripe.** Having developed full flavor and sweetness; ready to eat. (Ch. 26)

## S

**salmonella** (sal-muh-NELL-uh). A type of food poisoning that can make you so sick you may have to go to the hospital. Raw poultry, raw eggs, and other foods may carry salmonella. (Ch. 17)

**sanitation.** Keeping harmful *bacteria* down to as small a number as possible. (Ch. 17)

**saturated fats.** Fats that tend to raise the amount of *cholesterol* in the blood. Usually solid at room temperature. Found in all animal foods and in the tropical oils (coconut, palm, and palm kernel). (Ch. 5)

**sautéing** (saw-TAY-ing). Method used to precook foods such as onions, mushrooms, and green peppers before they are used in a *recipe*. The chopped or sliced foods are quickly panfried until they soften. (Ch. 14)

**scorch.** To turn brown from overheating; burn. (Ch. 23)

**season.** A certain time of year when the supply of a particular fruit or vegetable is greatest, quality is highest, and prices are generally lowest. (Ch. 26)

**self-confidence.** Your belief in your ability to succeed. (Ch. 1)

**short-term goal.** A task that can be accomplished in the near future. It may help you reach a *long-term goal*. (Ch. 1)

**shortened cakes.** Cakes that contain fat, such as shortening, margarine, or oil. (Ch. 40)

**shucked.** With the shell removed. Some shellfish, such as clams, can be bought already shucked. (Ch. 30)

**sift.** To put a dry *ingredient*, such as flour, through a fine sieve or sifter in order to separate the particles. (Ch. 13)

**simmer.** To heat a liquid just until bubbles form slowly, but do not reach the surface; or to cook food in simmering liquid. (Ch. 11)

**simple carbohydrates.** One of two types of *carbohydrates*. Also known as sugars. (Ch. 5)

**spread.** A seasoned mixture of meat, poultry, fish, beans, or cheese. Can be spread on another food, such as crackers. (Ch. 36)

**standing time.** The short period of time that food is allowed to stand after microwaving. Standing time allows the food to finish cooking and heat to penetrate all areas of the food. (Ch. 15)

**stemware.** Beverage glasses that have a stem between the base and the bowl. (Ch. 21)

**stir-frying.** A method of frying food quickly in a small amount of oil while stirring constantly. (Ch. 14)

**stock.** Flavorful *broth*, usually made from bony pieces of meat or poultry combined with seasonings and cooked slowly in water. Used as a base for soup. (Ch. 34)

**stress.** Emotional and physical tension caused by changes in your life and the way you react to them. (Ch. 4)

**surimi.** Product made from chopped fish, flavoring, and seasoning; used to make imitation shellfish. (Ch. 30)

## T

**tender-crisp.** Tender but still firm; used to describe properly cooked vegetables. (Ch. 27)

**tofu** (TOE-foo). A custard-like product made from soybeans. It is very high in *protein* and has a mild flavor. (Ch. 28)

**translucent.** Semi-clear. Raw fish is translucent. (Ch. 30)

**tumblers.** Beverage glasses without stems. (Ch. 21)

## U - V

**UHT (ultra-high temperature).** Term for milk that has been processed using extra-high heat to kill all *bacteria*. (Ch. 23)

**unit price.** Cost per ounce, pound, item, or other unit of measure. (Ch. 8)

**unsaturated fats.** Fats that tend to help lower the amount of *cholesterol* in the blood. Usually liquid at room temperature. Found mainly in vegetable oils, except the tropical oils (coconut, palm, and palm kernel). (Ch. 5)

**unshortened cakes.** Cakes that do not contain fat or oil. (Ch. 40)

**vacuum bottle.** Insulated bottle that keeps foods at their original temperature. (Ch. 22)

## W

**wellness.** Physical, emotional, and mental good health. (Ch. 4)

**whey.** The thin, watery liquid that is separated from the curd after milk has been thickened. (Ch. 24)

**whip.** To add air and increase volume by beating food rapidly. (Ch. 11)

**whole-grain products.** Products in which all three parts of the grain kernel are used. Examples include brown rice, oatmeal, and whole-wheat bread. (Ch. 25)

**wholesale cuts.** Large sections of a meat animal; later divided into retail cuts. (Ch. 31)

**wok.** A large pan with a rounded bottom; used for *stir-frying*. (Ch. 35)

**work plan.** A list of what you have to do to prepare food. (Ch. 18)

## X - Y - Z

**yield.** The amount or number of servings that a *recipe* makes. (Ch. 11)

# Index

## A



## B



## C

## D



## E



## F

## G



## H



## I



## J



## K



## L



## M

## Q



## R



## S